RACE

IN PLAY

RACE

IN PLAY

Understanding the Socio-Cultural Worlds of Student Athletes

Carl E. James

Canadian Scholars' Press Inc.
Toronto

Race in Play: Understanding the Socio-Cultural Worlds of Student Athletes
by Carl E. James

First published in 2005 by
Canadian Scholars' Press Inc.
180 Bloor Street West, Suite 801
Toronto, Ontario
M5S 2V6

www.cspi.org

Canadian Scholars' Press gratefully acknowledges financial support for our publishing activities from the Ontario Arts Council, the Canada Council for the Arts, and the Government of Canada through the Book Publishing Industry Development Program (BPIDP).

Portions of this work were supported with funds from CURA (Community Diversity Research Alliance), SSHRC.

Library and Archives Canada Cataloguing in Publication

James, Carl, date.
 Race in play : the socio-cultural worlds of student athletes / Carl E. James.

Includes bibliographical references.
ISBN 1-55130-273-X

 1. High school athletes--Ontario--Toronto. 2. School sports--Ontario--Toronto. 3. Minority students--Ontario--Toronto. 4. Academic achievement--Ontario--Toronto. I. Title.

GV346.J34 2005   371.8'09713'541   C2004-906150-X

Cover design by Aldo Fierro
Cover photos: "Child's Eye," by floop/istockphoto.com, and "College Track," by sylvanworks/ istockphoto.com
Page design and layout by Brad Horning

05 06 07 08 09   5 4 3 2 1

Printed and bound in Canada by AGMV Marquis Imprimeur, Inc.

To

Kai,

Nia, and Kito

TABLE OF CONTENTS

ACKNOWLEDGEMENTS

This book has been in the making since I started work as a youth worker in downtown Toronto more than 20 years ago. It was from the recently immigrated Black Caribbean youth of Regent Park that I received my seminal and enduring lessons about the role of sports in navigating, negotiating, and maintaining interest in high school. It is appropriate, therefore, that I extend my gratitude to those youth for their individual and collective contributions to this project. I must here also acknowledge my friend and colleague, Denny Hunte, for his role in this work with the youth, and for his continuing support and assistance over the years by showing interest, giving his time and knowledge, sharing literature and other resources, and engaging in conversations—all of which have been sources of inspiration. To Denny I am sincerely grateful.

I am particularly grateful to the young men and women who willingly and generously volunteered their time to be interviewed, and made every effort to respond to my follow-up requests for additional information and clarification, and for their feedback on draft copies of the chapters. Their cooperation in all this has enabled me (with them) to produce a piece of work that I think will make a significant contribution to how we think about the schooling and education of student athletes. I appreciate the participants' trust and confidence in me to give voice to their ideas, experiences, aspirations, and analyses, so that others might benefit.

Very significant to this project are the cumulative support and assistance I received from a number of research assistants. Yazmin Razack played an invaluable and instrumental role in recruiting and interviewing participants, conducting literature search, and providing editorial feedback and critical comments. I am deeply indebted and sincerely grateful to Yasmin for giving generously of her time, energy, knowledge, and information, and for her initiative and resourcefulness in tapping into resources like her sister, Sabrina—to whom I am also grateful. In a similar way, Roger Saul made a significant contribution to this project. He brought his knowledge and insights from his student athlete experience to the editorial comments he provided on earlier drafts of the manuscript. I very much appreciate his counsel, encouragement, and suggestions. My appreciation also goes to Alice Wong for her research assistance.

I acknowledge with gratitude the assistance and contribution of Kai James and Sharon Sandhu, not only for their work with the literature, but also for sharing their student athletes experiences, thus enriching the work. I must also say a special thank you to Kai, who put aside his ambivalence (of course, I am sure that at times while in the library, he would think that he could be doing something "better") to contribute to yet another of my projects.

To my long-time friend, colleague, and now co-author, Everton Cummings, I say a special thank you for collaborating on Chapter One. His treasured contribution to this project has enabled us to get to know about, and to hear from, middle-school student athletes regarding their educational and athletic experiences and aspirations—a topic about which there is a dearth of information. I acknowledge also Susy Dabovic for her contribution on the subject of coaches. Her generosity in sharing her information, time, and interpretation is much appreciated. Both Everton and Susy gave to this project their valuable knowledge and insights as teachers, coaches, action researchers, and former student athletes.

The support and interests of colleagues are always important to any process and task. In this regard, I express my appreciation to my colleague Didi Khayatt for her comments on an earlier version of the chapter that I shared with our graduate class 5210 (Theory and Research in Language Culture and Teaching, 2003/2004); to the members of the class, I say: thanks for their feedback. Thanks also to Bruce Kidd for his consistent encouragement, counsel, and inspiration; to Brenda Hart for her support and thoughtfulness; and to Carol Reid and Jock Collins of Sydney, Australia, for helping me in my research during my visit there. To my faculty colleagues on the Minor Research Grant Committee, I say thanks for the funding support for this research project; thanks also to Elma Thomas and Debbi Sinera for their administrative and word processing support.

It is very pleasing to work with a managing editor who believes in your project and shares your excitement about the work you are trying to produce. Althea Prince is this person, and I treasure the support and counsel I received from her by way of conversations, critical comments, alternative perspectives, challenges; and her checking in to ensure that I was indeed working to deadline! While it is true that I would have completed the manuscript eventually, it certainly helped that Althea was there to offer encouragement and share her astute intellectual ideas and critical scholarship. For example, it was in one of our many exchanges that together we came up with the title of the book. Thanks, Althea. Let this be yet another tribute to your commitment to advancing knowledge and transforming ideas—and, as they say in Jamaica, "Nuff respect." Of course, the production and presentation of this book is due to the interest and support of Jack Wayne, as well as the outstanding editing work of Rebecca Conolly and Jennie Rubio. To all of you I remain grateful.

Finally, my continuing indebtedness is to many student athletes, former student athletes (like those with whom I worked as a youth worker), as well as Denny, Yasmin, and Roger, from whom I have learned so much as they helped to address the questions that I explore in this book. However, chief among these student athletes is Kai, who brought home, so to speak, the issues, and forced me to confront what it means to be a racialized student athlete attending school in Toronto. For all of you, I hope that the contents of this book provide some insights and assurances.

Carl E. Tonge James

INTRODUCTION
RACE, SPORTS, AND SCHOOLING

ARE STUDENTS REALLY LIKELY TO BENEFIT FROM THEIR PARTICIPATION IN ATHLETIC or sports activities in today's schools? According to studies the answer is both "yes" and "no." Studies indicate that participating in sports can help students to develop self-confidence and discipline, inspire high educational and occupational aspirations, and foster a sense of identity, through which they come to understand their relationship to others and the world around them (Coakly, 2002; James, 1995). But there is no decisive evidence that participation in sports has a significant effect on high school students' educational achievement. As Eitle and Eitle (2002) point out, "one cannot easily adjudicate on the matter of whether any finding on the association between playing sports and students' achievement represents a causal effect or whether such finding are simply an artifact of preexisting differences" (p. 124). Nevertheless, there is an enduring belief in Canada, especially among marginalized male high school students (and at times their coaches and parents) that participating in sports does produce educational benefits. The belief that sports can help students to negotiate and navigate school, and eventually win sports scholarship to study at American universities, is often put forward as one of those benefits. That such thinking exists at all indicates the role of race in student athletes' schooling experiences.

A cursory glance at the wall displays at high schools with a racially diverse student population will often reveal racial differences in the recipients of the academic and athletic awards, and further differences in the types of sports in which students participate. In some cases, there are over- and/or under-representation of students of particular racial and ethnic groups in such sports as hockey, basketball, soccer, swimming, football, track and field, volleyball, badminton, and tennis. These over- and under-representations on sports teams, or in athletic activities, cannot be explained simply by friendship groups and students' familiarity with the sports. And neither does the ethno-cultural background of students adequately explain students' affiliation. Indeed, in addition to parents, schools "play a fundamental role in structuring and promoting sports among adolescents" through teachers, coaches, and principals (Eitle & Eitle, 2002, p. 123), and does so along with the media, sports clubs, community organizations, and other social institutions.

This book examines the role played by race in the schooling experiences of student athletes in Canadian schools, with particular reference to schools in the metropolitan Toronto area. Specifically, I investigate the schooling experiences, athletic participation, and academic achievements of Blacks and other marginalized students. As well, I consider the schooling experiences of dominant group student athletes in order to explain how race informs the differences in students' experiences, participation, and achievements.

In this book, I address questions such as, How do students think of, and use, sports in middle- and high schools? In what ways do sports or extracurricular athletic activities serve the needs, interests, and aspirations of students generally, and racial minority students in particular? What opportunities and possibilities do sports or athletic activities offer students as they dream of becoming socially, academically, and financially successful?

I also examine the role that schools play—through their programs, activities, and curriculum, as well as through principals, teachers, coaches, and counsellors—in the lives of students. In this regard, I probe the ways in which schools structure, facilitate, and promote academic and sport activities for their students, and what resources are provided to students to address their needs, interests, and aspirations. Therefore, our inquiry into students' schooling experiences and educational outcomes necessarily involves giving attention to the school's culture—its values, norms, beliefs, and expectations. This culture reflects the dominant cultural discourse of the society—a discourse that schools inculcate in students. And depending on the degree of variations between the school's cultural values, repertoires, and expectations, and those of students, students will either "fit in" or dissent. The extent to which students assimilate or not will also reflect the school's (and society's) representation of them based on their racial, ethnic, immigrant, class, and gender backgrounds.

I bring to this work my understanding of how students are positioned, and how they respond to schooling and socialization. In so doing, I pay attention to the fact that the educational system is part of a stratified society with structures that maintain and re-inscribe racial, social, and gender stratification and inequities. Within the framework of critical theory, I dispute the notion that Canada's multicultural policy has produced educational policies, programs, and practices that make the race of students irrelevant to any consideration of their schooling and achievement. The reality is the opposite. In fact, multiculturalism in Canada has evolved a discourse that constructs some people as "having race" and others not. For instance, when I described this book, many people assumed that a book about race, sports, and schooling would be about Black students (my own racial identification notwithstanding): this is, in part, a representation of the racialization of Black students. That is, within the context of urban schools in Canada, and Toronto specifically, Black students are often constructed as athletes. My discussion will clarify the evidence behind this conceptualization of racial and ethnic group members. First I present a brief synopsis of my more than 20 years' experiences, which have allowed me to study the schooling experiences and academic achievement of racial minority youth, and African Canadians in particular. The partial autobiographical information that I provide below is not to assert my authority, but to indicate the limits and strength of my location, and to be a constant reminder of "the specificity of my perspective" (Thornton, 1998, p. 6). Moreover, it indicates some of the subject positions from which I have been observing and studying the social and cultural worlds of student athletes.

THE BACKGROUND TO MY QUESTIONS

My interest in the educational achievements of student athletes, and Blacks in particular, came from my experiences in working with youths in downtown Toronto. Initially, I worked as a tutor with the Black Education Project helping Black-Caribbean youth, most of whom were newly arrived immigrants, "with their school work." This was a time when there was a significant increase in the number of immigrant youths from the Caribbean entering the school system—a system that was ill-prepared to address their academic, social, cultural, and familial needs and issues. An immigrant adolescent myself of Caribbean origin, socialized with the expectation that I was to apply myself "to my studies," and to take all the opportunities that Canada afforded us, I was quite curious about how students negotiated the school system to enable themselves to fulfill what their parents (like mine) and other community members expected. One thing that struck me then was the intense commitment on the part of these immigrant youths to playing sports. And not just any sport, but basketball, interestingly, not cricket or soccer, even though they had experienced these sports growing up in the Caribbean. Hence the questions: Why? And wouldn't such substantial involvement in sports distract them from their school work, and hence from fulfilling their educational expectations and aspirations, and those of their parents? Was playing sports, in fact, a way of coping with the system, and with their social and cultural situation? And what understanding did they have of the school system, and the role that basketball could play in helping them to succeed academically?

These questions remained with me for years, and my curiosity to find answers piqued in the early 1980s, when I was a youth worker at a neighbourhood centre in a low-income/working-class neighbourhood in downtown Toronto. It was a culturally diverse government-housing neighbourhood made up of many new immigrants to Canada, many of them from the Caribbean, as well as European residents who had been living in the area for generations. There were two youth programs at the centre: one attended by mostly White European youth and a few Blacks with long-time roots in Canada (coordinated by Mary Anne MacArthur); and the other (which I co-ordinated) attended mostly by Black youth of Caribbean origin. Sometimes as many as 200 youth attended my program, and were mostly immigrant youth of Caribbean origin, aged between eight and 16 years (the average age was about 14 years). Almost all of the older youth were immigrants from Jamaica, while the younger ones were Canadian-born. Many of them lived in single-parent (typically mother-run) households, where the parents were either in low-wage jobs or on some kind of social assistance. The reasons for having two programs had to do with the differences in the interests of the two groups of youth. While the White youth (mostly males) came to the centre one night to play floor hockey, the Black youth (also mostly males) came to the centre on another night to play basketball. At one time there were three basketball teams connected to the program, coached by Denny Hunte.

As we worked with the youth, it became clear over time that basketball was the main reason for their regular attendance at the centre. And it was the activity that seemed to have enabled them to tolerate school, and to have their presence at school recognized. So the centre provided them with the chance to display their abilities and skills among their neighbourhood peers, to cultivate the "good ball player" reputation, and to gain respect from their male peers and attention from the females, who came to the centre largely to watch the males play. In addition, playing basketball at the centre was, in a way, a form of practice, a chance to "become better" at basketball so that they could maintain their place on their respective schools' basketball teams. I remember Sammy (not his real name), a six-foot-two centre player, saying in a documentary video of the youth program that he expected to "someday play for the NBA." I am not sure if he believed it, but what he said stayed with me for a long time. For I questioned then: how could Sammy expect to make it to the NBA when he was not doing well in school? Furthermore, he was in a vocational program at the school he was attending. Nevertheless, among his peers, Sammy's aspirations were never questioned.

It should be said that I was very skeptical of the athletic ambitions of the youth with whom I was working, and of the amount of energy they were putting into their athletic activities at schools. Like the parents who shared their concerns with me, I was concerned that the "basic" and "general" level education that most of the youth were receiving would be inadequate, especially if they were to fulfill both their and their immigrant parents' educational and occupational expectations and aspirations. I agreed with the parents that these youth should be putting their efforts into "studying their schoolwork" rather than playing sports. On this basis, and with the support of the youth's parents, I chose not to run an exclusively recreational or sports program. Hence, in addition to basketball, other activities were introduced into the program such as tutorials for participants who needed help with their school work, educational counselling, and workshops aimed at assisting students in their planning for high school and for post-high school. But despite the youth's need for academic assistance, this was not something they expected the centre to provide them. From their perspective, the centre was to be a social and cultural space where they could culturally bind together and hone their athletic skills, and where they would not be reminded of their limitations.

My experience at the centre was the motivation for my first major research on the schooling lives of Black/African-Canadian youth in Toronto. In that investigation, I interviewed 60 young people (33 males and 27 females) between the ages of 17 and 22 years old; among them 36 (or 60 percent) were born in the Caribbean or Britain (of Caribbean parents), 20 were born in Toronto, and five in Halifax. Twenty-nine lived with both parents, 21 with a mother only, and 15 were on their own. About 15 of these youth were of middle-class backgrounds (that is, had parents in professional or white-collar occupations), and the reminder were working class (i.e., their parents were in blue-collar, skilled, semi-skilled, unskilled jobs, or on social assistance). I also conducted ethnographic observations. The findings indicated that these African Canadians had high educational and career aspirations (such as becoming doctors, lawyers, accountants, technicians, counsellors), and, like most youth, they were quite optimistic about life. They also believed that their strategies of hard work, having the "right attitude," and aspiring to be "the best" would enable them to counter the "hurdles" of racism and discrimination and ultimately realize their aspirations (James, 1990). For many of these youth, primarily the males and, to a lesser extent, the females, participation in sports was a strategy they used to get past the "hurdles" of school participation and educational achievement, to compensate for their academic failures, and to actively participate in the construction of their schooling processes. Participation in sports was also an avenue for them to develop friendships, gain recognition, challenge stereotype, and exercise leadership. And for the most part, they believed that their efforts, abilities, and skills would be sufficient for them to overcome systemic barriers to their success (see James, 1995).

Over the years, this optimism of Black students, and Black student athletes in particular, continues to be in evidence in many of the studies of their schooling experiences, aspirations, and achievements,[1] in magazine articles (Higgins, 2003) and newspaper reports (*Toronto Star*, 1998; 2003). And there are the weekly articles about high school athletes in the *Toronto Star* and the *Toronto Sun* newspapers that report on their athletic activities, academic attainments, aspirations, and successes. What remains consistent—and for me, curious—are the race, gender, citizenship/immigrant status, and social class identifications and representations of student athletes by sports in school and the media. For instance, the pictures of the many athletes featured in articles indicate that a significant number of the basketball players are Black males; football players also tend to be Black, while hockey and swim stars tend to be White. In one article (*Toronto Star*, November 5, 2002, p. E7), a Black "family"—a brother (six-foot-seven) and two younger sisters (six-foot-one and five-foot-eleven respectively)—is featured. The two older siblings have scholarship offers, and the article notes that the coaches believe that the Grade Eleven younger sister "might be the best of the three, [and] is already the subject of attention from recruiting schools." At times the article tells us about the birthplaces of the athletes as if to indicate that there is a connection between birthplace and athletic interests, abilities, and skills. Take, for example, the high school athlete featured in the *Toronto Star* on Friday, May 10, 2002 (p. D11). With the accompanying picture we are told that he "boasts major talent," and that the "Cuban-born star hopes to follow grandpa to [the] pros."

There are also the feature articles by *Toronto Star* reporter David Grossman about high school basketball "academic" stars of Greater Toronto. Appearing on the front page of the sports section, February 18, 2004, was a picture of the five "high achievers" of 2004 (p. C1). The five Grade Twelve, Black male students, aged between 17 and 19, who won this title had academic averages ranging from 65 to 75 percent (one had an average of 65 percent, two had 70 percent, and two had 75 percent). One is said to have had a scholarship offer, and another a "verbal commitment to scholarship" from two different US universities. Two others had "interests" from one or more US universities. Only one, a 17-year-old with an average of 75 percent, said that he would return to school the following year to "boost his academic grades hoping to pursue a career in medicine" (p. C4).

The profile of the previous year's (2003) Black "academic stars" is no different: four Blacks and one White. With the exception of one Black who was 17 years old and in Grade Twelve, they were 18 years old and in Grade Thirteen (February 25, 2003, E1 & 4). Reporter David Grossman tells us that the panel of judges who selected these five were comprised of representatives from Basketball Ontario, the Raptors, and university and high school coaches. The four Black students had academic averages ranging from 71 to 75 percent, while the White student athlete's academic average was 98.5 percent. In terms of their plans for the coming year, all four Black students were said to be either looking for, or exploring, were already recruited by, or "could end up at" NCAA schools. The White athlete was said to be heading for Cornell University. Interestingly, and probably not surprisingly, the five "academic stars" of 2002 were quite similar to those of 2003. Of the five Grade Thirteen players, three were Black, one was born in Jamaica, the others in Canada, and four were aged 18 years and had academic averages of 72 to 75 percent. One of the two White players was 17 years old, with an academic average of 98 percent and an aspiration to study microbiology (Grossman, 2002, February 15, 2002, p. C18).

I wonder about this picture/profile of these so-called "basketball brains": high school students who "excel in the classroom as well as the court" and have "high marks" (Grossman, February 25, 2003, p. E1, E4). While grades do not fully represent the potential and abilities of students, and they are subjectively assigned based on a number of factors, the *Toronto Star* article nevertheless leaves us to wonder about the educational future of student athletes, particularly Blacks. It is indeed possible that with their academic averages of 70+ percent, the Black students could get into a university or college, but should we not expect them to have higher grades if they are to beat their competition and win athletic scholarships? There is no doubt that involvement in extracurricular athletic activities takes time and energy that student athletes could otherwise be devoting to their academic work. For those who are not fortunate enough to win scholarships, the concern for many parents is how their children might fare against those non-athletes when it comes to gaining entrance into universities.

As a parent of a student athlete, I share the concern of many Black/ African parents who wish that our children—often sons—would not invest an inordinate amount of their school time in playing sports, for doing so is sometimes, if not often, at the expense of their academic work. I remember reluctantly expressing my concern to my own son, Kai, when he was in Grade Eleven and playing on his school's basketball team, as he had been doing since entering high school (he had also been a member of the volleyball team a year earlier). I say "reluctant" because I was well aware of the social and educational benefits of his participation in sports, not to mention the satisfaction it was providing for him. But I was still concerned with the fact that he was investing much time in sports, sometimes even missing the last class of the day because of games. He responded to my concern by saying that he did not wish to stop his involvement in sports, since doing so "was an important part of his school life." Why was I concerned when, after all, he continued to do well in school and he seemed able to effectively negotiate high school and cultivate good relationships with his coaches and teachers? Further, he was able to build and maintain good friendships with his fellow Black players, most of whom were not in the same level of education program. Possibly, my concern had to do with my desire to encourage him to disrupt the stereotype that he walked into when he first entered the school in Grade Nine: within weeks of starting, a teacher/coach, seeing a tall Black male student, met him in the corridor and invited him to be part of the basketball team (James, 2000).[2]

Indeed, I was concerned with Kai's racialization and marginalization in a schooling system in which the discourse of multiculturalism within a stratified

Canada operates to enable or limit his opportunities based on his race, gender, assumed social class, and athletic abilities and skills.

MULTICULTURALISM, MINORITY STUDENTS, ATHLETIC PARTICIPATION, AND EDUCATION[3]

In a society with a federal (or official) policy of multiculturalism, and with schools purporting to operate on principles of multicultural education (and in some cases anti-racism education), it should follow that all youth, regardless of colour, race, ethnicity, and citizenship/immigrant status, should be able to fully and equally participate in schooling activities in ways that enable them to realize the educational and occupational goals to which they aspire. But, contrary to the promise and "good intention" of Canada's multiculturalism policy, individuals are identified by ethnicity and race, and this in part determines their opportunities, as well as their educational and occupational outcomes.

For the most part, those considered White tend to be identified as citizens or "Canadians," and others, the so-called "visible minorities," are identified as members of "cultural groups"—the "Other"—people with cultural practices and values from elsewhere.[4] This "Canadian/Other" configuration within the school system is re-inscribed through school programs, educational materials, curriculum, and pedagogical approaches. All of these contribute to the marginalization of some minority students, including their disengagement from the schooling process, poor educational performance, a lowered self-concept, poor educational choices leading to concentration in particular areas of school programs, and finally, resulting in few making it to university or college.[5]

In the context of Canada's multiculturalism discourse, with its emphasis on "culture"—the beliefs, values, and behaviours of group members and individuals—what is communicated is that people "with culture," specifically ethnic and racial minority group members and immigrants, are governed by and indulge in prescribed beliefs, values, and behaviours. This culture is perceived to be a set of observable practices and characteristics that fulfils specific functions in the lives of minority group members. As such, it is believed that they all share the same ideas, values, and aspirations because of their group membership (James, 2003a). The resulting educational participation, and the ultimate educational outcome of minority students, then, is understood to be a reflection of their culture and not of any systemic inequalities within educational institutions. Further, ethnicity is often understood as a reflection of how students see their opportunities and possibilities in the society and how they accordingly construct their aspirations. This "cultural" explanation is premised on the idea that the society, and by extension the education system, is "colour-blind," and that students' abilities and interests will take them wherever they wish educationally and occupationally, regardless of their colour (James, 2001).

Educators often encourage Black students to play sports because it is often believed that their athletic skills are better than their academic skills (Entine, 2000; Codjoe, 2001), and sports are likely to be their most productive avenue of school participation (see D. Grossman, *Toronto Star,* June 9, 2000, pp. E1 & 4). Educators do this in the belief that it is in the interest of the students, as well as being an act of respect for their culture. So, if through sports Black students might win educational scholarships, then teachers and coaches may feel a responsibility to promote athletics as the pathway to educational and occupational success. Similarly, in the case of Asian students, there is the notion that they are hardworking, intelligent, with strengths in sciences and math (Lee, 1996; Li, 2001; Pon, 2000). According to Pon (2000), this stereotype might seem to be positive, but in fact "it is quite often harmful" (p. 223). Pon goes on to recall how in high school he was particularly passionate about English and writing, while mathematics was his "weakest subject." "It took me years beyond high school," he continues, "to figure out that my essay-writing skills, which were quite strong for my grade-level, ruptured the dominant stereotype of Chinese students, particularly the belief that we are all math whizzes."[6]

The practice of encouraging Black students in athletic activities, and Asian students in science and mathematics, are racializing and essentializing processes, and are also evident in schools where teachers and coaches purport to base their work on principles of anti-racism. As I discuss elsewhere, anti-racism education, implemented in a context informed by the ideology of multiculturalism, often results in an education that does not recognize the inequality and inequity leading to the stereotyping and marginalization of students, their alienation, and/or disengagement from the schooling process and, in some cases, eventual drop out (James, 2001). In fact, this multiculturalism discourse has inhibited the implementation of anti-racism (and other critical approaches to education), which could examine the complex and interlocking relationship of race, class, and gender. These factors together inform the experiences, interests, and aspirations of racial minority students.

What is termed "anti-racism education" as practised in schools is what I refer to as *race culture discourse*. In this discourse, race is acknowledged because of its "visibility," and the behaviours, practices, values, attitudes, and aspirations of racial minority students are considered to be part of their race culture. In other words, as in the discourse of multiculturalism, the cultural pattern of racial minority students' interests and successes, in particular school activities (for example, in the case of Blacks, sports, and for Asians, science and mathematics), are considered to be related to their culture. This re-inscribes the notion that culture and particular abilities are evident in particular bodies. And like multiculturalism, race culture discourse unwittingly fosters the notion that the social system is open and that individuals can attain whatever education, occupation, and careers they wish through hard work, motivation, abilities, capabilities, and applications. This belief can be witnessed in teachers', coaches', and others' references to and use of, for example, athletes as role models for Black working-class students, and artists, scientists, and engineers as role models for other students. So, in denying that race plays a role in their perceptions and constructions of students as good athletes or scholars, educators argue that "it is not race (not any physical or biological characteristics) but culture." What is missed in this conceptualization is the fact that culture is continuously being created and re-created by everyone within that environment in relation to space and time. Hence, in the context of schooling, teachers, coaches, counsellors, parents, students—in short, the composition of the school—as well as the principles and ideology upon which the school program is based, all contribute to the educational outcomes of the students. So too do the messages communicated to students about who they are and about their relationship to school.

In the absence of anti-racism and other critical approaches to education that recognize and affirm students' differences and lived experiences while also encouraging their empowerment, students will continue to struggle over their essentialization, marginalization, and "absented presence"[7] in school and in society as a whole (Walcott, 1997/2003). In response to this essentialization and marginalization, minority student athletes will participate in the schooling process in ways that enable them to construct possibilities for their lives, and to open up opportunities through which they might realize their aspirations. In so doing, they construct subcultures or group cultures with well-defined systems of meanings, symbols, norms, values, beliefs, expectations, and group actions. These group cultures are the students' responses to how they are constructed and treated in school, and how they assert themselves, as well as their interests and aspirations. The group cultures also represent the ways in which minority students attempt to differentiate themselves from the middle-class Eurocentric cultural structures of school, and at the same time function within it, in order to acquire the cultural capital needed to attain their educational, athletic, and/or scholarship goals.

Ostensibly, these group cultures are created with the knowledge of institutional and societal inequalities, which privilege those students with resources (economic, political, social, and cultural) and related power. Those with resources have the benefit of cultural capital—defined by Pierre Bourdieu as the set of useful resources (e.g., attitudes, behaviours, preferences, credentials) and powers that individuals derive from the social (including educational, economic, political) structure of society—which enable them to succeed in society (Anisef et al., 2000; Eitle & Eitle, 2002a). But while characteristics such as their race, ethnicity, class, gender, citizenship, and geographic residence could operate to limit students' participation in school, it is possible that the efforts they put in could open up possibilities and opportunities for them. These efforts, particularly for students with limited material resources, will draw on ideas and knowledge that students gained through their interactions in the various marginalized communities—related to race, ethnic, gender, class, geographic—in which they participate. Arguably, these students could be called multicultural, if not bicultural (i.e., they have knowledge, beliefs, and experiences of the different cultures they traverse and the capacity to interact within them). This is, in effect, a form of "cultural capital" that is likely to benefit them in their negotiation of school structures, their construction of aspirations, and accessing opportunities.

A lack of cultural capital is commonly used as an explanation for the unequal academic achievement found among the children of different social classes.[8] It is suggested that the middle-class norms, values, and expectations of the educational institution benefit students of middle- and upper-class backgrounds who have the cultural capital it takes to succeed in that system. Students of working-class background, on the other hand, are perceived to lack the knowledge and understanding of the system, and are thereby disadvantaged (Anisef et al., 2000; Brantlinger, 2003; Davis, 2004; Mayers, 2001).[9] Critical theorists[10] also suggest that the class culture of educational institutions is based on a Eurocentic ideology, which further disadvantages students from racial, ethnic, and immigrant backgrounds; this compounds the efforts necessary to seek their educational aspirations. Further, while the middle-class, Eurocentric curricula of schools are more likely, by design, to serve the needs and interests of urban students, those living in middle- and upper-class urban communities are more likely to be the beneficiaries.[11] In the case of immigrant children and those of immigrant parents (particularly new arrivals), the capacity of parents to pass on the capital—cultural, economic, and social—needed to negotiate the educational system is likely to affect their schooling experiences, opportunities, and achievements.

Relevant to this discussion are the situation and experiences of immigrant students (those born elsewhere). Accordingly, a differentiation must be made between immigrants and racial minority students; contrary to the common construction, being a racial minority person does not necessarily mean that the person is an immigrant. Nevertheless, within race culture discourse, the athletic interest of "immigrant" students is perceived to be representative of their national origins or the countries from which they or their parents come. With this view, little or no consideration is given to the cultural diversity among group members in relation to, among many other factors, class, ethnicity, race, and/or gender differences, or to the fact that in many cases, they are Canadian-born. This approach has the effect of not responding to the differential academic and athletic or sporting needs, interests, potentials, and aspirations of racial minority group students.

Because immigrant and racial minority students are usually believed to be one and the same, similar issues do apply—like the expectation for such students to assimilate into the dominant or mainstream culture of society and that of school. In other words, the expectation is that marginalized students will abandon their "old" cultural values, languages (including accent), and behaviours to adopt the "new" ones of the host society.[12] The underlying premise here is that unless immigrant and/or racial minority students can acquire and understand the "cultural capital" of the society, they will continue to be marginalized. "Assimilation" also infers that immigrant and minority group members will come to recognize where and how to access the dominant cultural characteristics that are necessary to succeed in society and schools. This understanding of the assimilation and settlement processes, along with paths to educational participation and social mobility (for it is believed that most of these students are of working-class backgrounds), leaves unquestioned the fundamentally important networks and social ties, in essence the "cultural structures" that immigrant and ethno-racial minority group members provide for each other (James, forthcoming). In fact, it is possible for such ties to strengthen, instead of limiting, the educational aspirations and achievements of such students (see Portes & Macleod, 1999; Zhou, 1997).

Furthermore, networks and social ties help to build a form of solidarity among the members of the various minority and immigrant groups, particularly as they struggle against discrimination, lack of recognition, or the devaluation of their skills and other barriers to their schooling and achievements. Through banding together for moral support, educational success, and cultural survival, student athletes will use their "social capital" (Portes & MacLeod, 1999; Eitle & Eitle, 2002a)—that is, their athletic abilities and skills—to command resources and colonize spaces[13] within schools. They do so in their efforts to gain access to coaches, teachers, principals, and scouts, and to ensconce themselves in the sports networks of their schools and community with the hope of winning scholarships (James, 1995). Typically, this hope pertains to winning athletic scholarship to study at universities/colleges, as well as to play on college and/or university teams in the United States on their way to eventually playing on national teams of their chosen sport. This aspiration, evident within the group culture of student athletes, especially males, is not only inspired by role models, parents, and media presentations, but also by the encouragement of coaches and other educators alike (principals, teachers, guidance counsellors). These educators tend to operate with the assumption, in other words with the stereotype, that particular groups of students make good athletes, and their role as coaches and educators is to make it possible for these students achieve their cultural destiny.

In essence, this work is informed by critical theories that contend that the multicultural discourse, which helps to frame the ways in which schools accommodate the needs—educational, social, and cultural—as well as the interests and aspirations of its diverse student population, has primarily served to reproduce Canadian social stratification system. This includes gendered opportunities favourable to males, "colour-blindness" ("race doesn't matter"), and inequitable educational outcomes for students. In this regard, students' racial differences are conceived of in terms of "culture," which is seen as "stable and homogeneous" (see Dunn, 2002). In such a context, participation in high school athletic activities could have some positive effects for some students in terms of popularity, pleasure, friendships, mentoring relationships, and academic achievement (Ewing et al., 2002; Gatz et al., 2002; James, 1995).

14

However, this will not be the case for all because race, class, gender, and other demographic characteristics will operate to affect the level of participation and hence educational outcomes. Student athletes, particularly minority student athletes, will develop strategies, construct aspirations, and take initiatives to counteract the race-based differences in educational and athletic achievements. In doing so, they can expect to be constantly negotiating educational and cultural structures, structures that do not always address their collective and individual interests, competences, and aspirations.

SOURCES

I used information from a variety of sources to explore the ideas in my discussion. In addition to literature from books, journals, novels, and magazines, I also used information from research studies I conducted (sometimes with research assistants), and from newspapers articles that I collected over a period of time. There were also times when I solicited information from individuals via email exchanges and short reflections. Through the information I collected, I sought to capture the experiences, comments, stories, and insights of student athletes, parents, coaches, teachers/educators, and youth/community workers. Essentially, my aim was to have this work be a story about the lives and experiences of student athletes, and so I went to the sources that would enable me to produce the story. As Weiler (1995, p. 34) notes, in sharing experiences through stories or personal narratives, individuals gain an understanding of the structures and/or agents that have shaped the experiences of those who tell the stories or about whom the stories are told. Stories also have a way of pulling the receiver—listener or reader—into the story, causing them to engage in a process of reflection about their own lives, experiences, and stories (see Conway, 1999; Garrod et al., 2002). Further, Errande (2000, p. 16) makes the point that "all narratives, whether oral or written, personal or collective, official or subaltern, are 'narratives of identity' ... [and] are representations of reality in which narrators also communicate how they see themselves and wish others to see them." And the satisfaction that is gained through autobiographical narratives, writes Conway (1999, p. 6), "comes from being allowed inside the experiences of another person who really lived and who tells about the experience of another ...." Complete or significant portions of individuals' comments, reflections, stories, and/or responses provide direct access to their outlooks, highlighting how they articulate, interpret, analyze, and address the issues with which they live and/or struggled; such comments also allow us to engage in dialogues and conversations.

I conducted individual and group interviews with, and solicited reflections and comments from, present and former student athletes, parents, coaches, and educators in metropolitan Toronto and surrounding suburban areas. The purposeful selection of these informants or participants was guided by the logic that they were good informants who were "information rich" (Morse, 1994). According to Morse (1994), "a good informant is one who has the knowledge and experience the researcher requires, has the ability to reflect, is articulate, has the time to be interviewed, and is willing to participate in the study" (p. 228). The term "information rich" reflects how these student athletes were likely to have experiences with many of the common, and seemingly significant, issues, incidents, and people that are typical or representative of many of their athletic peers. Moreover, as Blumer (1967) notes, with reference to the importance of interviewing a select group of individuals, "a small number of [well informed] individuals brought together as a discussion and resource group is more valuable many times over than a representative sample" (cited in Fontana & Frey, 1994, p. 365).

In the various information gathering processes, particularly in my facilitation of (as opposed to leading) the individual and group interviews/ discussions, I was careful to develop both trust and a rapport in order for all the participants to help make the information gathering process as active as possible.[14] For the most part, I accomplished this objective. Individuals were willing and ready to talk about questions and issues that were highly significant to their lives, issues about which they felt they had answers, and about which they had strong opinions based on their own experiences. In the cases of the group interviews, at times individuals would expand upon each other's points, "bounce" ideas back and forth about some of the rules, mechanics, or workings of the sport, and provide supportive and alternative viewpoints about similar incidents and experiences. Such engagements represent the fact that collectively, as Carspecken (1996) would say, they were living within the same culture. And as Fontana and Frey (1994, p. 364) point out, data gathering through the group interview method provides "a perspective on the research question that is not available through individual interviews." At times, the interviews and email communications were presented to me as if I were a student getting a lesson about the sport from a coach or educator.

ORGANIZATION OF THE BOOK

CHAPTER 1: "THAT'S WHY I COME TO SCHOOL": THE SIGNIFICANCE OF SPORTS TO THE HIGH SCHOOL PLANS OF GRADE EIGHT STUDENTS
Chapter 1 explores the role of sports in the educational and occupational plans and aspirations of a group of 12 Grade Eight students—males and females, representing Black, White, and South Asian students—from Westville Middle School in Peel region, west of Toronto. Specifically, with middle school teacher Everton Cummings, we explore these students' choice of high school and high school programs, noting the emphasis they place on the academic, social, athletic, and emotional factors in terms of constructing their educational and career plans. We examine the extent to which the significance of sports varies according to race, class, and gender; we also examine the role and influences of "significant others" (i.e., parents, teachers, and siblings) in how these students made plans and took decisions. The parents of the Black students participating in the study were interviewed with the intention of comparing parents' and children's outlook.

The study reveals important similarities and differences in the ways the various groups of students (in terms of race, ethnicity, and gender) use and understand sports, the value they placed on sports as part of their education process, as well as their perception of its potential in enabling them to successfully negotiate and navigate high school, and attain their educational and occupational plans and aspirations. Having experienced the benefits of sports—which gave them confidence, popularity, and interest in school—during their middle school years, most of the participants were quite confident that sports would continue to benefit them in their high school years.

The chapter provides important insight into the thoughts, ideas, and "constructed selves" of middle school students before they enter the high school system. The information from the parents of Black students also provides important insights, reflecting the active and tacit support and encouragement they gave their children.

CHAPTER 2: RACE AND THE SOCIAL/CULTURAL WORLDS OF STUDENT ATHLETES
Chapter 2 opens with an email I received from a former student athlete, in which he reflects on his experiences playing sports in high school. He tells of his reluctance to continue playing basketball in his later years in high school because, as he said, he was not very good. But in those later years, the

basketball team had become predominantly Black and he would have been the only White player on the team. I refer to David's experience in my discussion of the place of race in students' decisions to participate or not to participate in sports and the role that coaches play in these decisions. With reference to a *Sports Illustrated* article (Price, 1997) on the dominance of Blacks in sports, particularly basketball and track and field, I discuss the extent to which this might also be a perception in Canada among players and coaches. In exploring this idea, I shared the article with some White student athletes, and I use the responses of two of them as well as literature, interviews, email responses, and newspaper articles to discuss the perceptions and issues.

One respondent, in his email, noted that hockey "is central to mainstream life" in Canada. I use this as a premise to discuss how marginalized and racialized students are able to access hockey, and when they do, what some of their experiences are. I use newspaper reports of marginalized students, and information given to me by marginalized students, to discuss their experiences.

CHAPTER 3: THE LONG SHOTS: GOING SOUTH ON BASKETBALL TICKETS

Chapter 3 begins with the stories of four Black male working-class high school student athletes in Toronto who, in the mid-1990s, were aspiring to attain basketball scholarships to attend colleges in the United States. The stories, published in the *Toronto Star* newspaper (Duffy, March 23, 24, 25, 1996), show how much of the experiences of these Toronto student athletes parallel the experiences of their African-American counterparts. I also reference the *Toronto Star* 2003 series (Campbell, 2003) about a Toronto high school basketball team. Based on these newspaper reports, I discuss the implications of students relying on their high school primarily as a means of providing them with the opportunities and chances to obtain scholarships to American universities. I give particular attention to the roles of coaches, teachers, and recruiters as gatekeepers in the scholarship attainment process, and how systemic and institutional structures operate to define, construct, enable, and limit students' opportunities. In addition, I consider how race, social class, and gender intersect to influence these student athletes' experiences, aspirations, and perceptions of their chances to attain their scholarship goals.

Building on these newspaper reports, and using data obtained through a focus group interview of five working-class high school basketball players (four African-Caribbean Canadian and one Indo-African-Caribbean Canadian),

I examine how these youths negotiate the structures of school in their bid to obtain the coveted college and university scholarships. The interesting questions here are: Why do these young men think of "going south" rather than seeking the opportunities in Canada? And how do these Canadian student athletes believe that they can surpass their American counterparts who live "next door" to the post-secondary institutions and recruiting scouts and coaches? Is "going south" the best chance for social mobility for these students, some of whom are expected to live the dreams of their immigrant parents and realize their aspirations, hence "make it" for their parents/family? Is attaining an education really the goal, or is it a means to their financial security?

A key issue in this chapter is the extent to which young African Canadians, and athletes in particular, perceive that the "North American dream" of "making it" is less elusive for Blacks in the United States than in Canada. In analyzing this issue, I refer to Canada's history of racism and discrimination, which has facilitated the construction of some Canadians as "Canadians" while others are "outsiders." As a result, the perception exists that things will be better elsewhere for these "Others" or "outsiders," especially in places where, according to media information, many Black people are "free" to attain their aspirations.

CHAPTER 4: THE GENDERED EXPERIENCES OF FEMALE STUDENTS IN SPORT WITH SPECIAL REFERENCE TO ALICIA

Alicia is a 24-year-old African Canadian who was attending a US university on a full athletic scholarship, and who, at the time of the interview (May, 2003), had just completed her second season with the WNBA. Using a life history approach, I provide an interpretative account of the ways in which Alicia makes sense of her schooling experiences as a female student athlete in Toronto schools. I explore the circumstances and structural factors that have shaped her life and informed her path toward becoming a professional athlete. This life history presentation also illuminates the complexities of Alicia's athletic experiences, particularly with regard to race and gender, and assists in proving a contextual understanding of how historical, political, cultural, societal, institutional, familial and personal circumstances, and events have shaped her life and role as an athlete.

An important consideration here is how far Alicia's experiences as a female differ from that of her male counterparts, who hold the same aspirations and experience the same Toronto school system. As in other cases, I will explore the role of parents, coaches, teachers, and peers in supporting Alicia in her athletic and academic aspirations. But while I do not set out to make direct comparisons of Alicia's experiences and those of male student athletes, the insights that her story provides do highlight some interesting differences.

CHAPTER 5: SET DREAMS, FAILED PLANS, FRUSTRATED TRANSITIONS, AND LESSONS LEARNED

What happens to the student athletes who never realize their aspirations? What happens to the "sport-identified self," which at one point informed student athletes' expectations of, interests in, and engagement with school, as well as their aspirations? In what new ways do they think of their schooling, and what new aspirations do they construct? What happens to their "interest" in post-secondary education? In short, what new "life narrative" (Sparkes, 2000) do these student athletes construct in relation to their educational, social, and occupational goals and outcomes after events forced them to think of their future differently? In this chapter, I take up these questions using the stories of Amir, Devin, Lori, and Greg; these four students were unable to secure athletic scholarships or the chance to play their sport professionally in North America—aspirations that had special relevance to their identities. The stories that these student athletes tell of their experiences provide insights into how they dealt with their forced role transitions to, and disengagement from, the educational and athletic pathways around which they had build their future life stories.

My interest in examining how student athletes deal with frustrated aspirations and unrealized dreams is related to a number of observations and concerns that have emerged through my years of studying the educational experiences of students for whom specific "sport identification" (for example, in the case of Black students it is basketball) played a major role in their experiences. Following Sparkes (2000), I examine the consequences associated with having a strong athletic identity for, as Sparkes points out, a strong athletic identity can "act as either 'Hercules' muscles' or an 'Achilles heel.'" Specifically, individuals could benefit from their "development of a salient self-identity or sense of self, positive effects in athletic performance, and a greater likelihood of long-term involvement in exercise behaviours." But there are also the potential risks for individuals with a strong athletic identity: he or she may find it particularly difficult to alter his or her original plans as a result of failing to reach their goals (such as attaining an athletic scholarship).

CHAPTER 6: TEACHING ATHLETES/COACHING STUDENTS: ON THE ROLE OF COACHES

This chapter discusses the role and influence of coaches in the lives of student athletes, especially as students balance academic studies with athletics. I argue that coaches have a significant role to play in helping to address the barriers faced by student athletes as they attempt this balance. I suggest that coaches play a pivotal role in helping marginalized student athletes to negotiate school structures for, in many cases, they might be the ones who are closest to these students. And as "role models" (assigned, earned, or adopted), they have the responsibility to be advocates for these students, working to transform the schooling system so that they succeed academically, as well as athletically, from their schooling. In working with marginalized student athletes, coaches need to pay attention to their social and cultural backgrounds, and should not be just priming students to be "just an athlete" intending to win scholarships to US universities and colleges. They must encourage students to think about the long term.

In this chapter, I also discuss how school coaches can help student athletes work creatively and effectively to satisfy their athletic interest while paying equal attention to their academic work. To understand how coaches think about their roles and their influence on student athletes, I spoke with a group of four coaches, and I present my research here. I also discuss literature and newspaper articles that feature comments by coaches about student athletes.

CHAPTER 7: PARENTAL CONCERNS, ATHLETIC PARTICIPATION, AND ACADEMIC ATTAINMENT

The role of parents is central to the educational, athletic, and career outcomes of student athletes. This chapter begins with the concern of Dane's mother about the negative impact of her son's participation in sports on his academic performance and achievements. I raise the question of whether withdrawing Dane, and other students like him, from sports is an appropriate alternative. This chapter speaks to the concerns expressed by many minority and immigrant parents, and takes up the questions: Should these parents discourage their children from participating in athletic activities? Is this an appropriate way to ensure that their children redirect their energies into their academic work, hence addressing the problems of academic failures?

In discussing these issues, I argue that there are certainly valid reasons for parental concerns regarding academic success, athletic participation, and the common idea that excelling in sport results in poor academic performance.

However, disallowing participation in sports will not necessarily help or reverse the situation. In fact, research shows that involvement in sports can help marginalized students, and Blacks in particular, gain respect, build self-confidence, and cultivate peer support. This enables them to cope with the otherwise alienating school environment. As a result, many students manage to productively negotiate the structural constraints due to inequalities and racism within the school system. On this basis, I assert that what is needed is for athletic activities—physical education and extracurricular activities—to be regarded as a necessary and integral part of the schooling process, along with academic subjects. Also discussed are the roles of concerned parents, educators, and community members in ensuring that marginalized students' academic performances are not compromised as a result of excessive involvement in athletic activities.

Conclusion: Toward More Inclusive Schooling for Student Athletes

Here I return to my belief that schools need to develop an equitable approach to education. Educators (including coaches) need to be cognizant of the systemic and institutional barriers that all students (and in my present focus, student athletes) face as they navigate and negotiate the education system. I argue, with reference to newspaper reports, interviews, and other sources, that if equity is going to be realized within the education system, then educators (and other stakeholders) should not merely be keeping students in school via activities that are perceived to be part of their cultural repertoire. Instead, schooling should be about recognizing the inter- and intra-diversity among the student population (in terms of factors such as gender, social class, ethnicity, religion, birthplace, and language), their differentiated and dynamic social realities, and how all these might be addressed through the education process. If all students, and student athletes in particular, are to receive a fair and just education, then the concern of educators and coaches should not be about using sports to keep marginalized youth in school merely to obtain a high school diploma, or to make it possible for them to be exposed to scouts and coaches. And providing students with scholarship information so that they can gain entry to American universities is not the solution. What good are these opportunities if they re-inscribe students' disadvantages, and do not serve to provide life-long skills and opportunities to the youth? In the end, the only beneficiary will be the school. Educators must think of how much the opportunities that students gain from their participation in sports really do make a difference in the students' lives. Are they indeed achieving equity and equal opportunity in education?

NOTES

1. BLAC, 1994; Codjoe, 2001; Dei et al., 1996; James, 1990; Kelly, 1998; Spence, 1999; Solomon, 1992.

2. I too have fielded questions about my playing basketball, and not about volleyball, which is the sport I played at one time. (Most likely, my height also had something to do with the questions.)

3. A version of this discussion appears in James (2003), "Schooling, basketball and US scholarship aspirations of Canadian student athletes." *Race, Ethnicity and Education*, 6(2), 126–129.

4. See Clarke, 1998; Day, 2000; James, 2003a; Walcott, 1997/2003.

5. Dei et al., 1997; Brathwaite & James, 1996; Contenta, 1993; Cummins, 1997; Gabor et al., 1996; Haig-Brown et al., 1997; Henry, 1998; Johal, 2002; Mayers, 2001; Pon, 2001.

5. Dei & Calliste, 2000; Graveline, 1998; Henry, 1998; Kell, 2000; Roman & Stanley, 1997.

6. Pon, 2000, p. 224; see also Lee, 2003; Li, 2001; James, 2003a, p. 146.

7. That is, while minority students are physically present in school, and are recognized for their abilities and skills, they do not fully engage with the resources that shape the school's overall program and activities.

8. Wilson (2002) points out that there are class-based differences in sports involvement, preferences, and tastes. These differences are linked to cultural and economic capital, which "enable upper class involvement in expensive sports, leaving prole sports (tougher sports with more physical contact) largely relegated to the lower classes" (p. 6; see also Armour, 2000).

9. Anisef et al., 2000; Brantlinger, 2003; Davis, 2004; Mayers, 2001.

10. Dei & Calliste, 2000; Graveline, 1998; Henry, 1998; Kell, 2000; Roman & Stanley, 1997.

11. With reference to the US context, Ewing et al. (2002) make the point that urban minority youth tend to grow up in poverty, a situation that is likely to be seen in Canada. And as Honora (2003) asserts, in light of the composition of many urban schools, minority students, in his case African Americans, tend to be vulnerable to an emotional detachment from school, hence jeopardizing their educational career (p. 59).

12. Not surprisingly, the host society is typically constructed as a homogeneous, exclusive group of people with a culture that immigrants or minority group members should recognize, digest, and eventually practise. Interestingly, it is the "same culture" that tends not to be acknowledged by the same "host" group when questioned about their culture. The idea is that they "have no culture," or that there is "no Canadian culture" (see James, 2003a, p. 33). It is important to point

out that a more appropriate construction of "host" society necessarily includes Aboriginals and minority groups who have existed in Canada and contributed to its constantly evolving culture.

13. In his discussion of the "racialization of space," Cohen (1996) argues that Whites (for instance, those in working-class communities) may feel in control of that space, but in recognizing that there are certain spaces within the larger society that are "colonized" by marginalized groups, they might come to resent such development and see the colonization as a threat or something dangerous. Borrowing from this notion, I argue that a similar trend may be found in school, and for minority group students who colonize spaces such as the school gym, hallways, classrooms, etc.; such space may represent a warm and friendly environment through which they can escape the larger perceived hostile racist school environment (James, 2002b).

14. In addition to being convenient and inexpensive, group interviews, as Fontana and Frey (1994, p. 365) write, have "the advantage of being data rich, flexible, stimulating to respondents, recall aiding, and cumulative and elaborative, over and above individual responses." And as was evident in our group discussion, in prompting each other, participants were able to use information that was unavailable to me (Hammersley & Atkinson, 1992).

"THAT'S WHY I COME TO SCHOOL": THE SIGNIFICANCE OF SPORTS TO THE HIGH SCHOOL PLANS OF GRADE EIGHT STUDENTS

with Everton Cummings[1]

MEET DWAYNE[2], A GRADE EIGHT STUDENT OF BLACK-CARIBBEAN CANADIAN background who lives with both parents and two older brothers. An excellent student athlete, Dwayne was on several of his school's basketball teams. He was described by his teachers as an average student who did not "always work to his potential," and as someone with "a great deal of leadership potential." His peers described him as a very bright student who was particularly good in mathematics. In early 1999, Dwayne, like most of his Grade Eight peers, participated in choosing the high school he wished to attend the coming fall term. Everton Cummings, his Physical Education teacher, interviewed Dwayne and 11 other student athletes at Westville Middle School about their choice of high schools and their educational and career aspirations. As the following interview reveals, sports was pivotal to Dwayne's choice of high school and how he thought of schooling.

E.C.: What high school are you planning to go to?

Dwayne: I am planning to go to either [Rainyside] or [Markway].

E.C.: You are supposed to go to [Westville] because of the boundaries. How are you going to get into [Markway] or [Rainyside] if you live here?

Dwayne: I think my parents are planning to move to the Markway area or I'll be living with my aunt. I have an aunt near [Markway] and

[Rainyside], so I'll probably be living with them in time. I think
I would want to go to Eastborough ... I heard things about it for
basketball ....

E.C.:   Do sports or playing basketball have a major part to play in terms
of the high school you want to attend?

Dwayne: Yeah. That's the point of me going to school. First basketball and
then I have to do the academic things to play basketball—like do
my work. That's the only reason I can play basketball. That's why
I come to school.

E.C.:   What do you want to do after you finish high school?

Dwayne: Go to university in the States. The big ones ....

Dwayne's comments indicate that his choice of high school was very much
related to his constructed aspirations and the reputation of the high school. In
fact, as Everton has observed from his eight years of teaching Grade Eight,
Dwayne is similar to many other student athletes who, because of the benefits
(e.g., recognition by peers and teachers) they derive from sports, choose to
attend high schools with a appropriate athletic program,[3] and hence maintain
their interest in school. This expectation, especially for male student athletes,
is well documented in both Canadian and American studies.[4]

Generally, as Everton observed, the vast majority of public school students
choose to attend the high school into which their middle school fed because
they felt it would provide the most comfort and familiarity, particularly because
that is where siblings and friends, who share interests, values, and aspirations,
have gone or will go.[5] And just like student athletes, there are those students
who base their choice of high schools on the subjects in which they have special
interests or strengths. For instance, those who were interested in Arts tended
to apply to a school with a strong Arts program, and likewise those with an
interest in business and/or technology.

We explore here the role sports play in school participation, and in the
educational and occupational plans and aspirations of Grade Eight students.
Specifically, we look at the students' choice of high school and high school
programs, and the connections they make between the high school they wish
to attend and their post-high school plans and aspirations. We consider the
importance of academic, social, athletic, and psychological factors on these
racial minority (particularly Black), Grade Eight student athletes' schooling
and educational plans. We also consider the role of race, class, and gender in

the constructed significance of sports in their educational lives, as well as the role and influence of significant others in their decision-making.

The chapter is organized as follows: (a) a brief review of literature pertaining to minorities in high school; (b) discussion of the methodology; (c) analysis of the findings; and (d) conclusions. In our discussion of the significance of sports to the high school program plans of respondents, we provide in some detail a discussion with Kabir and Dwayne. We make reference to their interview with Everton as way of demonstrating how these two student athletes talked about and conceptualized sports as part of their schooling.

SPORTS AND THE EDUCATIONAL AND CAREER/ OCCUPATIONAL PLANS OF BLACK STUDENTS

A majority of the studies of Black students in Canadian schools have focussed on those attending high schools.[6] Many of these studies report that among Black-Canadian high school students, especially males, sports are considered to be a significant aspect of their schooling, their future plans, and their lives in general. Specifically, the studies show that students, particularly male student athletes, sought to participate in sports not only for the educational possibilities, but also for its capacity to enable them to acquire athletic scholarships and eventually careers as professional athletes. For this reason, they chose to attend high schools where they would get exposure to university and college scouts.

Sports often serve as a context for important experiences in the lives of some youth, and sports participation can produce positive developmental outcomes when it expands the number and types of connections with others, broadening young people's ideas about who they are and how they are connected with that world. When sports programs teach skills, develop competence, and give young people opportunities to display that competence, self-esteem is promoted (Coakly, 2002). Further, involvement in sports provide many student athletes with opportunities to develop self-confidence and self-esteem (Eitle & Eitle, 2002a), something that some Black student athletes tend not to experience in their classrooms (where they are often subjected to low teacher expectation of their academic abilities) (James, 1995). Many of these students claim that it is in the gymnasium and on the sports field that they had the opportunity to display the superior skills, abilities, and competence that contributed to their self-confidence. Sports were also identified as a "hook" that not only served as an incentive for some student athletes to stay in school, but that also made school interesting, relevant, and challenging to them (James, 1995; Spence, 1999). Through sports, students would demonstrate their superior athletic skills and abilities, and the extent to which they can dominate an important and prestigious aspect of school life. Honora (2003) writes of African Americans in "urban school settings" who are "vulnerable to the development of an emotional detachment from school"; for students such as these, involvement in sports and other extracurricular activities affords them a way of identifying with their school community (p. 59).

The term "coping mechanism" is sometimes used to characterize the role that sports play in the lives of Black high school students for whom the school environment is alienating and discriminatory (James, 1990). In such an environment, sports have been used in ways that provide strategies for resisting the alienating and discriminatory school system (Milne, 1998; Solomon 1992). It is clear that Black students exercise agency in their attempts to make their schooling work for them. At times this exercise of agency takes the form of resistance, as Solomon (1992) found in his study of Black high school students. Participating in sports was so important to some of the "jocks" in his study that they would transfer from one high school to another if necessary. One of Solomon's respondents, Roy, was cited as an example of a student for whom playing sports was so important to his schooling that he refused to accept a promotion to an academically oriented school because he could not fit physical education into his timetable.

For many Black students, participating in sports is a means of countering the negative stereotypes existing within both schools and society. But while this approach may have reinforced the stereotype that Blacks are good athletes, many students place an over-reliance on sports to counter the negative stereotype that "Blacks are not good at anything." Therefore, participating in sports is one way that some Black high school students, and male student athletes in particular, feel they can assert themselves and gain the status and credibility in an institution that otherwise does not provide sufficient respect and recognition.

Eitle and Eitle (2002) found that it is difficult to pinpoint the exact relationship between participation in sports and students' academic achievement. They note that while some research indicates that participation in sports is associated with high educational aspiration for Blacks (see also Braddock et al., 1991; James, 1995), there is no evidence of corresponding high grades. In fact they argue that there is no "clear and consistent positive relationship between participation in sports and students' achievement, especially when racial and class difference have been considered" (p. 126). And based on their own study, they found that participation in sports such as basketball and football may limit students' academic achievement.

In terms of middle school students, Braddocks et al. (1991) found that Black students' involvement in intramural sports assisted them in developing a high degree of academic resilience and persistence. It helped them to reduce and control risk, establish and maintain self-esteem and self-efficacy, and create new opportunities for success. The researchers further established that there was a positive relationship between involvement in sports and academic resilience. For instance, sports participation was found to be positively associated with many of the respondents' aspirations to enrol in academic or college preparatory programs in high school, and their attainment of high social status among peers. The data also showed some positive connections between sports participation and pro-academic behaviours and attitudes. Specifically, student athletes were less likely to misbehave in school, less likely to be judged by teachers as not giving a full effort, and more likely to look forward to core classes.

Similarly, Hawkins et al. (1992) found that sports are very significant to the academic lives and educational aspirations of Black middle school students. This study focussed on sports participation and Black-American eighth-grade female students, and revealed that, like their male counterparts, females also derived many benefits as well as social status from their involvement in school sports, such as popularity and a sense of importance. Those involved in intra-mural sports were more likely to have plans to complete high school and attend college. In terms of pro-academic behaviours and attitudes, the results also showed that female student athletes were "less likely to miss classes and more likely to look forward to their core curriculum classes" (p. 22).

Writing of the four New York student athletes who saw basketball as a "ticket" out of their Coney Island housing project, Frey (1994) notes that being motivated to play basketball because of their athletic scholarship ambitions, they excelled at the sport. In that regard, when Stephon was ready to choose the high school he wished to attend, he was actively recruited by "every high school within a thirty-mile radius" of their neighbourhood—a practice that was contrary to the public school system (p. 156). Frey observes that it is not unusual to see student athletes "crisscrossing the city to play on their favourite teams" (p. 157).

Researching middle school male and female students demonstrates that, similar to their high school counterparts, sports play a significant role in their attitude and behaviour toward school, their academic performance, and their educational and career plans and aspirations. Sports provide them with important satisfaction in terms of their personal needs, as well as significant amounts of social, academic, and athletic success. Therefore, among Canadian middle school student athletes, we find that, like their high school counterparts, they perceive participating in school sports or extracurricular athletic activities to be useful and relevant to their current and future schooling and educational plans. Within this context, we discuss the extent to which opportunities to participate in athletic activities—in particular, to play on school teams—are likely to influence the student's choice of high school. It is important for educators to establish the significance of sports to middle school students (and Blacks in particular) because it is through sports that some students come to feel less alienated from the schooling process, and therefore engage more effectively with their school.

OUR STUDY OF WESTVILLE MIDDLE SCHOOL STUDENT ATHLETES

In exploring the relationship of athletic interests among Grade Eight students and how this may affect their choice of high school, Everton interviewed respondents and their teachers, as well as observing them in various athletic and academic activities and settings (e.g., the classroom and gym) in the middle school in which he taught. And since we were particularly interested in the experiences and aspirations of the Black students, he also conducted interviews with their parents. The research site, Westville Middle School, is a public Grades Six to Eight school that is located in a suburban area west of Toronto. It is a school where students participate in 130 minutes of scheduled physical education during every six-day cycle. They also have the opportunity to get involved in lunchtime and after school intramural program and school team activities. The teachers also contribute to sports programs by creating impromptu opportunities for sports participation.

Approximately 500 students, of which about one-third were in Grade Eight, attended the school. The population of the school was mostly White students of mainly European heritage (about 50 percent), South Asian students of Caribbean and Indian backgrounds, and Black students of Caribbean and African backgrounds (the majority of whom were Canadian-born of Caribbean origin). The predominance of Blacks, some 30 percent of the student population, made the school an appropriate site for examining the views, experiences, plans, and aspirations of Black students against those of other racial group students. In terms of social class, Everton notes from his observations and experiences with students that the school is located in a community that represents the spectrum of Canadian workers—from blue-collar workers who work on assembly lines, to white-collar workers, such as engineers. The students came from rented and family-owned households including apartments and single-family dwellings.

In our attempt to ascertain the extent to which race and gender influence the educational plans and choices of middle school students, 12 student athletes (six males and six females) representing Black (Dwayne, Courtney, Joan, Tania), White (Craig, John, Karen, Amy), and South Asian (Kabir, Naseer, Mona, Rashmit) were selected after being observed by Everton in their physical education and core subject classes. Following consultations with their core subject teachers who provided information about the students' academic work, personal strengths, and interests, measures were taken to choose respondents who were from the same socio-economic status, had similar academic abilities (as perceived by their teachers), demonstrated a strong commitment to sports, and were good or very good athletes.[7] Having respondents of different backgrounds participate in this study enabled us to compare and contrast how each student thought of her- or himself as a high school student, and the kinds of decisions regarding high school and educational future each was making. Once the respondents were selected and consented to participate in this study, two of their core-subject teachers were contacted and asked to participate in the study.

Eight one-hour sessions were spent observing each of the 12 students. Four sessions were spent observing each of them in their core subject classes, and four sessions observing each of them in physical education classes. Core subjects (language arts, math, and science), rather than rotary classes (art, music, design and technology, and family studies), were observed, which provided an opportunity to note differences in the students' behaviours and attitudes in a more academic environment. Observing the students' behaviours in their core classes also provided interesting and relevant information that could be compared to information from parents and teachers; many parents and educators value core subjects over physical education, and expect a higher level of commitment, performance, and seriousness on the part of students (James, 1996, see also Chapter 7). After completing the observations, in-depth interviews lasting about one hour were held with each of the 12 respondents and his/her core subject teacher. In many instances, what was said in the interview with students confirmed or clarified what had been observed in the gym or the classroom.

A second set of interviews were held with the four Black students, our focal respondents, their teacher, and one parent. In these interviews we sought to elicit their experiences with, and perceptions, insights, and assessment of the students' plans and aspirations. We also wanted to establish the differences, if any, in the parents' aspirations for their children. These interviews with the students and their teachers and parents contributed to a "triangulation" (Bowen, 1978) of the data, and created space for a variety of voices and a diversity of perceptions, which enabled us to view events in a complex and integrated way (Anderson et al., 1994).

Indeed, in the tradition of qualitative investigation (Denzin & Lincoln, 1994), we aim to show the complexity, diversity, and variability of the students' experiences, choices, plans, and aspirations. As Denzin and Lincoln (1994) write:

> Qualitative research is multi-method in focus, involving an interpretive, naturalistic approach to its subject matter. This means that qualitative researchers study things in their natural settings, attempting to make sense of, or interpret, phenomena in terms of the meanings people bring to them .... Accordingly, qualitative researchers deploy a wide range of interconnected methods, hoping always to get a better fix on the subject matter at hand (p. 2).

A further important aspect of our research methodology is the "teacher as researcher" approach, which we believe enabled us to not only obtain a "thick" description (Geetz, 1973) of the routines, stages, and meanings of the students' lives, but also get a "better fix" on the issues. In his role as teacher-researcher, Everton observed and interviewed students, parents, and teachers whom he knew and with whom he had previous relationships. Indeed, as Anderson et al. (1994) point out, "there is no way an outsider, even an ethnographer, who spends years observing, can acquire tacit knowledge of the setting that those who must act within it daily possess" (p. 5).

This familiarity with the research site and participants engendered trust and helped to reduce reservations that respondents may have had about disclosing personal information.[8] And as Everton commented: "In many instances, the formal interviews I had scheduled resembled the very candid and informal conversations that I engaged in with students on a regular basis" (November, 1998).

THE HIGH SCHOOL PLANS AND ASPIRATIONS OF WESTVILLE MIDDLE SCHOOL STUDENTS

Like many of their peers, the Grade Eight students who participated in this study indicated that they spent a significant amount of time thinking about their coming high school years and expressed a variety of ideas, concerns, and plans when they were asked about the high school they were planning to attend. Several of them identified the need to be close to friends and home as important criteria in their plans and decisions to attend a given high school. A few students described the ideal school as providing them with what they, or their parents, believed was a superior education compared to that of the local high school they were expected to attend. They expected the high school to provide an environment in which they would be academically successful, and to effectively facilitate their post-secondary and occupational plans and aspirations.

With the exception of two students, the factors that seemed to most influence the choice of high school were friends[9] and the proximity of the school to their homes. Mona suggested that she planned to attend Eastborough High School "because the majority of my friends are going there." Having siblings at the high school was not as significant as having friends. For instance, when Rashmit was asked if she was going to the high school her sisters attended, she said: "Kind of, but mainly all my friends are going there." Other students, such as Craig, felt that "not having to go too far to school" was an important factor to consider in his decision regarding which high school to attend. Of his two options, Craig chose the one that he could get to by "just having to walk down the street." Identifying location and friends as key factors in the students' choice of high schools may be related to their anticipation of the new school as being stressful and strange (see Balk, 1995; Kelly, 1998).

Significant to the students' choice of high school was the quality of the education and the learning environment of the high school. They wanted high-quality education, as well as an experience that was conducive to productive work. But while most of the respondents focussed on what the high school could offer them toward their future successes, one student, Amy, considered to be an average student, suggested that the high school's academic program was not the real concern; rather it "depends on the individual, how they [sic] put themselves in a situation to learn or not to learn."

For the most part students such as Tania (also described as an average student) felt that they could not achieve what they wanted at high school unless they placed themselves in an environment that was conducive to learning. For instance, when Tania was asked why she was not planning to attend the same high school as most other Westville students, she said that the less popular local high school was "a school where you want to learn and where you would find people working .... If I went to [Eastern—the more popular school] I think I would goof off and not focus on my work and not achieve what I want to achieve." Other students like Karen talked of the advantages of going to a School of the Arts to further her desire to become an artistic director. Dwayne, on the other hand, indicated that his choice was influenced by access to college scouts who offered basketball scholarships.

While all of the respondents reported that they enjoyed physical activities and their gym classes,[10] few said that sports were a significant aspect of their choice of high school and future plans. Others indicated that sports do influence their choice of high school. Craig, for example, claimed that he was going to Eastborough "for the sports," and Rashmit, when asked if she would choose an academically oriented school over one with a strong sports program, said that she "would choose the other one with physical education." Even Joan, who was probably less athletically active than most of the students, revealed that sports had some influence on her choice of high school. As she put it, "I like having phys. ed. I like taking part in sports. If I can't do sports, that's one thing, but I still enjoy it." And Tania, who earlier had expressed that she wanted to attend a high school with an academic environment that was ideal for learning and studying, indicated that she would "feel kind of bad" if there was too much emphasis on academics at the high school she chose to attend.

Interestingly, the students, mainly males, who were considering a career in athletics suggested that they did not give much consideration to friendships (specifically their non-athletic friends) when choosing their high school. As Dwayne remarked, "friends are not a priority; there will always be time for friends." When asked how he felt about separating from his friends and going to a different school, Dwayne replied that "it does not matter" because he could visit the schools that they were planning to attend.

For the most part, the students in this study believed that school sports were important because they provided an opportunity to have fun while interacting with peers. Dwayne suggested that participating in sports was a motivation for academic work, and this is why it was important for him to have physical education as part of his high school program. Mona also valued sports, which provided students with an opportunity "to learn good sportsmanship" and "to work co-operatively with others." She thought learning about an important issue was best accomplished in a fun and enjoyable learning environment. Both Naseer and Joan indicated that sports were important because they provided students with an opportunity to be active, something that was necessary in order to maintain good health and fitness.

Most of the students who participated in this study indicated that they were planning or hoping to attend a university or college. In explaining this, some indicated that their university plans were closely related to their occupational plans. For example, Kabir expected to attend university "so I can have a career." Rashmit revealed that she had been investigating university as a post-secondary school option because she "wanted to go into journalism," and Karen indicated that she might go to York University so that she could "get into directing" (i.e., become an artistic director). With regard to their occupational or career aspirations, the students talked about becoming police officers, mechanics, engineers, teachers, doctors, lawyers, or professional athletes. But generally, they seemed to have what might be termed "a bank of career options;"[11] specifically, they all identified at least two occupations of interest. For example, when Carlton was asked about his aspirations, he responded by saying, "I want to be a doctor, or I want to be a police officer." One of the two careers to which four of the (not surprisingly) male students—one White (Craig), one South Asian (Kabir), and two Blacks (Dwayne, Courtney)—aspired were athletics. However, the significance of sports to the plans of the White and South Asian students did not appear to be as great as it was for the two Black male students, who appeared to have a greater commitment to this goal.

Interests in particular careers or occupations tended to be based on whether they were "fun" and whether they "paid well." For instance, Kabir stated that he would not mind being a mechanic like his father because "it looks like fun, it's not boring, and you get paid." Similarly, Dwayne was interested in a career in basketball because it would be "one of the funniest jobs to do, play basketball and get money for it." Some students, such as Joan, brought up the fact that they were not interested in a teaching career because "teachers' money starts in the sink [low]."

THE SIGNIFICANCE OF SPORTS AND ATHLETIC ACTIVITIES TO THE PLANS AND ASPIRATIONS OF STUDENTS

Nine of the 12 students who participated in our study thought that sports and physical education were important to their high school program because they provided them a "break" from their "academic subjects" and the "boredom" of the classroom (see Spence, 1999). Some students indicated that school would be difficult to endure without sports. As Dwayne said, "Without sports or physical education, school would be boring. Kids would get tired of doing the work ... [and] people would get bad grades because they would skip school more." Thinking that a change of pace from their academic classes will be necessary and indeed beneficial in high school, many of the students suggested that they have valid reasons for having physical education as part of their high school program. Even Karen, who was least interested in physical activities, felt that taking physical education in high school was worthwhile because it provided "time to relax ..., do something energetic and not just sit down to do school work." Earlier, Karen had said that friends were "very important" to her and they were one of the reasons why she participated in sports—"it's why I do it [sports] the most. To be with them [friends] ...." So for Karen and others, physical education provides opportunities to play sports and interact with friends. But according to Amy, compared to middle school, physical education during high school would not be as good because "they split up the classes, girls and boys, and they say you have to do a lot of writing. Not as much playing basketball or going out and playing soccer. Stuff like we have here [in Grade Eight]."

Some of the students, particularly the Black students, anticipated that high school would be just as disaffirming as middle school, and they would need to use sports as a way of counteracting alienation and low teacher expectations, and to gain recognition and respect. For instance, Tania, a Black student, observed that "they [Black students] think school won't help them [and] won't get them through anything." And referring to conversations she has had with "Black friends," Mona, an Asian, suggested that Black students were not as respected in classes as Asian and White students, and were not "getting the rights they deserved." Referring to his experience of teachers' expectations, Dwayne pointed out that teachers did not expect him to do well in classes: "they expect me to do bad things in the classroom, and they'll look at me more than the other students, like keep a watch on me." However, when it came to basketball, teachers reacted differently to him. He was respected "for basketball, but not for academics." Karen concurred in her observations that Dwayne and other Black male student athletes like him were recognized and respected differently when they were in the gym compared to when they were in the classroom. She said: "When they're in the gym, it's like they're bigger! It's like they're a superstar! When they're in the classroom it's like they're a nobody."

In terms of their involvement in sports after high school, five of the six male students indicated that athletic scholarships and careers in sports athletes would be exciting, but as two of the five noted that the chances of these opportunities becoming a reality were "slim." These two students (Kabir and Craig) also indicated that they would not be disappointed if they did not receive scholarships or attain athletic careers. For example, when Kabir was asked if he envisioned himself with a career in athletics, he replied: "I doubt I am going to make a professional career in sports."

None of the female students claimed to be interested in athletic scholarships or careers in athletics. Nevertheless, like their male counterparts, a few acknowledged that a scholarship or a career in athletics would be a welcome opportunity, but it was not a goal that they would actively pursue. However, several of them indicated that sports would continue to be an important part of their lives, if only, as Rashmit made clear, for recreational purposes or as a means of securing a job. Tania, on the other hand, indicated that she would like to run in the Olympics for the fun of being an Olympic athlete.

Craig, a White student, and Dwayne and Courtney, both Black, were the only students who indicated that sports were a significant component of their educational and career plans. They indicated that they were currently active in sports, and had aspirations of attaining athletic scholarships and careers as professional athletes. However, of the three, Craig seemed to be the one who would be least disappointed if his plans and aspirations did not materialize. This was evident during the interview with Craig. A number of times he indicated that he would "drop off" a team or "ease off" on sports if it was interfering with his school work. In contrast, while Dwayne and Courtney acknowledged that participation in sports might undermine their academic work, at no time during the interview did they indicate that they would curtail their involvement in sports in order to concentrate on academic work. This difference in the role of sports in the lives of these student athletes might be explained by the fact that Black student athletes tend to "carry a greater burden than your White counterparts" with regard to expectations (Shropshire, 2002, p. 136).

Evidently, while all of the students who participated in this study were actively involved in school sports and physical activities, understandably, sports had different meanings for them and their futures. It is not surprising that the females did not see the possibility of achieving educational scholarships through sports nor an occupation in sports. Indeed, from the media as well as their own personal experiences, they hear of athletic scholarship being won mostly by males (and in fact, were unable to name any females with athletic scholarships). For their part, the males, and Black males in particular, understood and hence constructed sports as an activity that would enable them to cope with and to eventually complete high school, to acquire a post-secondary education, and to eventually obtain a high-paying career. This was possible only if they obtained scholarships. As demonstrated by Craig, Dwayne, and Courtney, race, among other factors, seemed to mediate their perceptions of the opportunities and possibilities that sports can provide them.[12] Consider how Kabir and Dwayne, two of the most celebrated student athletes, think and talk about (in their interview with Everton) their expectations and aspirations related to sports. We discuss their comments to show how they process what they believe that sports can offer them. Here is a a brief background of both students.

Kabir was born in Canada of South Asian parents (from India) and had been living with his parents, brother, and sister. He was described by his teachers as a very active and talented student athlete who had represented the school on several sports teams, and had enthusiastically participated in his physical education classes. Kabir also played on an ice hockey team in the community. Academically, Kabir was described as "an average student who did not always work to his potential." His mathematics teacher said that he was sometimes disruptive in classes, especially when he was uninterested in the work. Rather than attend the high school into which Westville fed, Kabir planned to attend the other local high school that his older siblings attended. And like most of the students in this study, Kabir felt that sports were a source of enjoyment, an opportunity to be with friends, and a means of staying healthy and fit, but that sports did not play a major role in his future educational and occupational plans. He suggested that while an athletic scholarship and a career in sports would be ideal, it was not necessarily realistic. He was mainly concerned with doing well in school and working toward a number of career options.

E.C.: What are you looking forward to the most about high school?

Kabir: Getting good grades and sports.

E.C.: If you had to make a list of the most important things about high school, what would the list look like?

Kabir: Grades.

E.C.: Grades are first. What's second?

Kabir: Sports.

E.C.: How important is it that sports be a part of your timetable?

Kabir: I can have a professional career ....

E.C.: So do you see sports as part of your future career?

Kabir: I think I'll be playing it [sports] a lot, but I am not sure about getting paid for it .... If I don't make it to the NBA ... when my children—if I have a boy—when he's three I'll raise him [to] play a sport and he'll probably have a professional career. I have a big desire for my child to play in a league, a professional career in sports.

E.C.: What about you, though?

Kabir: Me? I doubt that I am going to make a professional career in sports.

E.C.: How far do you plan to go in high school?

Kabir: Academically, up to Grade Thirteen (OAC). Finish Grade Thirteen and go to university, and try to go to an American university. I am going to try my hardest to get a scholarship for basketball.

E.C.: Suppose you don't get that scholarship—how will you feel?

Kabir: I won't really care .... The only way I'll be mad is if I don't have good grades. If I don't have good grades, I am not going to be accepted at no university.

E.C.: Why do you want to go to university?

Kabir: So I can have a career.

E.C.: Have you thought about anything besides the sports career?

Kabir: I want to be a mechanic or an engineer.

Interestingly, while Kabir (like others in the study) did not believe that a sports career was realistic, he held out hope, however faint, of achieving an athletic scholarship to an American university. This reflects that at this age, students consider all of their options, with a focus on their strength, abilities, and the recognition that they receive from significant others like teachers and parents. But Kabir was pragmatic: he realized that he might never make it in sports, so in his youthful way, he speculated that if he did not, he would ensure that his son did. Evidently, Kabir understood, possibly through his family and friends, the idea of living vicariously through children.

Like Kabir, Dwayne also saw sports in his future. But unlike Kabir, he was optimistic that he would achieve his athletic ambitions. Described as an excellent student athlete, Dwayne was a member of several of the school's sports teams and an active participant in his physical education classes. He came close to winning the "Male Athlete of the Year Award" at one time, but because of his attitude toward, and performance in, his academic work, he was not selected. But for Dwayne, sports, especially basketball, not only provided enjoyment and a means of coping with school life, but through sports he also received recognition and respect from both his teachers and peers. It is understandable why the opportunity to play basketball would influence Dwayne's choice of high school and his future plans and aspirations.

We earlier quoted Dwayne's intention to attend one of three high schools, all of which were renowned for basketball, and all of which were in the suburban area of Toronto, outside his community, with one in downtown Toronto. Given the importance of sports to his education and career aspirations, he and his parents were prepared to re-locate near the school he chose to attend. But when he was asked to think about the difficulty of entering the high school he had in mind, Dwayne was undeterred and remained optimistic.

E.C.: Don't you think it will be difficult getting into Markway or Rainyside?

Dwayne: No, because people, the "superstars"—older students who play basketball well—who went to Eastborough and didn't make it, said if you are a good basketball player, don't make the same mistake I made. Try to go to a different school.

E.C.: Is the decision to go to these schools your personal decision? Is this is what you want to do?

Dwayne: Yeah. I have to make a decision. They [parents] are just giving me advice. There is just one chance in life to make it. I may as well go to the school that everyone is telling me. I just have to sacrifice and go to those schools.

E.C.: Do sports or playing basketball have a major part to play in terms of the high school you want to attend?

Dwayne: Yeah. That's the point of me going to school. First basketball and then I have to do the academic things to play basketball, like do my work. That's the only reason I can play basketball. That's why I come to school.

E.C.: What do you want to do after you finish high school?

Dwayne: Go to university in the States. The big ones, Georgetown, Kentucky[13]...

E.C.: Do you have any fears about the academic part of school?

Dwayne: Nah, 'cause if I am playing basketball, they say that will push me to do well academically.

E.C.: At what point during high school do you think you will know that basketball is not going to be a part of your future?

Dwayne: By Grade Twelve I have to be playing basketball. If I am not starting and I am not a "superstar," then I will know that basketball will not be my number one ...

E.C.: Are you thinking of any other occupation right now?

Dwayne: No.

E.C.: How determined are you? How badly do you want to be involved in basketball?

Dwayne: I want to make it far because if you play basketball for money that's a fun thing to do. That's one of the funniest jobs to do. Playing basketball and getting money for it.

Compared to Kabir, Dwayne was quite confident that through sports, he would succeed educationally and occupationally. Some reasons for this might be due to the fact that his parents (as we will see further in the next section) were supportive of his aspirations and the strategies for achieving them. Teachers and community members have also been known to be supportive of the athletic aspirations of students. For instance, while Mrs. Bethune, a Black teacher at Westville, did not say that she encouraged students in sports, she did agree that sports were useful for Black students because they afforded them the opportunity to experience success in at least one area of their schooling. Hence, sports can be a way of counteracting failure, frustration, and negativity. It is also likely that the recognition Dwayne received from sports, as well as the examples and/or role models of Black-Canadian youth who have managed to obtain sports scholarships to play for the "big" American universities, made it possible for him to believe that he can "make it" in sports.

PARENTAL ROLE AND INFLUENCE IN THE HIGH SCHOOL PLANS AND EDUCATIONAL ASPIRATIONS OF STUDENTS

Evidently, parents play an influential role in the students' constructions of their plans and aspirations, especially at this important transition stage of their children's lives. In this regard, we interviewed the parents of the Black and South Asian students in order to understand their roles, as well as their perspectives and involvement in their children's decision-making. They all indicated that they were supportive of their children's plans and aspirations, but some said that they tried not to deliberately influence their decisions. All of the parents were able to talk specifically of their children's educational and occupational plans, goals, and aspirations. For example, Mr. Brown, Dwayne's father, correctly indicated that "Dwayne is thinking in terms of [Markway] or [Rainyside]." Similarly, Mrs. Sidney, Tania's mother, demonstrating her knowledge of Tania's aspirations, said that she knew that Tania "has two dreams—she wants to be a teacher and she wants to go to the Olympics."

Compared to their children, parents seemed to be more concerned with the quality of education and the type of learning environment high schools provide. For example, Craig's and Naseer's parents believed that their sons should consider attending schools outside of the community, schools that they perceived to have superior "academic" standards to those of the high school into which Westville fed. For this reason, Mr. Brown (Dwayne's father) and Mrs. Sidney (Tania's mother) expressed some concerns about their children attending Eastern because they felt that the school would not provide the type of academic "challenge" that they felt their children needed. Mr. Brown said: "I think Eastern is ruled out. We don't want him [Dwayne] to go to Eastern. I don't think his mom wants him to go to Eastern and I don't think he wants to go to Eastern. He was thinking in terms of [Markway] or [Rainyside]."

The parents revealed that they had conversations with their children about their educational and occupational plans and aspirations. But in most cases, the parents seemed to have left it to their children to choose the high school they wished to attend, saying that it was "their children's decision to make." And while most of the parents expressed concerns about a particular high school or their preference for another, they still seemed to be allowing their children to make the final decision. Mrs. Sidney was concerned about the high school Tania would be attending, yet, despite her concerns, she left the decision to Tania. When asked why she did not insist that Tania attend Crawford, a denominational school that was her preference, as opposed to Markway, Mrs. Sidney explained: "I tried that but she doesn't want to go. She wants to go to [Markway]; she doesn't want to go to Crawford."

Several parents and students claimed that the decision about high school was based on negotiation. But it seemed that, as in the case of Tania, these negotiations did not always produce the desired results. So in settling their differences, and to ensure that their children approached their high school years feeling satisfied that they had played a role in the choice of school, parents reluctantly left the final decision to their children. But there were those students for whom there was no negotiating with their parents. In such cases, as with Amy, parents asserted their right as parents to make such decisions. Conversely, some students exercised their right to make the decision and, as in the case of Mr. Edwards (Courtney's father), the parents were unaware of his son's plans and decisions.

While some of the parents agreed that sports were an important aspect of their children's schooling that might help them to cope with the challenges of school, they did not all support choosing high school on the basis of athletic opportunities. Despite his assertion that school without sports would be "boring" and a "waste of time," Kabir understood that, given his parents' feelings, he should not choose a high school on the basis of sports alone. However, some parents, particularly those of the Black students, were willing to encourage attending a high school that would make sports participation possible, given this potential to inspire a greater interest in school. Some of these Black parents reasoned that a positive attitude toward high school would lead to good behaviour—which, of course, they welcomed.

This idea was evident in Mrs. Edwards's response to the question of whether the privilege to participate in sports should be taken away from Black students who misbehaved in school. She said: "It's going to make them worse. They're going to get angrier and they're going to hate the teacher .... They should punish them like sending them to the office or somewhere to do their work, but don't take away their sports ...." Mrs. Tate likewise suggested that sports have a beneficial effect on Black male students: "If they're frustrated because of the suspension, they kick the ball and get rid of their frustration." The implication here is that sports help students to cope with difficult school situations.[14]

Furthermore, what we might infer from these comments is that these parents were seeking to ensure that the relationship between students and school did not become more alienating than it was already. Hence, they advocated that opportunities to participate in sports should be something that teachers and administrator did not deny students.

Further, some parents (specifically those of Dwayne and Courtney) understood and supported their sons in their pursuit of sports as a means of attaining their educational and career goals. Recall that Dwayne was the student who confidently expressed his desire to win a scholarship and attend an American university; eventually, he hoped, he would have a career in sports. His father discussed with Everton his support for Dwayne's aspirations:

> Mr. B.: I would be supportive. If he can get a scholarship, even if he don't end up in pro[fessional] [basket]ball, he [can] get a degree or certificate. He can come back and get a job. The idea is to at least get something in his head. He is one of the few guys who I think would survive both as an athlete and an academic.
>
> E.C.: How supportive would you be if he wanted to play in the NBA [National Basketball Association]?
>
> Mr. B.: Well, as a parent, to me, even though academics come first, to me finance is more important .... The bottom line is finances in North American society, especially if you are a teenager. Five years from now he'll be an adult, so he also got to look after himself.

Like Mr. Brown, both Mr. and Mrs. Edwards (Courtney's parents) said that they would be very supportive of Courtney if it was possible for him receive an athletic scholarship. Mrs. Edwards suggested this would be an excellent opportunity because Courtney could get his education, and then possibly "get into sports big time and [earn] bigger money." With such support from their parents, particularly at this stage of their lives (see Larter, 1982, p. 133), it is understandable that student athletes like Dwayne and Courtney would be confident about their sports plans and aspirations.[15]

Generally, our research shows that the parents of the students in this study tended to give their children the opportunity to take part in the decision-making process about which high school to attend. Some parents even gave their children the responsibility of making the final decision. There are three possible explanations for the children's role in the decision-making process.

The responsibility for deciding might have been given to the child as a means of supporting her or his empowerment and development of independence. Second, limited communication within the family (Courtney being a case in point) left the child to make the decision without the expectation of consulting with the parents. Finally, it is also possible that the above two situations exist because parents, most of whom are immigrants, believed that they could offer little help in their children's decisions, given their limited knowledge of the education system. But even though the latter might have been the case, it is not clear that all of these parents really liked their children making such an important decision on their own; nevertheless, in some cases some of the parents reluctantly agreed.

Interestingly, the parents did not talk about asking teachers for input into the discussion of which high school to attend. Apparently, there was very little contact between the parents and teachers, and the students seemed unwilling to engage the teachers. This might reflect the fact that teachers had very little in-class discussion with students about their plans for high school. However, one teacher, Mrs. Bethune, did indicate that she provided students with information about high schools. As part of this information process, she invited former Westville students, who were now in high school, to come to her class to talk to the current Grade Eight students.

CONCLUSION: MAKING THE TRANSITION FROM MIDDLE SCHOOL TO HIGH SCHOOL

In this study we explored the role sports played in Grade Eight student athletes' choice of high school and their educational and occupational plans and aspirations. By way of comparison, we explored the role and significance of school sports to the plans and aspirations of White, South Asian, and Black students, and of the parents of the Black students.

Our findings reveal that sports were a significant aspect of this group of Grade Eight students' schooling. For most students, regardless of race or gender, sports were valued because they provided them with enjoyment, as well as the opportunity to socialize with friends,[16] to stay fit and healthy, and to cope with the boredom and alienation of school. The female students tended to value sports for the social aspects, as opposed to the competition that the boys sought. This competitiveness and serious approach to the game was quite evident in the observations of the boys' play in the gym. Most of the boys' games entailed scoring, where a clear winner was usually decided. Hence, several of the girls observed that boys took the game "too seriously." For the Black male students in particular, participation in sports was their way of gaining respect and recognition, and to counter some of the alienation they experienced in school.

Nearly all of the students indicated that they enjoyed school sports and physical education, and, if given the option, they would include sports activities in their future school programs. At the same time, most of them indicated that they were more concerned with getting good grades in order to attend university. Those for whom good grades were a concern said that they could tolerate decreasing their participation in sport activities. But many of these student athletes indicated that they would be upset if the high school they eventually attended were to restrict opportunity for sports activities. Both Black male students indicated that their academic work was important, but it did not appear to be as important as playing basketball and seeking an athletic scholarship. This finding is not overly surprising. Harris (1991), in a study that compared White and Black high school student athletes, found that Black students were more likely than White students to view basketball as an "opportunity to compete for a place in college and the professional world" (p. 147).

Based on the findings in this study, it would appear that issues pertaining to sports, race, and gender are often highly complex. Importantly, then, our findings underscore the influence of race and gender on student athletes' interests in sports. In this regard, therefore, we cannot conclude that sports are more significant to the schooling, plans, and aspirations of students belonging to a particular racial or ethnic group or of a particular gender (see also Eitle & Eitle, 2002a). More precisely, we infer that sports are more significant to Black Grade Eight male students. Such a conclusion could be perceived as untenable, since both the male and female students in this study, from each ethno-racial background, presented different, as well as similar, values, interests, and commitments to sports and schooling. These findings cannot be used as an indication of how they view the possibilities of sports in high school.

Of the 12 student athletes who participated in this study, only three males indicated that sports were still valuable components of their educational and occupational plans. These three males—one White and two Black—indicated that sports were important to their future plans. But at 14 years old, it is understandable that they would be limited in their articulation of the significance of sports to their future education and occupational plans. It is difficult to identify the outcomes of these students' plans and aspirations given this "haziness." For instance, Kabir indicated that he was very serious about sports and wanted to achieve an athletic scholarship, but at the same time he explained that sports was not a very serious component of his future plans (and hence did not think that obtaining such a scholarship was a possibility).

The Black student athletes, specifically the males, showed great interest in sports and were determined to make them a meaningful component of their high school career, but this is no indication of what will happen once they enter high school. However, it is understandable that because they have been able to negotiate sports in middle school, they would plan on the same in high school. Hence, given their middle school experiences and media images/information (Campbell, June 3, 2003; see also Chapters 2 and 4), it is logical that Dwayne and Courtney (compared to Kabir and Craig, who were similarly enthusiastic about sports) would emphasize a determination to use sports to help them realize their educational ambitions. And while the females were less inclined to give the same prominence to sports, they did see the value of sports, and as such used sports in beneficial ways. So while the males articulated their intentions of seeing how far sports could take them educationally, the girls did not see any future in sports.

Our findings are consistent with studies of Toronto high school students, which show that sports operate to connect some Black male students to school, provide them with opportunities to assert and empower themselves, and inspire their future educational and career plans and aspirations (Spence, 1996; James, 1990; Solomon, 1992). It is worth noting that, like some of his Toronto counterparts (see Chapter 4), Dwayne, with the support of his parents, was willing to move (see also Frey's [1994] discussion of New York City middle school students).

In schools such as Westville, where sports seem to be significant to a portion of the student population, teachers, coaches, and guidance counsellors should talk about post-secondary and career options in sports in order to help students make decisions about high school, the level of program, and the most suitable. Such an undertaking would not only be a relevant component of a teaching unit, social studies, or guidance curriculum, but would also help students to develop a more realistic outlook on the possibilities of sports participation. Moreover, a focus on the opportunities that students may derive from sports would be particularly useful for Black male students like Dwayne and Courtney who tend to rely, many times exclusively, on sports as their connection to, and means of coping with, school, sometimes at the expense of their commitment to academic work.

Like other parents, community members, and scholars, who have been following Black student athletes' sports participation and academic achievements over the years, we support the notion of finding ways to "infuse" sports within various areas of school curriculum. For example, topics such as "the science of sports" (nutrition, physiology, mechanics, etc.), "race and sports," and "sports and career opportunities" could be explored as a component of the language arts, social studies or guidance programs. We believe that there is some merit to the former North York Board of Education BASE (Balancing Athletics, School, and Education) Program, which was designed to help student athletes achieve a balance between athletic participation and academic performance (see also Spence, 1996). Wherever possible, since sports can be a positive aspect of many students' schooling, measures should be taken to encourage participation in sports, and at the same time insist on high academic performance and in the process reinforce students' connection to school. Schools, both high schools and middle schools, need to evolve a culture in which all students live with the belief that excelling in sports and academics is not contradictory; if anything, one complements the other. Indeed, academic success is not contradictory to athletic success.

NOTES

1. Everton Cummings currently teaches at Shortwood Teacher Training College in Kingston, Jamaica. Before this, he taught middle school for more than 10 years with the Peel Board of Education in Ontario. He holds a graduate degree in education, and an undergraduate degree in Physical Education and Geography. He has been a youth worker, as well as a school and community basketball and soccer coach.
2. All names of individuals and schools are pseudonyms.
3. By appropriate athletic programs, we mean ones that would provide opportunities to develop skills, adequate playing time, and chances to be exposed to scouts. Schools that do not provide these opportunities would be perceived as having an inferior program and therefore student athletes would refuse to attend these high schools.
4. Braddock et al., 1991; Eitle & Eitle, 2002a; Fredricks et al., 2002; Honora, 2003; Frey, 1994; Harris, 1991; Hawkins, 1992; James, 1995; Spence, 1996; Solomon, 1992.

5. Some students, usually with considerable influence from parents, chose to enroll in the local separate (or non-public) school system as a means of avoiding a public high school with a perceived "unfavourable" reputation.

6. Codjoe, 2002; Dei et al., 1997; James, 1990; Kelly, 1998; Head, 1975; Spence, 1999; Solomon, 1992.

7. While Everton had taught some of the students physical education in earlier grades, none of them were in any of his classes at the time. This made it possible to talk with students without fear of the discussion affecting their grades. But this is not to suggest that the students might not have thought of other implications. The important point here is that Everton was careful in ensuring that these respondents were comfortable in participating in this project.

8. Nonetheless, we are well aware that there are possible disadvantages to studying one's own school. While being an "insider" might have served to enrich the data we collected, there is also the possibility that a teacher—an authority figure in the school—could have influenced some students to provide what they perceived to be the correct answers—the answers they perceived Everton wanted to hear.

9. There was little to no gender and racial differences in the importance of friends. Males and females identified friends as significant to their schooling, and with the exception of one White and one Black student, all others identified attending schools with friends as significant to their choice of school.

10. All, except two, were members of at least one school sports team.

11. Both the Toronto Board of Education Every Secondary Student Survey (Cheng, Yau, & Ziegler, 1993), and the Community-Based Education for Work and Living (CAWL) Pilot Project (1994) found that early adolescent students were actively thinking about several career possibilities.

12. See also Honora, 2003; James, 1995; Frey, 1994; Shropshire, 2002.

13. These American universities are well known to the students for their basketball teams.

14. These ideas seem to concur with those of Mrs. Bethune, who, as we have already noted, viewed sports as something that could be used to help Black students cope with school.

15. Interestingly, according to Craig, while his parents were supportive of his sports aspirations, they were quite definite about him attending a high school that was known more for "academics" than athletics.

16. In some cases, the opportunity to be with friends was given as a factor that influenced their decision to attend a particular high school. This is consistent with other research findings that show that friends are very important to students at this age (Balk, 1995; Kelly, 1998; Slavin, 1991; Vappu, 2001; Woolfolk, 1990). Through friends students have familiarity and some comfort in dealing with the stress involved in the transition to a new school (Balk, 1995).

RACE AND THE SOCIAL/ CULTURAL WORLDS OF STUDENT ATHLETES

Hi Carl,

A quick glance through the pages of my old high school yearbook paints a picture of a school with a student population representing a variety of cultures. Page after page, the yearbook displays photographs showing a multitude of white, black, and brown faces. That is, of course, until you get to the sports team photos, where quite a different picture begins to emerge. If one were to randomly open my school yearbook at boys' basketball team's photograph, one would see a group of almost exclusively Black faces. By contrast, the school's hockey team photo is filled with White faces. Why such an obvious racial divide along sporting lines in a school with such a racially mixed student population? What follows is a short reflection about my experiences as a White male high school student athlete, and some possible answers to these questions.

I went to school in Montreal, where high school begins in Grade Seven and lasts until Grade Eleven (from 12 until about 17 years). By the time I got to high school, I was already serious about playing baseball (which I did during the summers), and I wanted to get serious about playing basketball, a sport that I had only played recreationally up until then. Although I don't remember much about my first day of high school, I do remember that on that day my most important concern was finding out when the school basketball tryouts were. The same was true for many of my friends, who themselves were representative of our school in the diversity of their collective backgrounds. When the day of basketball tryouts finally did arrive several weeks later, our coach made a surprise announcement. In an effort to increase enrollment for volleyball, which he was also coaching, he announced that any student who would agree to play volleyball would get an automatic spot on the basketball team. For that reason alone, several players, myself included, decided to play volleyball. Never mind that many of us had never even played the sport. It was worth learning if it could get us a spot on the basketball team.

That first year and the following year as well, I played both basketball and volleyball for my school team. Both teams were quite mixed racially, and we enjoyed a lot of success, particularly in my second year, when we won the Greater Montreal Athletic Association city championships in both sports. However, as the years went on, the racial demographics of both teams began to change significantly. To put it simply, the volleyball team started to get a lot "whiter" and the basketball team a lot "blacker." By my senior year of high school, only two Black players remained on the volleyball team. Conversely, on the basketball team the number of White players decreased to zero. My own choices regarding the sports I played reflected this pattern. Ironically, while I had only joined the volleyball team to ensure a spot on the basketball team, I decided to quit playing basketball after my second year of high school. As for volleyball, I continued playing throughout my five years of school.

Why did I choose to stop playing basketball? One reason had to do with my skill level. Although I had been one of the better players on the team during my eighth-grade year, I can remember coming back to school from summer vacation the next year and playing a game of pick-up basketball with my teammates. I had been playing baseball all summer and hadn't even touched a basketball during those months. It was obvious that many of my teammates had. As we played, I can remember getting the sense that others had caught up to me and, in some cases, surpassed me in skill level. That year I made the decision to stop playing basketball competitively in order to concentrate on my other two sports of choice, baseball and volleyball.

In retrospect, I can see that my motivation for playing the sports I chose as a youth was correlated to my perceived skill level. In other words, I came to enjoy playing baseball and volleyball because I felt I was good at it. Likewise, I enjoyed playing basketball early on for the same reasons. However, once others started to surpass me in skill level, I lost motivation. Perhaps this all has something to do with my own psychology, but I do believe that many youth make decisions about the sports they play based on similar factors. We play sports because we want to participate in something that we are good at, or that we aspire to become good at. When those aspirations toward a particular sport leave us, we often leave the sport.

So the question then remains, why did so many of us move toward or away from specific sports, based on what looks like predictable patterns based on race? While I do not feel equipped to completely answer that question, I can offer insight from my own experience: even during my first few years of basketball, I can remember feeling that while I was not at a disadvantage in terms of my talent, many of my teammates and I, both Black and White, all shared in a sort of acceptance that Black basketball players in general were far superior to Whites. Whether it was true or not, we all believed it on the basketball court, and spent a good deal of time joking about it. On the other hand, we never joked about that on the baseball field or volleyball court. We never operated under a notion of Black athletic superiority in playing those sports. What was different about basketball? Well for one, from all of the television and media images of professional basketball players, the reason for this perception seems rather obvious. At elite levels, Black basketball players are undoubtedly the top performers. And while the chances of anyone being good enough to play sports professionally are extremely remote, most young athletes will admit to spending a great deal of time thinking about and often working toward collegial or professional sports aspirations. In reality, those aspirations are a big motivating factor in the reason we are so passionate about playing our sports in the first place. With that in mind, it doesn't seem so farfetched that certain groups gravitate toward certain sports based on ideas and beliefs about race, when the images they see point them in certain directions. Perhaps I too made my own unconscious choices based on related factors. Incidentally, I never did play hockey, but I wonder if there is a reverse mentality given that at the elite level, White players dominate. Similarly, I wonder if the fact that Blacks and Whites often choose to play certain sports based on accepted notions of athletic superiority with regard to race has created a self-fulfilling prophecy. If this were true, one could easily see the evolution of a cycle in which different groups would favour participation in different sports.

Despite this seeming divide among races, I find it interesting that participation in sports can accomplish the opposite as well. For example, when I look back at my own experiences as a sports-playing youth, some of my best memories are of the lasting friendships that I made (and kept). Ten years after leaving high school, some of my closest friends are former coaches and teammates from my high school basketball, volleyball, and baseball years, whose backgrounds are very different from my own. If I had not participated in sports, I might never have enjoyed those friendships. On the other hand, this personal observation brings up a very troubling issue: if sports participation provides such important socializing benefits, what does it say about our society that now sports are so highly segregated among students?

A final note: in my senior year of high school, I tried out for the boys' basketball team again after staying away from playing competitive level for about three years. During the tryouts, I was the only White player in attendance. Although I was by no means one of the better players, I did make the team, only to later decline. In the end, I just did not feel like playing basketball on a competitive level. As had been the case several years earlier, the sport no longer appealed to me. And yet, in thinking back on it, my decision always seems somewhat peculiar: given that I had once been so passionate about basketball, why the lack of interest? Did I simply decide to stop playing for personal and unrelated reasons, or did other societal factors contribute? Although I would like to believe the former, those pictures in my high school yearbook tell a different story.

David

INDEED, THE PHOTOGRAPHS IN DAVID'S HIGH SCHOOL YEARBOOK SHOW A disconnection between the diversity of his high school population and the makeup of the hockey and basketball teams. These photographs provide clues to David's "sudden lack of interest in playing basketball" even though he had been playing on his school teams in the earlier years. He remembers having good relationships with his coaches, and he even now says that some of his "closest friends" are his former basketball teammates, some of whom "have backgrounds that are different from his" (i.e., Black). Evidently, skill level aside (something that could be improved with practice), lack of friendship or having difficulties with coaches were not the only reasons for David's lack of interest in playing basketball in his senior year of high school. In fact, as he implies, his disinterest in basketball likely had something to do with race.

That he was going to be the only White player on the basketball team in his senior year was probably a situation for which David was not quite ready, particularly when in his early years playing basketball, he and his teammates, as he discloses, "Black and White, all shared in a sort of acceptance that Black basketball players in general were far superior to Whites."

In this chapter, I take up this idea that participation in sports is related to "race." I reason that the "self-fulfilling prophecy" that David mentions, may indeed be so, but that a significant factor here is how the structures of schools produce and reproduce the "accepted notion of athletic superiority with regard to race"—in other words, racialize students. With reference to comments from young male athletes, I examine how race is used to explain students' interests, abilities, and skills in particular sports, as well as to account for their "political and cultural decisions about what to play and who to play with and against" (Booth & Tatz, 2000, p. 8; see also Hatchell, 2004). I concur with Booth and Tatz (2000) that it is important to scrutinize preferences in sport as related to race (as well as class, gender, ethnicity, religion, and sexuality) in order to determine "what a group represents, how it lives, its priorities and its values," and how this reinforces the group's "sense of exclusiveness and distinctiveness so as to enable groups to regulate their membership. Often this prevents the mobility of others who may want to join in and participate in the privileges they have built up over time" (Booth & Tatz, 2000, p. 8).

An important aspect of this discussion is the deployment of race to explain such things as the abilities, skills, habits, interests, behaviours, practices, aspirations, and outcomes of some students and not others. In the context of Canadian "colour-blind" multicultural discourse, people who "have" race (more appropriately, those who are raced) are those considered "visibly different" (that is, different from the "White norm") in terms of skin colour—in Canada, officially referred to as "visible minorities." These groups are also those that are constructed as having "culture" (see Introduction to the book). And educational and athletic activities, in which particular ethno-racial minority and/or immigrant group members excel, are perceived to be a product or characteristic of their "race culture."[1] I maintain that athletes' preferences, concentration, or dominance in a particular sport have more to do with the economic, political, cultural, and social conditions that promote or make possible their participation in a sport rather than any inherent talent they may possess based on ethno-racial characteristics (see Kell, 2000). In this regard, David and his teammates' (including Blacks) "sort of acceptance" that

Blacks are superior to Whites in basketball reflects how race is used to explain the athletic interests, talent, and capabilities of some athletes (in this case, Blacks) and not others (i.e., Whites), and reinforces cultural beliefs, ideas, and behaviours of individuals (Harrison et al., 2004; Sailes, 1991).

That they "joked" about the superiority of Black basketball players on the basketball court and not "on the baseball field or volleyball court" reflects how spaces also become racialized and identified with particular groups (see also Abdel-Shehid, 2003).[2]

RACE AND SPORTS PARTICIPATION: WHO PLAYS WHAT AND WHY?

The dominance of Black athletes in sports such as basketball, football, and track and field has been debated for years. In a feature article in *Sports Illustrated* (December 8, 1997), S.L. Price writes that in the United States, White athletes who had dominated the American athletic scene for much of the century do not want to play anymore. Distracted by other leisure-time pursuits and discouraged by the success of Black athletes, who have come to dominate sports in spectacular fashion, the White athlete, unlike his Black counterpart, is now less interested in playing certain mainstream games. He is increasingly drawn to sports that are primarily "White" such as soccer, or to alternative athletic pursuits that are overwhelmingly White, such as mountain biking or rock climbing (p. 30).

Price argues that Whites are "now tagged by the stereotypes of skin colour" (p. 33) and as a result are choosing to compete in sports like baseball, ice hockey, and in-line hockey in which they feel they have a chance of maintaining a competitive edge. High school coaches in urban areas complain that they can recruit White students for activities like baseball and wrestling but not basketball. The coaches also point out that in the early high school years, basketball teams tend to be racially diverse, but in the senior years the teams become "more Black." And when White students are asked why they do not participate on the teams, they say: "I can't run with those guys" (Price, p. 34).

A *Sports Illustrated* youth poll revealed that "while many young Whites are unsure of their place in athletics, young Blacks, brimming with self-confidence and certain that sports are one of the few professions in which they can make it big in America, are pouring heart and soul into team sports" (Price, 1997,

p. 34).[3] But this situation is not only about race, for race intersects with social class, gender, and other demographic factors to influence the sports in which students participate and the use they make of it (see Varpalotai, 1996; Kell, 2000; Nakamura, 2003; Paraschak, 2000; Armour, 2000). Price also points out that while affluent White urban students tend to play basketball "for the fun of it," Blacks, particularly those living in "inner cities," look at basketball as a means of financial security. As one coach said, "the White athlete is not as hungry as the black athlete—period" (in Price, 1997, p. 35). From a coach's perspective, "hungry" athletes (typically from "inner city projects") are more likely to be "coachable" and hence make good basketball players (Frey, 1994).[4] Frey gives the example of an occasion (at a Nike basketball camp in Indianapolis) when he heard a coach, after enumerating the various life circumstances of an athlete—"orphaned at a young age, living in a foster home, searching endlessly for authority figures"—said "with enthusiasm," "Bet he's *extremely* coachable" (p. 67, italics in original).

Linked to social class and race is immigrant status or citizenship. In my study (James, 1990) of African-Canadian youth (mostly of Caribbean immigrant background, either born there or of parents born there), sports helped them negotiate educational structures that were culturally new to many of them (see also Solomon, 1992). Capitalizing on the opportunities and possibilities that came through basketball and track and field (since soccer[5] and cricket, to which they were accustomed, are not popular sports in Canada), these first- and second-generation African Canadians quickly learned the rules and skills of these athletic activities to fit in; in the process, they were recognized, valued, and respected in the school community. This would, in part, account for such notable players such as Denham Brown, Jamaal Magloire, Tammy Sutton Brown, and many others making it to the NCAA, NBA, and WNBA, and for track and field stars such as Ben Johnson, Donovan Bailey, Angela Bailey, Angela Taylor-Issajenko, and Bruny Surin, who have represented Canada in the Olympics. Members of other immigrant groups have also used sports to make their way in Canadian society. For instance, in a longitudinal study of the 1973 and 1974 Ontario high school graduating class, my colleagues and I identified three study participants of working-class Italian-born parents, who used sports to serve their needs and interests through high school. One participant, Ray, who was a chartered accountant when he was interviewed in 1995, was involved in football and basketball during his high school years, and credited his athletic involvement with making his school years among "the best time of his life." Sam, another participant in the study, had an MBA. He had obtained an athletic scholarship to an American university after he completed high school in Toronto, but he completed only one semester at the scholarship university. With reference to these study participants, we wrote that "sports operated as a cultural resource, whereby they were able to learn the norms and values of Canadian society. It also provided an emotional benefit, in that it helped them to relieve their tensions and stresses" (Anisef et al., 2000, p. 168).

Members of recent immigrant groups in Canada, as in the United States and Britain, have used sports to negotiate the economic, cultural, and social structures of society, and ultimately to better their lives. In other words, they tend to capitalize on the space provided by athletics and establish themselves in the "mainstream" of the society, believing they will eventually attain their educational and occupational goals. But there is also a perception—if not a belief—among many, including Blacks, that their dominance in certain sports is much more than an attempt to advance in society. In fact, what Price (1997) says of African Americans could be applied to Canadians:

> many people find it hard to believe that economic incentives alone account for Black athletic dominance. These observers offer a simple theory: Blacks dominate sports because they are faster, quicker, better ..., they possess superior athletic skills and have thus transformed the way sports are played (p. 36).

Individuals, including coaches and, in some cases parents, who subscribe to this belief cite the Black athlete's "mobility, toughness, and physical ability" to run fast and jump (most of us know of the movie *White Men Can't Jump*) (see also Kell, 2000). These individuals ignore the many factors (socialization, role models, stereotyping, provision of opportunities, etc.) that channel Black students into athletic activities and play positions (i.e., "positional segregation" *à la* Lapchick in Price, 1997, p. 38); instead they claim that it is a result of genetics. In such a context, then, it is understandable that Blacks would, as Isiah Thomas said, "always want to keep the stereotype that we're better than whites; it's an advantage" (in Price, 1997, p. 37). And as Price further points out, "mix the notion of white athletic inferiority with the comfortable suburban culture in which many young white males live, and the result is an atmosphere in which commitment to a sport such as basketball or football become ever rarer."

While conducting research for this book, I asked a number of White male university students and former high school student athletes to read Price's (1997) *Sports Illustrated* article: "Whatever Happened to the White Athlete?" I asked them, on the basis of their experiences as student athletes, to comment on the points that Price raises about White athletes. Did they agree with his representation? Did they see themselves in his representations? I will share two of the responses I received. The first is from David, whose reflections we read in the introduction to this chapter, and the second, is from Craig.[6] These responses also came to me via email after our conversations.

David:
I just read the article you gave me, "Whatever Happened to the White Athlete?" I was completely fascinated by it. The author brought up a lot of issues about a subject that I think a lot of athletes and former athletes have been captivated by for quite some time. Perhaps most interesting to me is the question of whether Black athletes seem to be outperforming Whites because of innate ability or outside influences, and how that affects the choices that young athletes make in choosing what sports to participate in.

I can see how socio-economic and cultural differences have an effect on the choices that youth make regarding what sports to play. The article points this out very effectively. However, I really do believe that there is something to be said for the "innate" argument. From my own observations as a former student athlete and as an avid professional sports fan, there is absolutely a difference in the way Blacks and Whites "play" certain sports (and not just at the professional level but at amateur levels as well).

"You play White" has become a common term in basketball vernacular. When someone says it to you, it of course implies that you're probably not a very good leaper, you're probably a little on the slow side, and your overall set of skills is not all that exciting. There's a basketball player in the NBA right now named Jason Williams. His nickname is "White Chocolate." His teammates (predominantly Black) gave him the nickname because he's a White player who plays a "Black" style of play.

But is playing a "Black" brand of basketball or playing a "White" brand innate? Let me argue both sides for a second. If I watch a basketball game at any level I am quite confident that I can pick out each player and with some level of success determine whether that player learned to play basketball in an urban environment or in the suburbs. I've seen Black players who play "White" and White players who play "Black." Really, the more appropriate term would be, "He is a city player," or "He is a suburban player." I think people just use the terms "he plays Black" or "he plays White" because that's what they see—and it so happens that most Black players come from and learn the "city" game and vice versa for the White players.

Now let me refute what I just said. Despite the effects of culture on the way we play sports (and ultimately on the sports we choose to participate in), there is quite obviously a superiority among Blacks in many sports where culture and geography might not have anything to do with it. I think culture definitely enters the equation in this debate, but it does not exist alone. There is something to be said for innate athletic ability (as much as I hate the term "innate," I have yet to be convinced that environment acts alone here. I'm open to the fact that it might, but like I said I have yet to hear a convincing argument ...).

Craig:
During my 16 years of playing organized and competitive hockey, I have never worn the same jersey as a Black person. I did, however, play on a team with a girl for a few years .... She was the most talented player on the team. Aside from hockey, baseball is the only sport I have played outside of the school context. I played one year of "rep" baseball and there was only one Black player on the team. He was the most talented .... The rest of my sporting career took place on school teams.

Before I respond to the issues raised in the *Sports Illustrated* article, it is necessary that I share my own background and experiences. I attended [one of Canada's prestigious high schools] in Toronto.[7] During my high school, I played on the volleyball, rugby, football, hockey, and baseball teams. When I was in my senior years, I focused on athletic endeavours on the varsity football and baseball teams. There was only one [Black] player on the varsity team; he was also the only player on the team who was faster than me. My sporting experience at [high school] epitomizes the notion that Blacks are simply better athletes than Whites.[8] The few Black students that there were in the school did excel in their respective sporting careers ....

It is a virtual impossibility to find an area in the life of any athlete that is not shaped or influenced by socio-economic factors. The harsh reality in North America is that ... competing in sports costs money. Of course, different sports require different amounts of money in order to participate. When understanding school sports, it becomes a question of which sports certain school boards are willing to pay for in terms of equipment and insurance for their students. For example, traditionally hockey is a sport for which school boards in North America are not willing to pay for students' equipment. Football, however, is .... All one needs to play soccer and basketball are the appropriate footwear and balls, while hockey skates alone cost in excess of $200. It is inevitable that these types of socio-economic circumstances will influence who plays which sports. When I was in high school, there was a prevalent belief that Blacks were "better" athletes than Whites .... When I was an active athlete, I was certainly more comfortable playing on an ice surface than on a basketball court. The main reason for this was due to my mastery of hockey as compared to basketball .... While I was growing up in an affluent and White context in Toronto, hockey was a central part of mainstream life .... As a White Canadian male, instilled in me was a desire to play hockey, not basketball. The majority of Black friends growing up did not play hockey. Either they could not afford to, or did not have the desire to strap on a pair of skates ....

Part of my reason for not picking basketball as a child was influenced by my country's obsession with hockey, but this does not completely account for my not wanting to play basketball. In my childhood, when I watched the NBA slam-dunk competition on the television, I did set up a trashcan on a shelf with an ottoman positioned beneath it to play the role of a launching pad. I rented the ever-so-popular video games, "NBA Jam." I occasionally watched games. I had friends, mostly Black friends, who played basketball. I could have joined in the hoop action with my friends had I wanted to, and I did have White friends who played basketball .... However, there was an invisible and mysterious barrier that kept me and the majority of my White friends from stepping onto the basketball court with any substantial amount of confidence ....

However, this does not answer the question of whether Whites are intimidated by Black prowess on the basketball court. I have no credible answer to this question other than "probably." Is this intimidation supported by biological evidence? Are Black people more genetically predisposed to excel in athletic pursuits? .... Could it be that throughout these centuries of physically demanding lives that Blacks genetically adapted to their environment in order to cope with the demands put on them? It is impossible to say with certainty what the answer to this question is. However, it is something that should be considered in this debate over racial dominance in athleticism.

I share at length David and Craig's reflections to indicate the process they used to assess the sociology vs. biology debate. Interestingly, while both of them agreed that sociology has something to do with Blacks' athleticism, they both insist that biology cannot be ruled out. Their reasoning probably has to do with their exposure to Black athletes—both have played with "very good" Black athletes. For example, Craig relates that there was one Black player on his baseball team and that he was "the most talented." And the only Black player on his football team was the one who was "faster than him." It seems that participating on teams with Black players, as Craig did, or attending racially diverse schools, as David did, contributes to their beliefs about the superiority of Black athletes. In fact, according to a *Sports Illustrated* poll, Whites in the US who attended racially diverse schools were found to be more inclined to believe the athletic stereotypes, while Blacks in similarly diverse schools (compared to "all-Black" schools) also believed that Blacks are athletically superior to Whites (Price, 1997). The same could be said of African-Canadian students.

In my earlier study of the experiences and perceptions of Black student athletes in the Toronto area, although most attended racially diverse schools, I found a tendency to believe that participating in sports was "natural." For instance, when one participant, Brian, was asked about his involvement in school sports, he responded:

Do you believe in God? Do you believe that everybody is here for a reason? I believe that everyone has a talent and I believe that my talent is sports. So when I was born I was naturally an athlete. So it would be pretty dumb for me to go into science (James 1995, p. 28).

I wrote then that the problem with this logic is that

it contributes to the self-fulfilling prophecy ...; and ignores the complex social mechanisms that are responsible for his participation and success in sports in the first place. In fact, this social construction of Blacks as naturally superior in sports is a stereotype based on racism (James, 1995, p. 28).

However, it should also be pointed out that other participants reasoned that sporting success was due more to practice than to genetics. For instance, one participant asserted that "Blacks are good because they spend many hours a day playing basketball. The more you do something, the better you get at it. It's not a natural thing. It is something they work at …. They've been running for a long time, so it accumulates" (James, 1995, p. 28; see also Sailes, 1991).

Beliefs about the types of athletic activities that best suit particular ethno-racial group members are part of the racist discourses and practices found in Canadian society in general and schools in particular. This sports discourse also tends to polarize and compare Whites and Blacks. Whites are represented as people whose skills in athletics come through learning, interest, motivation, talent (not "raw talent," a term that is often used with reference to Blacks), and exposure to a particular sports: they "choose" to participate in sports, suggesting that they have alternative means of participation and paths to success in society. Blacks, on the other hand, are represented as people whose athletic skills, abilities, and interests are integral to who they are: they participate in sports because of their physicality/biology. For instance, in a study of race broadcasting at US college basketball games, Billings et al. (2002) noted that White athletes were frequently praised for their perceived "intellect" and "leadership capacity," and Black athletes were often praised for being "naturally talented." It was also observed that "Black athletes are expected to succeed athletically; conversely, White athletes are expected to have an innate ability to overcome seemingly insurmountable odds to accomplish their 'athletic stature'" (p. 1). So for Blacks, sports are perceived to be an "easy" means for them to participate in society and ensure their success. For other racial minority groups, their athleticism is related to perceptions of their physicality, their intellectual abilities, and the historical and contemporary roles that they have played, or are expected to play, in society.[9] This paradigm of athleticism can be seen in the raced culture of, for example, basketball and hockey, and manifested in the values, behaviours, habits, aspirations, and activities of student athletes. In the following two sections, using newspaper and magazine articles, and data from in-person and email interviews, I discuss the experiences, socially constructed images, identifications, material and athletic interests, and aspirations of minority youth in basketball and hockey.

THE SOCIAL AND CULTURAL WORLDS OF YOUNG BASKETBALL PLAYERS

In an eight-part series of a Toronto high school basketball team featured in the *Toronto Star* recently, reporter Morgan Campbell (2003) describes not only the skills and achievements of the players, but also their athletic culture: their habits, attitudes, ideas, and aspirations. The series highlights the raced aspect of the school basketball culture, a culture informed by the African-Caribbean background of the players. Describing how identity was forged among the basketball players, Campbell (June 1, 2003, p. A8) writes:

> Basketball is a tool—like fashion, music and language—that they use to forge a Black identity in a White country. This identity is Caribbean by heritage, American by choice and Canadian by default .... It doesn't matter that they were born here. They identify with the country [Guyana, St. Vincent, Jamaica] in which their parents grew up (p. A8).

Campbell explains that Jamaican culture is very pervasive among the basketball players, and that while the players might claim to be Jamaican (some of them listen to reggae) and talk "Jamaican patois" (e.g., "whapm tyuh"—what's happening), "nobody wants to be too Jamaican—because they'd be freshies" (June 1, 2003, p. A8)—a term meaning "'fresh off the boat' from a Caribbean island usually Jamaica" (p. A1). Being a "freshie" is also understood to mean that the individual is an immigrant, and therefore unlikely and hence not likely to be very a good player. So, on the one hand, the language and habits of Toronto basketball players might, to an extent, portray a Jamaicanness (or Caribbeanness). On the other, the hip-hop music, the Black Entertainment Television (BET), and the clothes (i.e., the jerseys, jewellery, caps, and shoes[10]) are all part of a culture of African-American basketball and baseball players, which indicate their link to American culture. Add to this student athletes' aspirations to win US college and university basketball scholarships, and/or to play eventually for the NBA. These various aspects of the constructed culture of student athletes are indicative of their Canadian identifications.

There is often an association made between "basketball culture" and "Black identification" of young athletes. For example, one Korean-Canadian undergraduate student identified the mannerisms, dress, and speech pattern—in short, the cultural pattern—of his "Korean friends" who played basketball as "Black culture." There is no denying that many basketball players—Blacks and non-Blacks alike—tend to act in similar ways that some people come to construct as "Black." Take the case of Drew, for example. He was the only White player on a Toronto high school basketball team, and as Campbell (2003, June 3, 2003) maintains, "Drew may have pale skin ... but his patois-inflected speech and hip-hop style make him as 'Black' as any other player in the gym" (p. B2). To illustrate how much Drew had become "Black," Campbell tells us that not only had he embraced the "hybrid" Black culture like his teammates, "in the summer, he wore his sandy brown hair in cornrows. He listens to hip-hop and reggae, and often laces his speech with Jamaican patois" (March 31, 2003, p. A19). Having demonstrated his ability to leap, catch, dunk, and score, Drew is said to have gained the required acceptance and respect of the Black players. In fact, once during an audition for a recruiting American coach, Drew so convincingly demonstrated these abilities that one of his teammates called out: "He's a nigger!" (Campbell, 2003, p. B2) And to further illustrate Drew's "blackness," Campbell tells of an interaction between Drew, his coach, and a recruiter: the recruiter, neglecting to show photographs that reflected the racial diversity on the prospective university campus, was reminded by the coach that Drew needed to see pictures of "dark faces" in order "to feel comfortable." To this statement, Drew responded, "Yeah, I've got to fit in." Then the recruiter assured him that they have "plenty of black students [and] plenty of sistas" (Campbell, 2003, p. B2).

Related to their aspirations to earn a basketball scholarship to US universities and colleges, or a place on an NBA team, a number of student athletes in the Toronto area would switch high schools (for example, Drew) to be on the basketball team they believed offered them opportunities (preferably a guarantee) of playing time and exposure to US college scouts. Some student athletes would even choose to complete high school in the US, where they envisioned their athletic ambitions would be better and much earlier realized. The thinking of these athletes, as Ro Russell verbalized it, is: "Go south sooner or threaten your future" (Leeder, 2001, p. S4).[11] There are also those athletes who, with the encouragement and support of few coaches and NBA scouts, dream of "jumping" (and few do "jump") directly from high school to the NBA (see Higgins, 2003; McCullum, 1995). But given that very few players ever actually manage this, many realistically elect to spend one to four years in a post-secondary institution where, as critics suggest, they get an opportunity to emotionally or physically mature, learn responsibility, develop the skills to successfully navigate the world of basketball, and to more adequately prepare themselves for playing on professional teams (McCullum, 1995).

But there are those NBA aspirants who believe that they are ready for the professional league and related demands. They would argue, as McCullum (1995) did with reference to Kevin Garnett who "jumped," that:

rather than take up someone else's space in a college classroom, what [they have] done is enlist in the real world. Every year hundreds of men—boys, really—younger than him head for minor league baseball and hockey teams, and few people are concerned about this. For that matter, teenagers make a full-time living digging ditches, working in steel mills, administering to the sick in hospitals and fighting wars. Bouncing a basketball and staying in nice hotels is tougher? (p. 67).

McCullum answers his question by saying that in some respects, becoming a professional athlete and going from having pennies to having millions when you are teenager is tough, especially when that young athlete is growing up "in the spotlight" and "making a lot of money while we watch." "Money," McCullum writes, "changes people, alters motivations, messes up priorities, attracts hangers-on, opens up possibilities with women for which [young athletes are] unlikely to be prepared" (p. 67).

Sports observers, coaches, educators, parents, and adults generally may question young athletes' readiness for the world of NCAA or NBA, as well as their low high school grades, their attention to athletic over academic activities, and their failure to receive qualifying scores on the SAT or ACT test. But these young athletes nevertheless maintain a culture of expensive and fashionable possessions that may anticipate the attainment of their social and economic goals. So we will find basketball players (as well as their fans) fostering an image that is consistent with material success. For as Campbell (June 1, 2003) found with the basketball players he investigated, "glittering earrings, new shoes and meticulously trimmed hair" was typical of how they dressed (p. A8); add to this their cell phones and headphones, which play hip-hop music. The picture that emerges is of a culture that indulges student athletes in expensive habits. Indeed, the jerseys that many of them wear can cost as much as $100, and the shoes up to $250. Describing the fashion habits of one basketball player, Campbell said: "Looking good was so important that [he] spends all of his money on shoes. He worked for a minimum wage at Food Basics, but buys new Nikes every month. Not just any Nikes. Jordans ... New models come out about once a month and they usually cost about $250" (June 1, 2003, p. A8). This look or image is as much about the athletes showing that they are aware of the fashion and can afford to dress accordingly, as it is about attracting women. Further, the hip-hop look of the low-wearing oversized pants and designer t-shirts or jerseys, low or shaved haircuts, are not particular to any one ethno-racial group. As I have already noted, young people of all ethnic and racial backgrounds and income levels dress in this fashion. One Chinese youth observed: "A lot of my friends are Chinese, and most play basketball. They listen to hip-hop music, wear their pants low, and like to wear jerseys (NFL, NBA, NCAA)" (March, 2003). Similarly, based on his observations of a Portuguese youth who attends the Toronto community centre in which he works, one youth worker remarked that Luis (pseudonym), nicknamed "White Chocolate" by some of his Black friends (evidently a reference to Jason Williams of the NBA), "is a flashy player and his attitude is more or less based in urban culture (baggy pants, cap worn backwards, his speech, etc.). He managed to gain the respect of his peers based on his 'urban' basketball skills" (May, 2002).

EXPERIENCES OF MINORITY ATHLETES IN HOCKEY: A SPORT "CENTRAL TO MAINSTREAM LIFE"

In his account (above) of choosing hockey over basketball, Craig explains that he was much better at hockey. But probably more significant is what is implied in his further statement about hockey being "a central part of mainstream life" and that as a "White Canadian male" he was instilled with the desire to play hockey (see Abdel-Shehid, 2000). In this statement, Craig gestures toward the significance of "mainstream" and how much hockey helps him build confidence and affirm his status as a White middle-class male. So, we might say that what hockey does for Craig and his White male friends, basketball does for racial minority youth: it builds confidence and a sense of community. But if hockey is a sport of the "mainstream," as Craig indicates, why don't racial minority student athletes seek economic and social privileges by getting involved in hockey? By extension, if through hockey racial minority (and immigrant) youth might be acculturated or integrated into the mainstream, and in the process establish networks that will enable them to negotiate the White structures, why not choose hockey instead of basketball? Or is their preference for basketball and basketball culture evidence of minority youth's resistance to the "mainstream," and a counter-culture where they can exercise agency, assert their presence, and take control of their sporting lives in ways that best represent their interests and aspirations? In considering these questions, I discuss below some of the experiences of racial minority youth in hockey, noting how issues they faced as players may account for their low participation in hockey, even though in some cases they grew up loving the game and wishing to some day make it to the NHL (National Hockey League).

ACCESS TO HOCKEY—"A SPORT THAT FEWER PEOPLE CAN AFFORD"

> More telling is that hockey is a middle-class sport. It costs serious cash to play. You need to buy the equipment (about $1,000); plus most games are all over the city—you need a car. This makes the sport one that fewer people can afford to play. Kids are no longer happy or able to become NHL stars by just owning skates and a stick playing on the outdoor rink .... Whereas basketball games are organized by schools, hockey, for the most part, is organized in private civil society leagues. This means that parents hang around more with hockey but let l'école [school] deal with basketball. This has an impact on access to the game (Howard Ramos, email communication, July 2003).

In the above comment, my colleague Ramos draws attention to the cost of hockey as one of the factors that makes it inaccessible to economically deprived youth and families. Many of them are recent immigrants or mainly racial and ethnic minorities who live in large metropolitan areas like Montreal and Toronto. It follows, therefore, that those racial minority youth who get the opportunity to play hockey beyond their neighbourhood streets will be those who can afford the necessary costs of playing (including equipment costs, team and league fees, etc.), as well as having access to teams and transportation. Furthermore, for youth of working-class backgrounds, their opportunities to play hockey are likely to be attained through sponsorship—i.e., obtaining financial support from interested individuals, organizations, or businesses—based on recognition of their potential, skill, and ability. Anthony Stewart of Scarborough, Ontario, is one example. According to the *Toronto Star* newspaper, he was a "Florida draft pick who overcame poverty to realize [his] dream"—a realization made possible by his "parents and important mentor" (Campbell, 2003, June 22, p. E8). That mentor, according to Campbell, "saw enough talent and nobility in the young man to pay the minor hockey registration and equipment expenses that Stewart's parents couldn't pay" (p. E8).[12] By way of illustrating the significance of Stewart's achievement, or as it was put, "Stewart's tough journey to NHL," Campbell writes: "After all it's a long way from the strip of seedy motels on Kingston Road [where Stewart's financially strapped family stayed at times] and long subway rides to the arena to the cusp of the NHL, but Stewart made the journey ...." (p. E8).

It was a journey that "made him stronger" and instilled in him a desire "to help his family out by playing hard and with the hope that one day he would be drafted" (Campbell, 2003, p. E8).

Stewart's story demonstrates the salience of economics in shaping and influencing the sporting activities and outcomes of youth (see also Devin in Chapter 5). Accordingly, when parents are unable to provide the resources to participate in sports, young people, particularly those of working-class backgrounds, will have to look for these opportunities in schools, community recreation centres, and youth service organizations. And given the significance and role of school in young people's lives, it is logical to think that it is not only the social and economic situation of families that determines the sports in which they engage but the situation of the school as well. In other words, the sports to which students will have access depend on the finances and willingness of school boards and/or particular schools to provide equipment and insurance for students. They also depend on having teachers who are willing and able to be coaches. In this regard, based on cost alone, hockey, which is much more expensive to play than basketball, baseball, and soccer, is a sport that is less likely to be found in many of today's urban schools, administered by cash-strapped school boards. But at schools in which parents are willing and able to finance such sports, hockey is likely to be a sport to which students will have access. By comparison, in urban area schools (often referred to as "inner city"), with youth of immigrant, racial minority, and working-class backgrounds, sports activities tend to be mostly basketball and baseball. Hence, it is in these sports that we often see a significant proportion of minority student athletes. But inaccessibility to hockey through school does not fully explain the low participation of racial minorities in the sport; it is, as some youth indicate, "the cruelty and meanness" that they experience that operate to keep them away from the sport.

"... Being a Visible Minority Requires You to Be Extra Special"
In talking about their experiences playing hockey during their high school years, brothers Gary and Troy,[13] of Chinese-Canadian background, said that in their early years of playing hockey they were treated like every other hockey player, but that was not the case in their later years.

> Gary: As a hockey player, I never felt discriminated in any way until last year [Grade Eleven]. Before, I was treated like every other

kid that played hockey with me. Hockey did not have such a big meaning until last year, which was the year you either go on (to the provincial or junior level) or not. In my last year of competitive hockey, I realized that my colour and size really mattered; I realized that I wasn't 6'2" and scouts look for size first. I felt my dreams crushed because of the reality that I would never be able to fulfill my hockey dream .... I know this is happening to a lot of talented people as well. I wish I didn't have to go through this, but it has helped me become who I am today (April, 2003).

Troy: Early on, it seemed that it didn't matter that I was Chinese, my skills in sports were sufficient enough for me to gain respect. This was true in high school. Even though I was shorter than most, I was working out, which allowed me to excel in football and rugby. My hockey experience was a little different. After playing competitively on a winning team (we were first in the league), I was released, so I went out and tried out for other sports teams. I wasn't the best goalie in the league but certainly had a lot to offer to a team. In the end, I was not chosen .... What I conclude is that being a visible minority requires you to be extra special .... I don't think I was ever meant to play in the NHL, but I was certainly capable of playing competitively (April 2003).

It is likely that the decision not to invite Gary and Troy to participate on their hockey teams, from the coaches' perspective, might have had to do with their skills and abilities. Nevertheless, we must consider Gary's and Troy's perception that their colour and size were factors—by inference, their race. Their comments imply that the decision of who plays hockey competitively is based not only on talent, skill, and dedication, but also on physicality and race (see Abdel-Shehid, 2000; Carnegie, 1997).

The ways in which race and racism operate to limit and eventually discourage racial minority youth participation (see Fernández-Balboa, 2000; Schempp & Olive, 2000) in hockey is captured in Rav Johal's (2002; 2003) reflections on his experiences growing up as a South Asian in a suburban area of Toronto. Johal explains that his immigrant father, who had grown to enjoy hockey from watching "Hockey Night in Canada," enrolled him in hockey school at the age of six years ("much to the chagrin of my mother, who was worried sick that I would get injured"). Johal recalls that he was one of three racial minorities (himself, a Black, and an Asian) in hockey school, and one of "a handful of ethnic minority kids" playing in the community league. This continued to be the case during the seven years (1982–1989) that Johal played organized hockey. And while he remembers most of his ice hockey coaches as supportive, he says that his "dad still reckons that my first coach was a jerk—I don't really remember" (he did not give Johal equal playing time, and this did not change until the coach was confronted by his father). Of his teammates, Johal says that for the most part they were "okay," but he remembers being occasionally ostracized:

> I do remember being called a "Paki" in the eyes of opposing players—that was their way of targeting me, trying to either identify me or get under my skin. I hated that term—like many other South Asians who have been labelled as such, I knew my family was from India, not Pakistan. I was born in England, so I had no clue why I was being called a "Paki." It really used to hurt at times, but I had my own way of coping. I remember being called a "Paki" when I first went to school and defending myself. It worked. Other times, I just ignored it, and that's what I usually did in hockey, hoping to hurt them by putting the puck in the net instead (Johal, 2003, p. 3).

He loved the game ("It was a fun sport—I really enjoyed it, and I was pretty good too. I always played everyday ... on our street with other kids") and his father's tried hard to make him a successful player by following "Walter Gretzky's model of building a rink for me a couple of times in the backyard"; however, by the time he entered Grade Ten, he "stopped playing hockey all together—playing soccer instead, as well as basketball" (p. 3). Johal (2003) suggests that his disinterest in hockey had to do with his development of a consciousness of ethnic identification:

> I remember going through a lot of issues regarding my ethnic identity. I began to feel somewhat distant from the White friends I had grown up with, choosing to hang around kids that were South Asian, West Indian, and Black .... I felt that hockey was a 'White man's sport,' and that as an ethnic minority, I should be playing sports that coloured kids played. For about 3–4 years, I rarely picked up a hockey stick, and hardly watched the sport on TV (p. 4).

Like Johal, Montreal-born Sean (July 2003), who identifies himself as "mixed-race Black" (because of his African-Jamaican, Chinese, and South-

Asian ancestry), started playing hockey at an early age. As he says: "At five, I was playing organized hockey. Everybody on my street played hockey. Everybody in my school played hockey. Everybody talked about hockey and everyone watched hockey. So not once did I ever think it was strange to play hockey." At school Sean would wear his hockey jacket to register that he played hockey, and to "show off his team affiliation" (his team was known for winning), but nevertheless his teachers questioned his skating ability. And during hockey games where he "played hard," Sean reports receiving "taunts" from other team members. But, he recalls,

> I was not surprised. What was strange, however, was the names I had only previously heard on the playground were now becoming part of the game I lived and breathed. It got to me, but I never said a word about it. I just hit them harder and often. My mother said I was impossible to talk to when I came home after a game.

However, despite his determination and best efforts, by the end of high school, while he was "still playing good hockey," Sean admits that his "dreams of the NHL were far away." This was because he had switched from playing hockey competitively to playing football. It was not because he preferred football, but because it seemed that he was better accepted as a football player. Sean recalls, "Other than the coach once calling us the 'running blacks,' the thing I liked was in the four seasons I played at high school, I did not hear the 'nigger this' and 'monkey that,' or the host of other ridiculously sad stereotypical comments that came with me playing hockey."

Toronto-born Ramish, of South-Asian background, captures well the sentiments and experiences of these former hockey players who, despite their efforts, skills, and abilities, found racism so demoralizing that they chose to stop playing competitive hockey:

> I love hockey and have been playing the game since I was young. I remember the name calling and repeatedly being told that I couldn't play hockey because I was not White. I was make fun of and laughed at, and I was the last one picked for teams. I grew up in a White neighbourhood, and as all the kids played hockey, I began practising the game in the hope that one day I could play with everyone else. After a couple of months of practice I became a better player as I was faster and much smarter than the rest of the guys. I was

asked to play for higher calibre teams because I excelled in the sport. I was always working hard, but was still made fun of by the opposing teams. My teammates learned to accept me. However, when another minority played on another team they taunted him with the same names used against me by the other teams. All I wanted was the opportunity to play and to be treated like everybody else. I finally learned to work harder and shield myself from the comments. Unfortunately, I would go home and feel the effect of the cruelty and meanness of some people (in James, 2003a, p. 131).

While youth like Ramish, Sean, Rav, Gary, and Troy were willing to pursue playing hockey, there are others, like Devin (see Chapter 5 for his complete story), who did not go beyond playing street hockey with their neighbourhood friends. For Devin, this was because of the cost of playing, and because at a young age growing up in his working-class, immigrant community, he did not see hockey as "fitting who he thought he was":

I couldn't identify with anybody in that sport. There were no role models for me because they were different cultures ... different backgrounds ...; things that I couldn't myself relate to .... Even the players that I played with had difficulty relating to, you know, some of the players .... None of my Black friends who were equally skilled ... were playing ice hockey .... We'd all play together on the street, but never on ice.

CONCLUSION

I have argued here that the preference, concentration, and/or dominance of particular ethno-racial group student athletes in specific sports is a product of the educational, economic, social, cultural, and political conditions in society and school that encourage their participation in a sport rather than any innate abilities. So the fact that Black youth often prefer basketball is not entirely a situation of their own making; instead, it reflects the opportunities available to them in a society where sports, in conjunction with other social structures, help to create and perpetuate inequalities. Indeed, as Armour (2000) declares: "Simply put, sport, in most manifestations, is not a 'classless' [or raceless] activity offering equal opportunities for all" (p. 79). In this context, therefore, the "basketball culture" that evolves reflects minority athletes' particular interests, priorities, values, and aspirations—a culture that represents their lived experiences as minorities, and their related social mobility ambitions. On the other hand, in a society where the discourse of athleticism represents particular minority groups as having "natural athletic abilities," sports such as hockey, which are dominated by White European players, will understandably be policed (just like basketball is) to ensure that its ethnic and racial membership and program remain consistent with the values, priorities, and aspirations of players. Further, there are mythologies within both cultures that serve to maintain exclusivity in memberships. For example, mythologies such as "White men can't run or jump," and "Blacks have weak ankles that prevent them from skating" (as Craig heard from his parent), have operated to restrict access to these sports. Fortunately, change is inevitable, and with every "different" athlete that joins a team or sport, we will see not only a change in the physical characteristics of players, but also corresponding changes in the cultures of the sports.

NOTES

1. Space restricts me from including the complex situation of Aboriginal peoples. However, it is important to note that in spite of some key differences, their situation is also in many ways similar to that of racial minority student athletes (see Gabor et al., 1996; Paraschak, 2000).

2. While the reference here is to David's high school, it is possible that in other schools, depending on the racial composition, social class, and school facilities, the racial make-up of the sports teams will be different. Nevertheless, the general discourse related to the social construction of one racial group's superiority in a particular sport will be in evidence. In 1997, Eitzen and Sage found that only 18 percent of professional baseball players were Black, while 77 percent and 65 percent of the basketball and football players, respectively, were Black. And more recently Dimmons identified a similar representation in the percentage of Black and White players on professional teams. And the presentations on divisional teams were as follows: Basketball (34 percent Whites, 56 percent Blacks, and 1 percent Latinos); football (64 percent Whites, 46 percent Blacks, and 2 percent Latinos); and baseball (88 percent Whites, 3 percent Blacks, and 5 percent Latinos) (*Toronto Sun*, 2002, December 8, pp. S14–S15).

3. The study found that young Black athletes, compared to Whites, were three times more likely to say that being successful in sports could earn them "a lot of money." And 51 percent agreed that Blacks cared more about sports because it was one of the few ways that they could make the money (Price, 1997). In a more recent

national survey of 865 high school students, Lou Harris found that "many African Americans still harbored unrealistic aspirations to stardom. Fifty-one percent of them compared to 18 percent of White student athletes believed that they would make the pros" (cited in Lapchick, 2001, p. 235).

4. Similarly, in her discussion of coaches' perceptions of what makes good football players, Armour (2000) makes reference to what her son's football coach said of the group of eight-year-old boys: "they were a joy to teach," but they would "never make 'real' footballers," which Armour took to mean "they were too middle class for football" (p. 77).

5. Today, soccer is one of the fastest-growing sports in North America and is played in many schools.

6. David and Craig were both in one of my classes, and I spoke with them individually. They were told that their email responses would be published; they received a copy of the chapter in its draft form.

7. The school is a privately owned and funded institution with tuition fees of approximately $15,000 annually, and a student population that is largely White Anglo-Saxon.

8. Craig notes that during his five years in his private high school, there were three Black students in the school and two of them played on the football teams.

9. Within this paradigmatic context then we come to hear of the academically gifted model minority students (Pon, 2000; Lee, 2003; Nakamura, 2003).

10. In a photograph of a closet with nine sports jerseys (which usually costs about $100 each), nine baseball caps, and over 13 pairs of shoes, the newspaper shows the kinds of clothes the players wear and, as Campbell writes, that looking good is important to them. Identity and group culture as Kai James (2001) would say.

11. Russell runs non-school-related basketball camps in Toronto and provides advice and assistance to basketball players to plan and secure US scholarships. In some ways, he is considered to be a resource and a role model to many athletes. Critics of the practice of students completing high school in the US (particularly coaches and educators) argue that these youth are simply misguided: they "have a warped sense of reality," and do not understand that there is "more to high school life than basketball." One concern is the likelihood of these athletes becoming "basketball commodities." It is important to note that this practice of migrating to the US to complete high school with the hope of winning a scholarship to college and university has been a practice among hockey players for years (Leeder, 2001, *Globe and Mail*, p. S4).

12. With reference to the support he received from his "mentor," Stewart said, "I wouldn't be here today if it weren't for him. There were families that took me in when my family wasn't in a great situation. I can't tell you how grateful I am to be here today" (p. E8).

13. Gary, a high school student, and Troy, a third-year university student, were participants in a discussion group on the subject.

3

THE LONG SHOTS: GOING SOUTH ON BASKETBALL TICKETS

A CONSISTENT ASPIRATION OF BLACK/AFRICAN YOUTH, PARTICULARLY MALE student athletes, is to win athletic scholarships to American universities, with the hope of eventually moving on to one of the national sports teams (in the case of basketball players, the NBA). For instance, in eight articles with accompanying photographs, the *Toronto Star* newspaper (May, 31; June 1–7, 2003) featured the lives, experiences, and ambitions of a Toronto high school basketball team, the Mavericks. Reporter Morgan Campbell (2003, June 7, p. E5) gives "an accurate—if sometimes unflattering—portrayal of a group of teenagers … [who] showed me ambition that bordered on delusion …." Campbell tells of Oliver, the six-foot-five "star player of the team"; Drew, the six-foot-seven "only White player" on the team; and Brian, six-foot-six, "a solid and reliable player," all of whom "form the tallest front line in Toronto." And then there was Nedrie, who at five-foot-seven, was "the team's shortest player … [and] determined to prove that basketball is his true calling." It appears that for this team, basketball was a major incentive for them to attend school, and with the encouragement of their coaches, two White teachers, they played to maintain their reputation as "the best basketball team in the city." As well, Oliver, Drew, and Nedrie in particular all expected to eventually win basketball scholarships. While Campbell does not provide much information about the socio-economic background or financial situation of the players, readers are left with the impression that it is primarily through scholarships that the teens were going to make it to a post-secondary institution.

The schooling experiences, motivations, and aspirations of this 2003 team of basketball players are not unlike those of the Saints, the basketball team of a school in downtown Toronto, which was also featured in a *Toronto Star* newspaper series in 1996 (March 23, 24, 25). The front page picture of the 1996 Saturday newspaper shows a team of 11 Blacks and one White. The reporter, Andrew Duffy, details the lives, scholarship aspirations, and academic achievements of three Black players: Jamaal (centre), Collin (guard), Aaron (forward), and their coach Simeon Mars. They all represented perseverance, dedication, commitment, and immigrant success. Duffy portrays a group of student athletes for whom playing basketball was significant to remaining in school in order to win scholarships, and an accommodating coach who was a "role model" to them in the absence of their fathers. We are told that the team had gone undefeated in Canada for two years, which seemed like a remarkable accomplishment given the condition of the gymnasium in which they practised. According to Duffy, the gym of the downtown school had

> warped floorboards that rattle under the basket. The backboards were stained by blank shots, the net frayed like old wigs. Red gym mats hung from the walls behind each basket so that players didn't mash themselves against naked cinderblock. Smaller than most elementary school gyms, the gym at this downtown high school was only two-thirds the size of a regulation basketball court. It's so small that the referees have had to change the rules in keeping with its size (March 23, A22).[1]

The descriptions of the players further underscores the outstanding accomplishment of the team. Duffy (March 23, 1996, p. A22) reports that Jamaal first played basketball with his friends in a "school playground where a speckled orange rim hung like a fractured branch. The rim sagged at an impossible angle 8 feet off the ground; it begged to be torn from its failing steel bolts by a monster jam." He is the "most talked-about player ever to emerge from Metro's high school basketball scene; he's been featured in *Basketball Weekly,* the *New York Times* and *Maclean's* magazine." He's been called "a dominant forward," "an unstoppable force," and "the best Canadian basketball player ever." Jamaal went to 1995 summer Academic Betterment and Career Development (ABCD) "basketball camp in New Jersey where 240 of the best high school players in North America auditioned in front of 700 college coaches."[2] Duffy describes Colin's life in the following way: "He lives with his grandmother in Metro Toronto Housing Authority building .... He hasn't seen his father in five years; his mother lives in the States" (March 24, 1996, p. A6). And in Collin's words:

> I've been living poor practically all my life, not poor, poor, poor, but money has been a problem in my family .... I'd like to give something back to her [his grandmother] because it has been hard for her. I want a successful career at something—whether it's NBA or communications.

Forward player Aaron is said to have "always been in trouble," and has a history of failing in school. He had been to six schools in over five years in three different cities. "Sometimes, he'd leave simply because he's tired of school; he'd hang out with friends in Detroit for a semester or cruise with his pals in Vancouver .... He hasn't seen his mother in almost a year; his father works in Toronto but might as well be across the country. He lives alone in a basement apartment ...."

Coach Mars is reported to have been a very significant person in encouraging the players to put "academic first, basketball second." Mars is portrayed as a sensitive, caring, trusting coach, concerned about the youths' academic as much as their athletic successes. His life seemed to be his major reference for how he understood the lives, needs, interests, and expectations of the players (March 25, 1996, p. A6). An immigrant from St. Vincent who moved to Canada with his mother in the early 1970s, Mars "turned to basketball in search of a challenge." Successful at the game, he "desperately wanted to play for the national basketball team, but an invitation never came—even after Mars became one of the only Canadians to play professionally in the Continental Basketball Association." He believed that he was not considered for the national team largely because of his colour. In the late 1990s, because of his reputation, student athletes, who, according to Duffy, aspired to "a US college scholarship figured it in their best interest to play for Mars." For this reason, many scholarship aspirants, like Jamaal, transferred to this downtown school to be coached by Mars. But we are left to ponder the implications of the subtle recruitment that goes on at the high school: because of the transfer policy of the Toronto Board of Education, student athletes were allowed to transfer without penalty.[3] The three Eastern Commerce basketball players—Jamaal, Collin, and Aaron—like participants in studies by James (1995; 1990), Spence (1999), and Solomon (1992), all dreamed of obtaining US college scholarships.[4]

Of the three, Collin had already passed his American College Testing (ACT) on his first try, averaged 79 percent in his school work, and had accepted a four-year scholarship to St. John's University in New York City. Aaron was expected to write the ACT some time in the future. And during the investigation, Jamaal, the six-foot-ten star athlete, received a letter indicating that he had passed his ACT. But he still needed five credits to complete his high school diploma, and while he was able to take four during the day, he had to complete the additional course at night school—certainly a significant task, but Jamaal said he was up to it, since $100,000 (Canadian) was at stake. (He needed a 65 percent average in 13 core subjects to be eligible for the NCAA Division One scholarship.)

The possibility of realizing their dreams of obtaining US college scholarships is made even more viable with the number of American scouts that visited their games, practices, made contacts with the coach and the school principal, and even called the players by phone. Of the three players, the coaches were the most interested in Jamaal. Rick Pitino, one of the many college coaches who had visited Toronto, showed interest in Jamaal. However, as Duffy reports, Jamaal understood "American college basketball is a business and that he's a commodity, so he comes to each contact with a shopping list." We now know that Jamaal was successful in attaining a basketball scholarship at the University of Kentucky, where he attended for four years before going on to play in the NBA on the North Carolina Charlotte Hornets team. In a feature article, published about five months after Jamaal had been at Kentucky, reporter Mary Ormsby (February 8, 1997, p. C1) revealed that Jamaal had passed all his courses in his first semester. Nevertheless, "Maglorie says candidly that he needs a firm guiding hand to help him with his studies." Jamaal's high school coach, Mars, at that time, had also moved to Kentucky where, according to the *Toronto Star* newspaper (February 8, 1997), he worked as an administrative aide to Coach Rick Pitino, and "informally as sounding board and friend for Maglorie." Evidently, Jamaal was successful in realizing his aspirations. But where are Collin and Aaron today? And what chances do Oliver, Drew, Brian, and Nedrie (the 2003 "team of stars" players) have of success? Will they get a US university or college scholarship? Will they eventually play in the NBA? Will they make the Toronto Raptors team?

BLACK STUDENT ATHLETES AND THEIR DREAM OF "GOING SOUTH"

This chapter considers the US scholarship aspirations of Toronto basketball student athletes. Within the framework of anti-racism theory (see Introduction),

I argue that this aspiration represents the influence of the "good athletes" self-image on these students to negotiate and navigate the inequitable school system, where they are marginalized, racialized, and rendered otherwise invisible. So, in the face of low odds and intense competition with their US counterparts, Black/African-Canadian male high school basketball players develop attitudes, habits, and behaviours (a subculture) related to their acquired perceptions of their abilities, skills, and capacities to gain recognition and a sense of legitimacy as active school participants and contributors. While such aspirations can be considered a "long shot" or, as Campbell (2003) notes, "borders on delusion," it nevertheless serves the interests of the students and parents as much as the coaches, teachers, and principals.

For Black male student athletes, aspiring to basketball scholarships has become part of their social world and their "group culture." Their group culture is a response to "the Other," through which they come to understand and develop their techniques for negotiating cultural differences and maximizing their opportunities. Through group culture, many Black youth learn to traverse the different cultural boundaries and structures of their respective societies and educational institutions. And while attending high schools in Canada, they learn to negotiate the differences between their group culture (informed by their racialized masculine experiences) and the middle-class Eurocentric academic culture of schools within which they must function in order to acquire the cultural capital they need to pursue their aspirations.

The constructed high educational and occupational aspirations of Black Toronto youth (most either born in Canada to immigrant parents from the Caribbean or Africa, or immigrants themselves) are a product of their immigrant backgrounds (James, 1990) and, to an extent, of their desire to satisfy some of their parents' dreams (Brathwaite & James, 1996; Dei, 1996). This is reflected in their group culture. So, too, is their identification with their American counterparts. For as with African-Canadian youth in general, student athletes fashion and live their blackness in accordance with their African-American counterparts. This "outer-national political identification" evident among Blacks, as cultural theorist Walcott (1997) argues, is a product of the "in-between position" they occupy in a nation state where the policy of multiculturalism contributes to a situation in which people have difficulty "imagining blackness as Canadian" (p. 42). In this regard, influenced by the media (among other sources), as well as by the sporting relationships between Canada and the United States, student athletes are likely to think that there is little or no difference between themselves and their American counterparts. They conclude that they have equal chances of winning scholarships. The geographic border may appear to be meaningless or invisible.

Before proceeding to discuss my research findings, I first return to the newspaper information about Oliver, Drew, and Nedrie, the four 2003 star players. Brian, who was one of the frontline players, was out of the early running for a scholarship: during the year, he became a father, began missing classes and basketball practices, and dropped out by March break (he later found a job unloading cargo for $9 an hour).

THE *TORONTO STAR* PLAYERS OF 2003

In the *Toronto Star* article aptly entitled "Short Sight, Tall Plans," Campbell (2003, June 2) tells us that Nedrie, the son of a professional boxer, struggled to follow the path of his father, who at one time "held the Canadian lightweight title in the mid-90s." It is said that Nedrie's father "only wanted him to box," but according to Nedrie, "the more pressure his father applied, the less he enjoyed the sport" (June 2, 2003). After recovering from a boxing injury, Nedrie recognized he could better excel in basketball, and joined the high school team, averaging about 30 points a game. By the end of Grade Eleven, Nedrie determined that he wanted a basketball scholarship to attend a US university, and realizing that "US scouts would not find him" if he stayed at his then high school, he transferred to his current high school where he joined the Maverick basketball team. As Campbell points out, at only five-foot-seven, "players so small rarely grab the attention of the US college scouts that Nedrie wanted so desperately to impress. He dreams of a career in journalism, but won't consider applying to [Canadian universities or colleges]" (May 31, 2003). "All through the season," Campbell writes, "he held out for a US scholarship offer, believing that his toughness and hustle on the court would compensate for his small size ...." At the end of March, Nedrie sent letters to more than 50 American universities, expressing his interest in their basketball programs, and asking for a "potential scholarship offering"—"strongly" suggesting that he "would be an asset to [their] program," and welcoming an opportunity to discuss his career goals with them, and assuring them of his "determination to succeed" (June 7, 2003). Nedrie did eventually hear from three American universities, and from two universities in Nova Scotia. The coach of one of the Canadian universities came to town and tried to recruit Nedrie.

Similar to Simmons, Oliver started his high school career in basketball at a high school in Markham, north of Toronto, and in Grade Eleven transferred to his current high school. Oliver is described as having a "6-foot-5 frame… [which] carries 215 pounds of sculpted muscle" (May 31, 2003). Marchione, Oliver's coach, stated that he "loves Oliver's natural athletic prowess, his ability to sprint down the court and finish a play with a big dunk …, [and] his incredible agility, leaping higher than other players" (May 31, 2003). According to Campbell, "before Oliver even entered high school, word of his abilities reached US college coaches. By the end of Grade Eleven, at age 17, considered one of the best high school players in the province, top American schools ... wooed him with recruiting letters." Campbell goes on to point out that in Toronto, "most players can only dream of receiving that kind of attention" (May 31, 2003). Oliver, who nearly two years earlier was in a serious road accident in which he suffered a brain injury and was temporarily confined to a wheelchair, is understandably admired for his tenacity and willpower, having overcome this incredible adversity to become "one of the brightest high school basketball stars in the city." And like the other members of his basketball team, Oliver played basketball with the hope that he would be recruited by a US scout, and win a scholarship to a US university or college. But by the end of the basketball season (and "increasingly strange behavior" notwithstanding, June 4, 2003), the only letters that Oliver had received were from College Prospects of America, a corporate headhunting firm, which at a cost of about $1,000 US, promised to pitch Canadian student athletes to US schools (June 2, 2003). However, Oliver claimed that he was not going to respond because he believed that NCAA schools would find him, especially if he continued with his strategy. By the end of the basketball season, Oliver—despite having US coaches come to watch him play—did not get any scholarship offers (they saw his "temper"), and as a result he decided to return to "school in the fall for another year" to make up for lost time. As Campbell said, "Another year would give him that chance to solidify his status as a top recruit for US universities" (June 7, 2003).

At six-foot-seven and 230 pounds, Drew is not only the biggest member of the basketball team, but also the only White player; and a website devoted to Toronto high school basketball said that he "is one of the best" (May 31, 2003). Similar to his other teammates, Drew transferred from his neighbourhood high school to his current school because he had "dreams of a career in the NBA," and being on the Maverick team gave him the opportunity "to prove his talents" (May 31, 2003). Interestingly, Drew is constructed as a White player with "Black" Caribbean cultural characteristics,[5] including, we might say, his scholarship aspirations. A number of US colleges made early contact with Drew, indicating interest in offering him scholarships. By March, knowing that his grades were too low to win a scholarship, Drew quit school, vowing to improve his grades by correspondence courses.

Despite his low grades, Drew did hear from a number of US universities, and had an all-expense-paid visit to Southwest Texas State University (SWT) where "he met a few guys from the team for some pickup ball" and was amazed at the tiring pace of the game with the players. Campbell writes that Drew's lessons in the recruitment process "ended on the dance floor of a night club near his hotel where he danced all night with a 22-year-old former student of the university" who "promised they would meet again when he enrolled in September. Drew didn't get her phone number, her email address or even her last name, but he was sure he would find her again. The basketball coach and all the players knew her" (June 7, 2003). It is suggested that sometime later, the same young woman sent a letter to Drew, encouraging him to accept the offer from SWT university. That scholarship did eventually arrive by early May, and Drew accepted, but he still had to pass the Grade Twelve English courses, which he was taking by correspondence. So as the coach had assured Drew when he visited the university, "his grades wouldn't be a problem" (June 7, 2003).

What we learn from the behaviours of Nedrie, Oliver, and Drew is the extent to which their aspirations of achieving a US university basketball scholarship operated to influence the high school they attended, keep them in school, and, as in the case of Drew, use alternative means of completing the necessary education requirements. For all three players, their desire to obtain a US scholarship offer was so important that they were unwilling to entertain any alternative. Nedrie was willing to hold off applying to a Canadian university (something he did later, likely as a contingency measure), and Oliver returned to high school for another year to get a chance at being "a top recruit" for US universities.[6] A logical question is: what is the pull for these student athletes? Is it simply a chance to get a university education in order to secure a good occupation afterwards? Is it to play on a university or college team? Or is it to be closer to the NBA scouts, so that they get a better chance at being drafted eventually into the big leagues, thus gaining celebrity status and correspondingly millions of dollars? The evidence points to the fact, and understandably so (given the capitalist society in which we live), that these students are seeking the big social and financial rewards. Indeed, not only do student athletes, as one community college coach put it, "bounce around from school to school each year, essentially creating high school 'dream teams,'" many of them, "seduced by the lure of a US college basketball scholarship" will even leave Toronto schools early to enroll in US high schools, or enroll in US high schools after graduating from school in Toronto (see David Leeder, 2001, *Globe and Mail*, "Growing Number of Basketball Players Leaving High School Early to Head South," p. S4).

That many African-Canadian student athletes would win basketball scholarships to US colleges seems like "a long shot," especially when, like them, many African Americans also hold similar aspirations[7] and are closer to the observing eyes of college scouts. In his book, the *Last Shot: City Streets, Basketball Dreams*, Frey (1994) tells of four student athletes who live in the inner city neighbourhood or "projects" of Coney Island, New York. According to Frey, all four players expected that "their talent and tenacity on the court will at least reward them with free college education, a decent job after graduation, and a one-way ticket out of Coney Island—a chance, in other words, to liberate themselves from the grinding daily privations of life in the ghetto" (Frey, 1994, p. 16). But as Sperber (1995) writes: "The lure of an athletic scholarship is similar to the appeal of lottery, with the chance of an individual winning almost as remote .... In any given year about 90,000 [US] Black male high school seniors play organized basketball at inner city or poor rural schools. About 1,100 of them are offered 'full-ride' athletic scholarships. Thus, about 1 per cent of such seniors win the basketball lottery" (p. 59). And as Simons and Butow (1997) write: "The odds that any high school athlete will play a sport on the professional level are remote—about 10,000 to 1. As far as probabilities go, there's a better chance of, say, taking a coin, flipping it, and having it land on heads 13 times in a row" (p. 46). With respect to Canadian student athletes, Higgins (2003) suggests that the ratio is likely to be more than twice that of those in the US (p. 27).[8]

THE STUDY OF FIVE STUDENT ATHLETES[9]

In the face of these odds, why then would African-Canadian students have US athletic scholarship aspirations, and think that it is possible for them to realize these aspirations? How do they navigate the educational and athletic structures of Canadian schools in order to attain their post-secondary educational goals? In exploring these questions, I conducted a focus group discussion[10] with five (Kevin, Colin, Charles, Saeed, and Gordon) male working-class[11] high school basketball players, all of them Black/African Canadians; one, Saeed, was African-South Asian (who identified as African). They attended different (both public and separate) schools in a suburban area west of metropolitan Toronto. All were of Caribbean background and were either born in Canada or immigrated here at young ages (before age eight). Four were 17 years old, and the others were 18.

Three of the four were in Grade Twelve, one in OAC, and one in Grade Eleven.[12] With the exception of Colin, all aspired to obtain basketball scholarships to study in the United States. Two lived with their mothers only, and three with their biological parents. They were all friends who played basketball together in their spare time, and I was meeting them for the first time.

My meeting and interview with the group was arranged by one of the players' mother, introduced to me by a mutual friend. And as her home was the usual "hang out" spot for the group members, it was volunteered for the interview. In my initial contact with this parent by phone, I explained the purpose of my research, specifying that I was "looking to interview student athletes, specifically basketball players, who were highly committed to the sport." I was interested in knowing about those who lived and attended school in the suburban area outside of Toronto, as I was familiar with studies and the *Toronto Star* 1998 articles (see above) that reported on the significance of sports to the educational and career aspirations of Black students in the metropolitan city of Toronto (Dei et al., 1997; James, 1990; Solomon, 1992; Spence, 1999). I sought to talk with "information-rich" student athletes (see Introduction; also, Fortana & Frey, 1994; Morse, 1994) who had key knowledge and experience relevant to my research; and in the group discussion, participants were able to aid each other through their questioning, prompting, and by elaborating and verifying points. In doing so, participants were able to use information that was unavailable and inaccessible to me (Hammer & Atkinson, 1992).

In what follows, I examine the recurring themes that emerge from the focus group discussion. First, I discuss the strategies that the participants employed in their bid to realize their aspirations. These strategies are: (a) attending the right school, and (b) getting exposure to college scouts who, these students believe, will help them to win US college scholarships.[13] Second, I discuss what the participants reveal about their interactions with their coaches and teachers; and third, about their perceptions of what winning a scholarship would mean to their parents. In a discussion section, I provide my reading of the participants' experiences, perceptions, and aspirations; I conclude by suggesting that the scholarship aspirations of African-Canadian youth can be understood in the context of their "outsider" position in society.

BASKETBALL, EDUCATION, AND SCHOLARSHIP OPPORTUNITIES

All five student athletes who participated in this study reported that they had been playing on their respective high school basketball teams for most of their high school years. I asked them, "What is basketball doing for you?"

Kevin: It is opening a lot of doors for opportunities, so I might as well stick with it ....

Carl: What are some of the opportunities that it is opening for you?

Kevin: People do stuff to help to go where you're going. I guess it looks good if you can do something that you're good at, and other people will respect you.

Carl: So what are you using your interest in basketball for?

Kevin: To get an education ... and try to get a scholarship so I can get my education without paying for it ....

Saeed: Same thing as Kevin. But I'm trying to play basketball and take it as far as I can go with it, and [at the] same time try to get a scholarship and use it as a way to pay for school ....

Gordon: Just like Kevin said, when people see that you can play basketball, [it shows] that you have potential to do something, they'll help you out ....

Colin: I kinda reached the end of the road with basketball, so I've got to look at other avenues. Fortunately, I have parents who put in other things. Concerning opening doors, basketball is not going do it for me. I have other things to fall back on .... like giving private piano lessons.

Charles: I can try to get a scholarship, and if I get a scholarship, I can go to school for free.

These comments reflect their optimism and their investment in basketball. And while none of them had yet been contacted by a college scout, they remained optimistic because they knew of people who had won scholarships. Specifically, two participants—Colin and Gordon—said that they had siblings who had obtained scholarships. Gordon explained that when his older brother (now on a football scholarship at a US university) was recruited, he was asked to give the names of his siblings. But even though at age 17, the university still had not made any contact with Gordon, the fact that his name was in a university file led him to continue believing that he would some day gain a scholarship if only to the same university as his brother. Why were they all so optimistic? What kept all five student athletes believing that basketball would "open the doors" they wanted opened? I think Gordon expressed the sentiments of the group best when he stated: "I guess it is determination and who has it more will get it, and that's the way you have to face life. You cannot sit back and wait for it to come to you, you have to go out and get it yourself."

For these young men, being determined,[14] committed, and optimistic was necessary if they were to realize their scholarship and social ambitions. And as they further indicated, in addition to being good at "playing ball," there were initiatives and strategies they had been using to achieve these scholarships. Some of these strategies involved attending the right school and getting exposure to scouts.

NEGOTIATING SCHOOL: "LOOK AT THE SCHOOL AND WHAT THE SCHOOL HAS TO OFFER"

In arguing that there is a relationship between the school one attends and the possibility of attaining an athletic scholarship, these student athletes argued that it was important to attend schools that were known to be supportive of their sport of interest. They commented that the school board where their current schools were located did not sufficiently support basketball; rather, as Colin said, the board "was more for other sports such as football and hockey." They went on to point out that schools and school boards in metropolitan Toronto were more supportive of basketball—"it is a year in year out thing for downtown schools," and some would "bend their rules a bit for a certain player." The Toronto school to which Jamaal transferred (described earlier) was cited as an example where the rules were bent in order to open up opportunities for student athletes.

The social and cultural mix of schools, and the schools' location, play a role in how much particular sports gain prominence. The communities in which these students resided, and the schools that they attended are in the middle-class suburbs outside of metropolitan Toronto, with largely White European residents who the students felt preferred sports "such as football and hockey." But while they attended schools that provided some level of support for basketball, this was not complemented with local school board support. Hence, they saw less opportunity for scholarships than that of their peers residing in metropolitan Toronto. As an example, they referred to Jamaal (and other Toronto players) as more likely to win basketball scholarships because of the schools they attended. And by way of demonstrating the better situation of Toronto players, Gordon explained that "the list of the top 50 players from all over Ontario ... is the most biased you will ever see. There are only three players from [this area] ... and the rest are from teams in Toronto. If you look at all of us here, I think that we could all make it in that top 50 .... They might have height ...." And, as Kevin added: "But they don't have the skills."

Conscious of the fact that having opportunities to play basketball and "getting exposure" to scouts are crucial to eventually winning scholarships, these students did their share of transferring from one school to another. Some acted on their own initiative, while others were recruited by a coach or other team members. And while none of them have actually transferred to a metropolitan Toronto school, they still believed that their opportunities would be enhanced if they had because (they claimed) university coaches "know these schools." In fact, one player, Kevin, considered transferring to a private boys' school in Toronto. He later decided against doing so, partly because of finances, but more because he did not want to go to "an all guy school."

At the time of our conversation, Saeed was thinking of changing schools. The first high school he attended was outside of his area. As Saeed explained:

> My home school, I did not go to it because of the basketball team. The basketball team and the program were not all that good, so I decided to go to Jack because they had a good basketball team and a coach. But how I really got on the team was playing street ball and some players from the school saw me play and they mentioned my name to the coach and when I got it, it was pretty easy.

Now he was in the process of transferring to Maple because, as he put it, "they have the exposure you want .... They just came back last weekend from

Syracuse [university]." And as Kevin added: "They won the championship for this area last year." When Saeed was asked what was influencing his decision to transfer to Maple high school, this was the response:

> Saeed: I looked at my school and what my team has to offer me ... [M]yself I have to do all the work, I have to play all five positions; and that's hard for me. And, then, plus, I have to go home when I am all exhausted and do homework .... That's so hard .... My school right now is giving no exposure whatsoever. I am scoring a lot of points and getting my name in the [local] newspapers but that is it. But if you go to Maple, they actually take you to some tournaments in Toronto. We don't even go to tournaments in Toronto. This school do not even go to Toronto, maybe we are scared of Toronto, so we go far away .... This [Maple] is going to help me, give me a lot of exposure that I need. This is a win-lose situation .... [Meaning?] It most likely will help me get the scholarship that I need, but then I'll probably be more focused on basketball and as such slackin' off a lot on my school work, and then once you start doing that, your marks will drop.
>
> Carl: How then will you balance your schoolwork and commitment to basketball?
>
> Saeed: That is something that I have to do for myself. I have to work hard, I guess.

What is evident in Saeed's comments is his expectation that the school he attends, and in particular the basketball team on which he plays, affords him the opportunity to attain his goals. To this end, all five athletes seemed to be engaged constantly in evaluating their situation. They felt that it was their responsibility to ensure that the school was not thwarting their strategies. Kevin remarks,

> ... getting onto the high school basketball team may look and sound great and all that, but in reality, are you going to play when you get there? Are you sure that he [the coach] is going to guarantee you the start? .... Some people get chosen just to be practice dummies, say they are like six-ten or whatever, and they have a centre that's like seven foot. They are just there to make sure that the centre is in shape and that he can do his moves against someone about the same height as him. Is that what he is going to be used

for, or are they bringing him to the team for his ability ... [or] to practise with other guys to make sure he becomes a better player?

It became clear later that Kevin's well-placed comments and questions were based on his own experience of having been recruited by the basketball coach of St. Elma Separate School. It happened that for Grade Nine, Kevin went to Audrey High School (a school, according to Kevin, that he didn't even know the location of) instead of St. Elma High School (both in the separate school board), which was closer to his house. He had planned to go into Grade Ten at St. Elma's, but the coach there, who was coaching Kevin's older brother, sent a message to Kevin via his brother, suggesting that Kevin stay at Audrey. The reason given was that the coach was moving to Audrey to be vice-principal, and was intending to become the basketball coach. According to Kevin, in the message the coach promised that he would give Kevin "the recognition and exposure" that he needed, and that the team would be going to "a lot of tournaments." But contrary to this commitment, the coach "did some stupid things" and Kevin returned to St. Elma. This can be regarded as a serious breech of contract insofar as the coach did not provide Kevin with the opportunity to play at one of the most critical times in his playing career. As Kevin explained:

> We were undefeated in the whole season .... We beat Davis twice and he benched me in the semi-final game against Davis at our school for missing a tournament that he said was meaningless. So I went to my rep because I was paying almost $200, so I might as well get my court time. So, he benched me in that game and we ended up losing ....

It is evident that these student athletes took seriously the opportunities to play basketball and to get the necessary exposure. They were prepared to put in the necessary efforts toward building their skills and securing opportunities through their selection of appropriate schools and school teams. And they understood that their coaches had a significant role to play in this process. However, they were unwilling to allow the school, coaches, and/or fellow-players become barriers to their success. School, as Kevin and Saeed made clear late in our discussions, and as Solomon (1992) has demonstrated, was merely a means to an end.

Kevin: First of all, I don't really care about school. I am in school so I can play basketball. I'll do my best at whatever, it is just like if you give a 100 percent on the court, you have to give 100 percent off the court, and that's what I do. But I am saying, if push came to shove, and I have to choose a school for academic or for basketball reason, I would definitely go for basketball ....

Carl: If you are not so keen on school, is it basketball that is going to make your decision to go on to university, more than academics?

Kevin: I could always become a stripper. Like $500 a night is not too bad, you know .... I wouldn't want to go to school just based on academics, 'cause I am not a study book guy. I'm not in the books. That's not me. I like to have fun, party, do whatever, and if basketball falls through, then I can become a dancer [laughing], a stripper. If not that, I want to become a historian, a history teacher.

Saeed: Same thing. School is just there for basketball basically. But I'm taking basketball as far as it can take me.

Carl: Would you be one who stays in school for a year longer so that the scouts can see you?

Saeed: Yes [jokingly and teased by the others], I might do that. No, but I would want to stay 'til I'm 21, but there is a limit. I'd say after five years for me, that's it ....

Carl: What about you, Kevin?

Kevin: No, because my parents would actually pull me out of school. I don't think if I'm 21 years, and I am playing great, scoring like 40 points a game, but it is against people who are 17, and if I went to play against someone who was my age, they would probably be doing the same thing I am doing to the other kids so I [would] feel like I was washed-up. I would just try to get my education.

These comments indicate that while these participants are willing to work hard to get basketball scholarships, there is a limit beyond which they will not go. They seem to be guided by integrity, self-pride, and the expectations of their parents. They claimed that unlike other student athletes, they would not deliberately fail a school year in order to return to school for an extra year to play basketball.[15] This is demonstrated by their concern that, unlike others, they do not want to play with younger players. This would be an indication that they are "not good." Interestingly, their parents' expectations that they get an education and finish school are not far from their consciousnesses; they discussed how far they would pursue these expectations. In the case of the student athlete in New York, Frey (1994) found that athletics more than academics was a major incentive for attending school, and coaches aggressively recruited young players, promising them, among other things, the chance to win a city title and be exposed to college scouts. This contributed to a situation where players were criss-crossing the city to play on their favourite teams, and others remained in schools where they continued to play even though their grades and ages should have rendered them ineligible (Frey, 1994, p. 157).

IMPORTANCE OF EXPOSURE: "YOU CAN'T JUST SIT BACK AND EXPECT SCOUTS TO COME WATCH FOR YOU"

I noted earlier that obtaining exposure to scouts is seen as crucial to winning basketball scholarships. And while these student athletes looked to the school and coaches in particular to provide them with the necessary exposure to recruiting American college scouts, they were not prepared to sit back and wait. Saeed remarked:

> You have to expose yourself. You can't just sit back and expect for scouts to come to watch you .... Either you write letters to them, or you make videotapes of the highlight of your year ... try and go to a school that actually goes across the border and play. You go halfway, meet them halfway .... As you [referring to me] said, there are so many people in the States that are just like us right now.

In talking about the initiative that he has taken, Kevin recalled sending around "profile sheets just last week" to some 15 colleges in the United States, but he knows that "they don't really look at you unless you have done your SAT, so I'll have to write those in January." Kevin was encouraged to do so by a young woman who recently received a basketball scholarship for a school in North Carolina.

In addition to these strategies, participants also said that they were taking other steps, such as playing on community leagues,[16] and going to camps and tournaments. As Colin said: "It is not just school that gets you the exposure. It's yourself. You have to go out there. Go to camps, go wherever. If you think you are good enough to compete with the rest of them, you go out there and do your stuff. You don't sit back ...." Exposure was named as the primary reason for participating in leagues. According to Kevin, playing in leagues helps "because we go to tournaments all over the place," places in both Canada and the United States. However, there was disagreement as to whether leagues provided more exposure than high school. Kevin noted that he knew of a league player who sent letters to a number of schools in the United States, pointing out that he was going to be representing his area and playing in a provincial championship with the "best" players of his age group. The scouts did attend the game to watch him, and later he received a college scholarship. From this Kevin concluded that if scouts know "that you are one of the top among your class, then they will come and look at you." But as Gordon adds:

> you have to be a good player to get scholarships. But a big thing, something that will help, is you have to know how to talk to people. If you can have a nice conversation after every game with the opposing team's coach, they going to think: "Yah that guy, he's a good player. I talk to him. He's a good kid." That's how people will begin to know you and recommend you more than just as a basketball player.

All five of these student athletes said that they have been to basketball camps both in Canada and the United States, but this was a year or two earlier when they were younger and unable to take full advantage of the possibilities that camp could provide for them. Nevertheless, they recognized as articulated by Kevin, that camps are "another avenue to a scholarship." All of them were well aware of the many camps, and in reference to elite camps like Nike, Kevin also notes that "people who go to those camps pretty much have a future in basketball." Understandably, while they would welcome the opportunity to attend these camps, they pointed out that money is a barrier. In Kevin's words:

> ... if you have the money and you want the exposure, and you want basketball to take you somewhere, do it. But if you're just doing for the sake of doing it, then don't even try it because if you go to one of those top camps, and you're just there for fun, you'll cry when you get home, because they will just make you look stupid.

And as Gordon adds, you must be prepared for the "competition" because "those guys will just jump right over you. They'll make you look like you just learned how to walk."

There was a strong sense of realism about their abilities and skills that seemed to permeate these student athletes' sense of how they will be able to perform in order to win a basketball scholarship. As well as the overwhelming confidence expressed in discussions, they also, at times, expressed reservations. Kevin, who claims to be in school for basketball, hopes to win a scholarship someday, and points out how the "five guys in the room" were much better players than many in metropolitan Toronto. Although he "went to the so-called best camp in Canada," he also said that it:

> ... was a piece of garbage. It's expensive. I'm thinking it's going to be some good athletes, but it was basically a bunch of little kids who could afford it. To be blunt, it was a lot of White kids. Half of them couldn't even play, but they thought that I was good. They thought that I was really better than I was.

THE ROLE OF COACHES AND TEACHERS

Teachers and coaches play a significant role in preparing students academically and athletically for the college and university athletic scholarships that they hope to win. In this regard, student athletes expect them to facilitate the process of school transfers, provide exposure opportunities, and demonstrate a willingness to accommodate their athletic interests. Charles, Gordon, Kevin, Saeed, and Colin seemed satisfied that, for the most part, their teachers and coaches were supportive in helping them maintain their goals. In cases where their coaches appeared unsupportive, they would change schools. This was what Kevin did: he left the school after the coach did not give him the opportunity to play what he considered was an important basketball match.

Interestingly, while these student athletes recognized that coaches and teachers in Toronto might have provided them with better basketball opportunities, they nevertheless did not transfer to Toronto schools. And while some, like Kevin, argued that they were in school for basketball, they were quite proud to point out that there was "a big difference between our school and metro schools" (Colin): the schools they attended were "academically oriented." Teachers in their schools, according to Kevin, were "there to teach you about life. Life is not going to be as easy as you think." They would try to demonstrate that their academic preparation was superior to that of the student athletes in Toronto schools. For example, Gordon pointed out that he knew student athletes in Toronto schools who failed courses many times because the schools they attended "do not preach academics; it's all about basketball." And as Colin added, "Teachers slack off on players just because they play basketball." My respondents felt that this was not the situation for them personally. However, the participants said that they knew of students on their basketball teams who failed subjects and, as a result, were on academic probation.

The discussion of the role of the coach in ensuring that they are in school to obtain a meaningful education and not just for the purpose of playing sports (see Lapchick, 1995; Sperber, 1995) precipitated a discussion of race. As if to assure themselves that they were not caught in a school system that constructed them mainly as tall, Black male youths who were more given to physical than intellectual ability and skill,[17] these students indicated that they would challenge rather than accept such a stereotype. They argued that such stereotyping was based on "ignorance." It seemed that their coaches were not part of such stereotyping for, as Kevin argued, his coach was "Black at heart." Hence, they insisted that their coaches realized that they not only needed basketball skills, but academic skills as well.

PARENTAL SUPPORT AND SCHOLARSHIP ASPIRATIONS

I asked the five student athletes what their parents thought about their plan to use basketball to secure an education, and also how their parents felt about the attention that they were giving to basketball (James, 1996; Simons & Butow, 1997). Their responses indicated that their parents were supportive of their educational aspirations and felt that a basketball scholarship was a means by which to attain them. Two of these athletes (Kevin and Saeed) said that they were from large families and that their parents could not afford to pay for their post-secondary education, so they felt that "if they were able to get a scholarship, then that would help their parents a lot." Kevin went further to say that his parents viewed a scholarship as providing him the opportunity "to become a pro," and since there was a lot of competition, then in college he could become the "exceptional" player he needed to be to succeed.

Having similar educational aspirations for their children, and recognizing the significance of high school in preparing them for that athletic scholarship, the parents understandably supported these student athletes in choosing to attend a high school based on their athletic interests and needs. Hence, with the support of their parents, these youths could respond positively to the offers made by coaches to attend particular schools. There was no evidence of their parents challenging or blocking their recruitment to attend schools in their suburban communities. But in the case of Kevin, lack of financial support from his parents prevented him, as he explained, from transferring to a private school in downtown Toronto. However, parents were not blind supporters of these student athletes' ambitions. Recall Saeed saying that while some student athletes stayed in school for up to seven years in order to develop their skills and eventually obtain a basketball scholarship, he would not be able to do so because his parents would expect him to leave school. As Kevin added, "... my parents would actually pull me out of school."

A READING OF THE STUDENT ATHLETES' PERCEPTIONS AND SCHOLARSHIP ASPIRATIONS

Interestingly, during our discussion, there was no explicit acknowledgement that their understanding of success through basketball was related to their construction of blackness. But hidden in their comments were references to racial identity, specifically in terms of their possibilities as tall, male Black basketball players (see also Greenstone, 2002). Recall Kevin's comments about the "White kids" at the basketball camp whom he described as "couldn't even play." This seems to represent Kevin's notion of who are likely to be good players; it was not the "White kids" at the camp. And while they denied that there is a connection between race and basketball skills, they told self-complementing stories of friends—all of them tall, Black males whom they encouraged to play with them—who are now successful basketball players. Still, all five contended that they were not living up to society's expectations of them as more capable at sports; at the same time they indicated that they would take advantage of sporting opportunities. Charles, for example, said, "I don't think that it is my duty, because I am Black, to live up to the expectations of society to be better than anyone else. I play my game, and if it is good enough .... I guess it is all about taking the game to another level when it is needed. It has to come from within yourself."

In his essay on the role of sports in the representation of masculinities, Abdel-Shehid (1997) recalls that, for him, sports was part of a Black nationalist struggle and a sporting contest that was a "mythical narrative" of Black masculinity and anti-colonialism:

> I felt that this "mythical narrative" would allow me a sense of belonging and an anti-establishment politics. This nationalist desire for certainty, and a homeland, in this case a heavily Americanized version of what Michelle Wallace refers to as Black Macho, informed the choices I made and the sports I played. For me, not only were sports political, the role models I chose and the styles I played corresponded to a belief that it was good to be *bad.* There was a connection between black athletic excellence and moral goodness. Athletic excellence, to me, meant the same thing as serving the community, being down with the struggle and speaking out against racism (Abdel-Shehid, 1997, pp. 2–3).

Like Abdel-Shehid, basketball contributed to these working-class students' identification of Black masculinity (a connection academics have failed to make). This might have been behind Kevin's desire to choose a school for athletic rather than academic reasons. Failing that, he would become a "stripper." Kevin said this in jest, but it conveys the image of the Black macho. Kevin was also concerned about attending an all boys' school in downtown Toronto because it would not be in keeping with the macho image. Ostensibly, the idea of winning a basketball scholarship is something that fits into a construction not only of blackness, but also of maleness, all within a heterosexist paradigm. It is a reflection of the performance of Black masculinity in the racialized society these students inhabit (Abdel-Shehid, 1997; McCall, 1997).

That all five youth are from immigrant families who have recently moved into this middle-class suburban area outside of metropolitan Toronto is a salient factor in how they construct their futures. Their working-class immigrant parents, who have attained some measure of financial success, have likely socialized these student athletes into the middle-class values and aspirations of attaining upward social mobility through individual efforts, abilities, skills, and education (Boyd & Grieco, 1998; James, 2002). And given the reality of racism and the "occupational glass ceiling" experienced by Blacks (Henry, 1994; Plaza, 1998), parents might have subscribed to the notion that US athletic scholarships provide the hope and possibilities for their children to attain the educational credentials necessary for financial security and upward social mobility. Security and status are often sought by immigrant parents themselves, but failing that, they seek to realize this through their children (Anisef et al., 2000). Further, insofar as the participants suggested that their parents were unable to afford to send them to college or university, then scholarships were their best option. This would explain why parents did not object to their sons' choice of schools for basketball-related reasons.

It is instructive that the participants' coaches expected them to work toward obtaining athletic scholarships. Is this because academic scholarships were perceived to be beyond their reach? And did their coaches, and possibly teachers, believe that there are more opportunities for Black student athletes if they follow the path of seeking US college and university scholarships? Studies have shown that teachers and coaches, based on their social construction or stereotype of Black males as athletes, often encourage them to participate in athletic activities at the expense of their academic program (Codjoe, 2000; Solomon, 1992). As a result, many student athletes have little opportunity to obtain the necessary grades that would enable them to win academic scholarships.

Additionally, there is the students' perception that they are unlikely to obtain athletic scholarships to Canadian universities and colleges, and the Ontario Student Award Program (OSAP) will leave them in debt (see Anisef et al., 1982). Colin explained:

> ... for Canadian scholarships, they give you OSAP, which you will have to pay back as soon as you finish school. Canadians emphasize that school comes first, academic-wise, but sports-wise, we suck. A lot of Canadian high school basketball players do not have good marks to get into Canadian universities because they are asking 75 percent and over, so you have to get in by basketball.

And Kevin added:

> For [entry to] Canadian universities six OACs [Ontario Academic Credits] are needed. For the first term you are still on probation if you are not at the recommended level with your average. They are just as crooked as any other university ... In the United States, universities would accept me with marks lower than average knowing that I would be playing basketball.

Evidently, this belief in the financial assistance available in Canada plays a pivotal role, not only in these youths' understanding of the route to economic and social success or mobility, but also in that of their parents. For example, Gordon pointed out that his brother had been offered scholarships to study at a college in Canada and one in the United States; his father, however, encouraged him to go to the United States because in Canada he felt he would still have "had to pay" even though the Canadian coach had said "that he would provide him with everything; he did not have to worry."

The initiatives and strategies that these suburban student athletes employed in order to win scholarships were influenced by the fact that they lived and attended school some distance from the hub of the basketball action—away from metropolitan Toronto and the schools that are known for producing good basketball players (and hence are the places where college scouts visit). Therefore, as these youth demonstrated, it was up to them to seek opportunities for exposure. So while they sought to attend schools in their suburban community that would provide opportunities, more importantly, it was in the city that they ultimately wished to live and attend school where they could play with their city colleagues (who they insisted were no more talented than they). Furthermore, they believed that city basketball players had advantages over suburban players: the teachers "do not preach academics, it's all about basketball," and they received the needed exposure to scouts.

Except for Colin, who was at "the end of the road with basketball [and was looking] at other avenues," the others were thinking seriously about attending a US university or college on a basketball scholarship. Two relevant questions here are: how much do they know about the situation or treatment that scholarship winners encounter once they arrive on college campuses? And how do they anticipate dealing with situations that might prevent them from realizing their aspirations? As Sperber (1995) writes, the majority of Black males who win basketball scholarships "are treated as 'black gladiators,' brought to campuses mainly to play sports, not to obtain a meaningful education" (p. 58).[18] They avoid focusing on limitations to their success (see James, 1995; Lapchick, 1995; MacLeod, 1987; Sperber, 1995) by asserting their agency, and trying to maintain their optimistic and hopeful outlook. The participants maintained, as Kevin said, "I am a strong person and I don't make other people make my decisions in life." Saeed added: "One has to know what he wants. Don't let someone else tell you what you want. It is your life, you have to go out and get what you want." When asked directly about the suggestion that scholarship winners sometimes end up being used mainly to satisfy the goals of institutions, Kevin responded by saying: "You can buy me for a fool, but you can't sell me for a fool .... They use you to entertain, but you use them to get your education, to get where you want to get in life." Concurring, Gordon added: "We have to learn to use people as we are being used."

There are many contradictions in the attitudes of these student athletes. For example, they claimed that the schools in the city of Toronto offered the best opportunities to win US basketball scholarships; nevertheless, while they claim to actively select their schools and coaches, they chose not to attend any of the Toronto schools. They suggested that the conditions were "not right." Other reasons might be parental influence. While this was not explored in our conversation, it is likely that their parents might not have agreed to them going into the city. After all, in moving from the city, parents made deliberate decisions about where they wish their children to live and go to school—in the case of these student athletes, their parents may have intentionally wished for them to attend suburban schools; these schools might have appeared to be more appropriate than those in downtown Toronto. Another apparent contradiction is the priorities that these youth place on academics vs. basketball. For most of them, school was not merely a way of negotiating and navigating educational opportunities, but was also a means of playing basketball; getting an education, as Kevin so eloquently articulated, was an ordeal they have to endure. Yet they criticize Toronto teachers, coaches, and their peers for their educational shortcomings. And they also respond to the possibility of being used by US universities and colleges with the claims that by obtaining an education, they will "beat them at their own game." If, indeed, education is the real goal (and not joining the big leagues to "play ball"), then why not simply obtain that education in Canada? They could continue to live with their parents, and if they lack finances, they could attend school part time. To understand these contradictions, it is important to consider the social, political, and cultural context of the society in which these youth have grown up.

CONCLUSION: SCHOLARSHIP ASPIRATIONS AND THE DESIRE TO "GO SOUTH"

The aspiration to win US athletic scholarships can be seen as part of the working-class Black suburban Toronto male subculture—a subculture related to the marginalization, racialzation, and assimilative structure of schools and society. In their subculture, athletic abilities and skills are constructed as signifiers of blackness, masculinity, and a means by which Blacks are able to gain respect, prestige, and acknowledgement. It is also seen as a means by which they can expect to achieve their educational, occupational, and career goals. This subculture is also interrelated to the hegemonic discourse of multiculturalism, which conveys a cultural image of Black people as good athletes (and tall Black males as basketball players), and more generally as "Other" Canadians—people who are "outsiders."[19] The resulting "outer-national political identification" (Walcott, 1997) of Blacks helps to socialize them into thinking that their means of attaining their goals exist elsewhere. In this case, their aspirations are directed toward winning US athletic scholarships and moving to the United States. Hence, these student athletes surmise that it is best not to look to Canadian colleges and universities for post-secondary scholarships or for general opportunities to obtain the necessary educational credentials for their occupational success and upward social mobility.

The odds of winning athletic scholarships notwithstanding, it is understandable that the black student athletes who participated in this study would cultivate strategies such as attending the "right" school, playing on winning basketball teams, and seeking exposure to college and university coaches. Their strategies, initiatives, and performances reflect their struggles against alienation within the school system, and their attempts to ensure that their schooling provides them with what they need. Further, the way these students exercise agency is in effect structured by a subculture in which sports play a key role.

As this study shows, coaches (who often are also teachers) play an instrumental role in helping to shape these students' US scholarship aspirations. But more than encouraging student athletes to win US athletic scholarships and go south, coaches and teachers have to be cognizant of and sensitive to the reality that their good intentions sometimes serve to reinforce the racialization and marginalization of these youth. They may be inadvertently communicating to them that educational opportunities lie outside of academics. Educators should instead assist students to negotiate and navigate the academic culture of schools while taking seriously the social and cultural situation and needs of the students. Coaches should hold access to US athletic scholarships as an option, but at the same time help student athletes to combine sports with academic activities. Furthermore, parents, teachers, coaches, and school administrators need to give critical support to student athletes, and need to advocate for changes to schooling structures and processes at the levels of high and middle schools, so that they may respond to the needs, aspirations, and interests of student athletes in an equitable manner.

NOTES

1. This gym is even smaller than that of the Mavericks' school, where, as Campbell (2003) notes, players "can't even shoot a three-pointer from the corner without stepping out of bounds." The Mavericks' gym is "a full 20 feet shorter than the standard 94-foot basketball court."

2. According to Darcy Frey (in the *Last Shot*, 1994, p. 50), this ABCD camp, sponsored by Nike, is passed off as "an academic program to get athletes ready for college," and tends to draw players from "inner city neighbourhoods."

3. While students are able to obtain permission to attend schools outside of their area, according to Duffy, compared to Toronto, other school boards ban students from playing sports if they transfer for "athletic reasons."

4. According to the rules of the National Collegiate Athletic Association (NCAA) to enter college at the time, student athletes need a combined minimum score of 820 on the Scholastic Assessment test (SAT), or 68 on the American College Testing (ACT) examination, and a 2.5 grade point average in 13 core high school courses (Sperber, 1995, p. 58).

5. Campbell indicates that it is understandable that Drew would assimilate some of the cultural attributes, given how Black student athletes dominate the sport by their presence on teams and with their subculture. In this regard, it is said that Drew's "skin colour doesn't stop him from fitting in. In fact, he embraces the same black culture his teammates do, a hybrid that draws from their Toronto upbringing, their Caribbean-island heritage and the influence of African American culture." Drew was said to be Oliver's "best friend on and off the court" (May 31, 2003).

6. The *Toronto Star* (2004, February 18) reported that Oliver had a "verbal commitment to a scholarship" for the 2004/2005 school year from a Division 1 university in the US (p. C4).

7. Frey, 1994; Harris, 1994; 1991; MacLeod, 1991; Simons & Butow, 1997; Sperber, 1995; Staples, 1994.

8. *Toronto Star* reporter Michael Clarkson reported (November 26, 2003) that some 38 student athletes (referred to as "stars") from high schools in Toronto and surrounding areas were rewarded US scholarships, and were studying at American universities and colleges (p. C2).

9. The discussion of the research study in this chapter appears in C.E. James (2003b) "Schooling, basketball and US scholarship aspirations of Canadian athletes," which is published in *Race, Ethnicity and Education* 6(2), 124–144.

10. The focus group discussion was tape-recorded and lasted for approximately two hours. My prepared areas of questioning elicited information about the participants' schooling experiences, athletic activities, and their aspirations. I asked about the school they attended, their classroom experiences, and how well they were doing in their academic subjects. To find out about their participation in athletic activities at school and in the community, I asked questions about the number of years they had been playing basketball, and in what ways playing basketball benefited them and helped to maintain their interest in school. I also asked about the roles that participants' parents, teachers, coaches, and peers played in supporting their educational, athletic, and occupational aspirations.

11. Social class is inferred from the claims of the five participants that their parents were unable to afford their post-secondary education. They suggested that this had more to do with their parents' limited incomes rather than a desire to socialize them into self-responsibility and social independence.

12.

Names	Age	Grade	High School
Kevin	17	12	St. Elma Separate
Colin	18	OAC*	Davis Separate
Charles	17	12	Davis Separate
Saeed	17	11	Jack Public
Gordon	17	12	Davis Separate

*formerly Grade Thirteen

13. Indeed, Black students are not the only ones who dream of winning US athletic scholarships. Many young White males have been taking advantage of these scholarships (particularly hockey, soccer, and football) in their bid to attain their educational and occupational aspirations—aspirations that include winning hockey scholarships as a route to playing on a team in the National Hockey League (NHL) (see Anisef et al., 2000; Gruneau & Whitson, 1993).

14. In talking about their need for determination, Colin added, "who has it more will get it, and that's the way you have to face life. If you want something in life, you cannot sit back and wait for it to come to you. You have to go out there and get it yourself."

15. The participants mentioned that they know of players who stay in high school for six or seven years in order to play basketball. However, it was pointed out that there are new rules that allow students to play for five years.

16. All five student athletes stated that they had played in community leagues; however, only two (Charles and Kevin) were playing on leagues at the time of the interview.

17. See Codjoe, 2000; Entine, 2000; James, 1995; 1990; Lapchick, 1995.

18. See also Fields, 2001; Gerdy, 1997; Lapchick, 1995; Siegel, 1994; Tate, 1993.

19. This idea of "outsider" is well documented in writings by Black Canadians who tell about being constantly asked: "Where are you really from?" with the expectation that they would *confirm* that they or their parents were born elsewhere, most often Jamaica (Palmer, 1997; Shadd, 2001).

THE GENDERED EXPERIENCES OF FEMALE STUDENTS IN SPORTS, WITH SPECIAL REFERENCE TO ALICIA[1]

We feel that the Olympic Games must be reserved for the solemn and periodic exaltation of male athleticism, with internationalism as a base, loyalty as a means, art as its setting and female applause as a reward (Pierre de Coubertin in 1896, founder of the modern Olympics, cited in Coakley, 1998).

Perhaps no other issue raises barriers to young people's participation in sport and physical activities than gender (Schempp & Oliver, 2000, p. 146).

THE TEXTURED NARRATIVES OF STUDENT ATHLETES REVEAL MUCH ABOUT HOW gender, race, and class have created, perpetuated, and even determined their educational pathways and educational and athletic outcomes. Notwithstanding the interlocking relationship of these demographic characteristics (not surprising in the patriarchal educational system in which today's students negotiate their educational and athletic needs, interests, and aspirations), gender operates to influence their athletic participation in schools, as well as their post-high school education and athletic aspirations. Male student athletes continue to enjoy the benefits, privileges, and support from their coaches, teachers, peers, parents, and the media, resulting in their high participation and achievements in sports (e.g., athletic scholarship and opportunities to play professionally). Female students, however, face a different situation: in particular those from ethnic and racial minority as well as working-class backgrounds, have had to struggle against the limitations and barriers posed by their gender (see also Varpalotai, 1996). It is little surprise that they have a lower rate of sports participation and educational achievements. Indeed, as Coakley and Donnelly (2004) indicate, this problem is rooted in the historical, social, cultural, economic, and political realities of society, and is evidenced by the fact that in many cases, there is an emphasis on boys' teams as being the most important teams in schools. Furthermore, they point out that "the sport programs that do exist in societies ... are grounded primarily in the values, interests, and experiences of [White] men ... and geared to the way men have learned to think about their bodies, their relationships to other people, and the way the world operates" (Coakley & Donnelly, 2004, p. 15; see also Lapchick, 1995, Chapters 9 to 16). By extension, in schools, it is common to find that young women and their coaches have limited influence in the athletic programs or in the use of the athletic facilities and other resources.

In this chapter, I examine more closely the situation of minority female student athletes in terms of their participation in sports, as well as their experiences, interests, aspirations, and educational achievements in relation to sports. In doing so, I review the literature and discuss the research findings of studies that inquired into the gendered experiences of female high school student athletes in the Toronto area. The last part of the chapter will be devoted to the presentation of a life history interpretive account of Alicia. This gives us insights into how one young Black female made sense of her experiences as a student athlete. This includes the circumstances and structural factors that shaped her life and informed her educational and athletic pathways, as well as her perceptions of the opportunities and possibilities that athletics provided her.

Feminist theories provide a useful framework for reading the educational and athletic experiences, expectations, and outcomes of female students. These theories posit that, in stratified societies, gender is a significant characteristic that interacts in varied and complex ways with other characteristics such as race, ethnicity, and class to structure relationships among individuals, as well as between individuals and groups, institutions, and society as a whole. As a system of complex institutional and patriarchal relationships between females and males, gender plays a significant role in the experiences, available opportunities, role expectations, and achievements of both females and males; this is not because of biological or physical differences, but because of the meaning attributed to these differences. As such, the performance of gender— specifically the performance of the socially, racially, and culturally constructed categories of femininity and masculinity—is regulated and circumscribed by the societal and institutional contexts in which females and males interact and come to learn about their gender roles and expectations.[2] And as Jordan and Weedon (1995) point out, these gender categories "determine the forms of subjectivity and social relations open to us as men and women" (p. 185). Integral to any discussion of feminism is the role that sexism[3] plays in denying access and opportunities to females while according men privileges.

While all feminist theories use the lens of gender to view the world (Rosser, 2001), the diversity and complexity of women's lives in relation to such characteristics as race, ethnicity, class, immigrant/citizenship status, etc., contribute to a number of feminist theories. One such theory is that of anti-racist feminism, which positions the lives and experiences of women of colour as the starting point for analysis, and in doing so—the interconnections of gender, race, ethnicity, and class notwithstanding—"attempts to integrate the way race and gender function together in structuring social inequality" (Dua, 1999, p. 9). As part of Canadian epistemology, anti-racist feminism gives attention to the historical, political, economic, and cultural context in which the process of racialization in Canada "has shaped and continues to shape women of colour's experience of gender, class and racism" (Dua, 1999, p. 24). And while it asserts that all women of colour are subjected to racism and sexism, it recognizes that their experiences differ depending on their social locations (e.g., class, ethnicity), as well as the institutional (e.g., school), and the societal (e.g., political, economic, cultural) contexts in which interactions take place (Dua, 1999; Wood, 2002). Indeed, as Henry (1993) argues, it is dangerous to homogenize the paradoxes and complexities of women's lived experiences. To this end, she contends that while it is important for scholars to acknowledge the commonalities in the gendered experiences of women, equally important are the specificities of their lives in relation to their historical, social, and economic contexts. For this reason, then, Henry (1993) advocates the centring of the experiences of Black women and girls, in order to fully grasp "the diverse historical, political, and economic forces within which Black lives are embroiled" (p. 214). It is this argument that is being followed in my exploration of the educational and athletic experiences of Alicia. Moreover, this examination of the educational and athletic experiences and outcomes of Alicia follows Wood's (2002) assertions that anti-racism feminism is a useful prism through which to view how schools, through their programs and activities, structure and facilitate the schooling experiences, and ultimate outcomes, of Black female students.

GENDER, SPORTS, SCHOOLING, AND THE SITUATION OF YOUNG MINORITY FEMALE STUDENTS

Today, girls and boys usually have equal rights in access to school physical education programs. This does not necessarily mean, however, that they also have equal opportunity "to learn and express themselves through physical activity" (Talbot, 1989 in Hall et al., 1991, p. 193).

As a major institution in society, schools play a central role in socializing young women and men into their respective gender roles. In so doing, schools, for the most part, continue to reproduce the inherent gender inequities of the society. Male students continue to enjoy privileges and opportunities through their access to, and accommodation in, school programs, including academic and athletic activities. Many of these opportunities are unavailable to female students. In such a context, therefore, schools are failing to provide female students with the knowledge, skills, and opportunities to critically engage the school system in ways that will ensure the achievement of their potentials and realization of their ambitions. Accordingly, as Wood (2002) asserts, "schools are implicated in the maintenance of gender inequalities and in the struggle to redress these inequalities" (p. 7). Indeed, studies (Hanmer, 1996; Henry, 1995; 1993; Wood, 2002) indicate that educators' interactions with, and expectations of, female and male students tend to reflect the gender norms and stereotypes of females as less physically and academically able than males. The result is that females tend to receive less support and encouragement from teachers, which in turn affects their self-esteem and self-confidence. All of this is further reflected in academic and athletic activities. Specifically, females tend to avoid certain activities that are dominated by males in their effort to escape being undermined by educators (teachers and coaches alike), or being stigmatized or sexually harassed by peers.

A major school activity that female students tend to avoid is physical activities or sports—not necessarily because of disinterest, but more importantly, because of inherent barriers. Their low participation rate in athletic activities occurs even though, as studies have shown, females understand the health, social, and psychological benefits of sports (Kippen, 1999). These benefits include higher levels of self-esteem and self-confidence, gained through the respect and recognition earned by some students. These psychological benefits in turn motivate students to keep up their level of athletic involvement and performance, and to do so they stay in school. Staying in school and actively engaging in their educational process has a positive effect on students' academic attainments and inspires high educational aspirations. In addition, through sports, students learn the skills of coping, problem-solving, decision-making, and leadership, as well as to value such things as respect, responsibility, friendship/camaraderie, and teamwork. For working-class student athletes, sports have been productively used as a "way out"—a means of achieving a post-secondary education scholarship, possibly leading to upward social mobility. Sports are also known to contribute to the development of self-pride, good physical health, and a general sense of well-being, and for females in particular, especially those in their adolescent years, sports contribute to increasingly positive body images.[4] Ostensibly, sports have provided student athletes with social, psychological, and educational rewards whereby they are able to develop positive relationships in schools, build on their talents, abilities, and skills, and actively engage in securing their goals.

But benefits aside, research findings indicate that, beginning at age 12, girls' involvement in physical activities declines steadily until by ages 16 to 17, only 11 percent of them are participating in physical activities (Hay & Donnelly, 1996). Furthermore, an Edmonton study found that of 42,000 young people under the age of 18 who played sports, about 67 percent were boys (Fenton et al., 2000). The reason for the low participation of females in sports can be explained, in part, by the fact that sports, as Kidd (1987) maintains, "perpetuate patriarchy" in that through sports, males obtain exciting opportunities, their achievements as "best male athletes" are publicly celebrated, and their tendency to view sports as a male domain is constantly being validated and affirmed. Females, on the other hand, are marginalized as cheerleaders and spectators, and excluded from the learning that males receive in the context of sports (p. 255; see also Dabovic, 2002; Hanson & Kraus, 1999). Similarly, Schempp and Oliver (2000, p. 146), write that:

> Sport often divides the sexes and perpetuates distorted definitions of masculinity and femininity (Coakley, 1998). For example, in high school there are "boys" teams and "girls" teams. In the community recreational programs, one often hears comments about "girls' sports," and "boys' sports." The divide due to sex appears too many—both females and males—as natural and normal.

They added that "while biological differences between males and females suggest separation for the sake of fair competition in some sports," gender differences nevertheless continue to be used to deny females opportunities and access to sport activities. In other words, it is difficult for females to escape the sexism that is embedded within the academic and athletic structures of schools and carried out by administrators, teachers, coaches, student athletes, and students generally (Schempp & Oliver, 2000, p. 146).

The scourge of sexism is also manifested in gender identification. Griffin (1996) points out that insofar as sports are considered to be an arena in which males learn masculinity—such things as competition, aggression, and perseverance—women and girls who participate in it, more so than men and boys, "endure intense scrutiny about their sexual identity" (cited in Schempp & Oliver, 2000, p. 147). Such scrutiny and accompanying stigmatization also stem from the fact that by participating in "the arena of masculinity" (Pronger, 1992; see also Davison, 2000; Katz, 1996), specifically White heteronormative masculinity (Abdel-Shehid, 2004), females are perceived to be violating the socially accepted norms of femininity. And as Griffin (1995) suggests, raising questions about the femininity of female athletes is one of the most potent strategies for discouraging their participation in athletics. So unlike male athletes, who are assumed to be heterosexual (unless something happens to raise suspicion or prove otherwise), female athletes have the task of proving their heterosexuality, or live with the suspicion that they are lesbians and face possible sexual discrimination (Griffin, 1995; Lenskyj, 2003). Consequently, the performance of gender roles is also shaped by the punishment of what is considered to be "gender-inappropriate behaviours" (Davison, 2000, p. 48).

In schools, coaches play a key role in re-inscribing or disrupting gender differences among male and female student athletes. In his study of gender issues as related to equity in high school athletic programs, Simmons (1999) interviewed 10 White[5] high school teacher-coaches (five females and five males) who work in three "racially mixed, working-class" high schools in "urban" Toronto. Two of the three schools are said to have a large Black student population. A teacher-coach himself, Simmons pursued his study in his attempt to, among other things, "develop a coaching philosophy that was both equitable and effective, taking into account the differences that he had perceived to exist between female and male athletes" (p. 4). He distinguishes between equity and equality, saying that "gender equity includes equal opportunity and equal access to resources that result in equal outcomes in a manner that respects both genders treating them justly and fairly" (p. 2). Reflecting on his "experiences and frustrations" as a coach, he writes:

> I found that I held beliefs that were dogmatic at their best and discriminatory at their worst. When I began coaching at the high school level in 1993, I made a conscious effort to treat the female athletes in the same manner as the male athletes. It was my opinion at the time, that this "equality of treatment" was appropriate and equitable. When one of the girls under my direction did not execute the instructions I had issued, I yelled at her as I would have yelled at a boy. She began to cry and I was left dumbfounded. I sought out the advice of a woman on staff who had 20-years of coaching experience. When I stated I was trying to treat the girls in the same manner as the boys, she reminded me that the boys and girls have been socialized differently. While I acknowledged the validity of this statement, I asked if modifying my coaching pedagogy to accommodate the gendered differences was not merely re-enforcing the very differences that have been used as a means of discriminating against women. To this my colleague relied: "It's a conundrum" (Simmons, 1999, p. 4).

Simmons mentions that the coaching pedagogy of many coaches like him has to do with being socialized by athletic programs that reward aggressiveness based on a "win at all costs" philosophy.

Simmons found that his respondents did not fully understand what is meant by gender equity. For them, gender equity meant giving the same opportunities to girls that were offered to boys. As one respondent said, "You provide the opportunity, but it is up to the girls to take them." And when the girls did not take advantage of the opportunities offered, the coaches did not think to examine the school conditions, resources, or even their own behaviours; instead they looked at the girls themselves. Hence, from three male coaches, Simmons heard:

> Girls do not push themselves as hard as guys. They definitely don't. They may be into the sport but they certainly don't push it. I don't know why not. I don't think they know what pushing it is. They give you the "girl thing" to get off the hook; you know, the "oh, I'm so tired." But for guys, that's not cool. They push and then push harder .... Ask a Grade Nine guy what the

most important thing in his life is, they'll say "basketball." Eight of the 10 guys will, in the regular school population. Only three girls, if that, will say sports are a high priority. Girls are looking at other things at this age, like guys and make-up .... A lot of people want to bring equality of the sexes into everything and it certainly doesn't apply (p. 54).

Girls are as competitive, as desirous at any given game as boys, but they may not want to get there in the same way. They may want to be more collegial than some of the guys are. I'll tell you, I find it easier to get four or five girls to go in one direction than I do the guys I've been coaching. Maybe it's me; perhaps I take more time to explain it to them (pp. 54–55).[6]

I think boys see sports as a means to an end. Here it is basketball. Boys come in dreaming of the NBA .... [They] dream of playing in college in the States or going to university in Canada. I try to steer them in the right way, not to give them delusions of grandeur. As for girls, I haven't been around any who want it to the same extent—an education via sports, that is[7] .... I find, even in class, the boys are willing to participate and be more active .... I don't know why. I guess it goes back to having strong coaches. I mean boys come into the school and all you have to do is roll a ball out to get them playing. The girls at this stage don't seem to want it as much; maybe because they just need direction—more encouragement. Also, who knows what backgrounds we are dealing with here or wherever (p. 55).

According to these coaches, it is the attitudes of the females—not prepared or not as motivated to work as hard as the males—and their aspirations that account for the differences in the opportunities they get to participate in their schools' athletic activities. But as one female coach stated,

The boys generally get better coaching, from the knowledge of the game perspective. Thus, the boys learn about the sport. As for the amount of play, the boys are in a tournament every weekend. They go to the United States twice a year. The girls may get away once. Maybe some exhibition games—that's it. Of course there are more boys' tournaments than girls' tournaments out there. On another level, the boys get more money to do things (pp. 73–74).

Even with such insight, we did not see this coach or any of the others substantially criticize how their schools (or themselves) were addressing the differences in opportunities received by the female athletes; neither did they attempt to examine from the female athletes' perspectives such things as why they did not take advantage of the opportunities. However, as one female coach speculated, the inequities that existed between the male and female student athletes were a result of their "social learning's outside of the school"—a way of referring to the lower socio-economic situation and the Black Caribbean-Canadian cultural background of most of the basketball team members. Yet, these "differences" were never considered in a way that would address the layered structural inequalities and the inherent sexism operating in their schools. In the absence of such consciousness, therefore, the coaches admitted that they treated the males and females differently based on the expectation that the females will "perform to a lower standard than the boys." As well, most of the coaches stated that "they held the same expectations and made the same demands of both genders." And while four of the five male coaches said that "the gender of the coach was of little to no significance," the females felt that it was "beneficial for the girls to be coached by a woman" (Simmons, p. 68).

With such limited recognition and absolute rejection of the significance of gender to students' experiences, it is understandable that these coaches would similarly see no correlation between the students' experiences and race, ethnicity, or class. And reading the study, one would miss out on the issue to which Simmons draws our attention near the end of the study: "Also significant is the fact that all of the coaches were White and all of the players were Black" (p. 77). Yet, the role of race and racism in the opportunities provided and the perceptions of the coaches were never taken up in any sustained way in the interviews or in the analyses of the coaches' comments (see also Dabovic's [2002] study, discussed below). If the objective is to provide equitable opportunities, then coaches must take into account the differences in the experiences, needs, interests, expectations, and aspirations of students. Treating all females the same will not result in them receiving equal treatment. So, just as gender has mediated the differential experiences of the female and male students, so too do the interlocking characteristics of race, ethnicity, class, and immigrant/citizenship status. This relationship of gender, race, ethnicity, and immigrant/citizenship status is explored in Nakamura's (2003) study of the journeys of nine (five males and four females) Toronto area South, Southeast, and East Asian university students enrolled in the physical education degree program. While the study does not focus on gender differences, it nevertheless alerts us to the role of gender, ethnicity, and immigrant background in the experiences, interests, interactions, aspirations, and parental expectations of these Asian student athletes.

In a substantive and useful review of the literature (representing studies conducted in Britain, Australia, the United States, and Canada), Nakamura documents the social, cultural, and familial factors that, in complex and varying ways, account for Asian females' participation in sports and physical activities. Parental influences and expectations play a significant role (see also Desai & Subramanian, 2003). Specifically, lack of parental support, parental restrictions, or constraints based on family and home responsibilities tend to circumscribe the participation of females in sports and recreational activities. For some immigrant parents (particularly newly arrived parents), there was the desire for their children to acculturate into the new society. To this end, parents value academics for the education of their children, rather than sports or physical education. The resulting schooling and athletic experiences of Asians can be explained, in part, by the degree of loyalty their parents maintain to the cultural traditions of their "home country" and by adherence to religion or religious conviction, as well as through language differences. But while parental and ethnic cultural factors (of course, taking into account within group differences) do affect Asian students' participation in sports, so too do the different cultural understandings of sports and physical activity,[8] and the socially institutionalized barriers of racism and sexism (Nakamura, 2003, p. 29). So not only do ethnic and racial minority students have to contend with and negotiate values of their parents as informed by their "home countries," but also those of the Canadian society as informed by racism, sexism, discrimination, and indifference to their minority status, cultural origin, and bicultural existence. Racism operates to construct Asian males and females as fragile (due to physical size). When educators, and coaches in particular, fail to take into account this reality of ethnic and racial minority students—that is, to acknowledge that racism, sexism, and stereotypes are inherent in the school programs and have a consequences on the attitudes, behaviours, and practices of the students—they are unlikely to develop and provide programs and facilities that adequately or appropriately appeal to such students. Because of the "absent presence" (they are there physically, but not recognized) of minority students, and specifically females, schools do not provide adequate facilities, supervision, and role models that would help to accommodate the needs, interests, and expectations of these students. Hence, they cope with such situations through avoidance and withdrawal.

With this background information, and drawing on her own experiences, observations, and assumptions, Nakamura (who is of Japanese origin) wanted to understand how her nine university respondents remained engaged in athletic activities, and eventually chose to major in physical education, in spite of their "model minority" immigrant label (and the other stereotype of them as high academic achievers). She found that many Asian parents believed that playing sports in school or majoring in physical education in university was not as important as taking courses in mathematics, science, and English. For these parents, sports were not only considered to be an extracurricular activity (and hence threatened to interfere with academic work), they were also concerned with the health risks and injuries that could result from sports. And while generally, the females, like the males, were discouraged from sports, there were differences in their experiences based on gender. Nakamura found that "the gender appropriateness of sports and muscularity was an issue for the parents of three of the female participants" (p. 94). For instance, one respondent said that her mother thought that she was "getting too butch" because of "lifting too much weight," and as a result she was pressured to lose the muscles. Another respondent said that a family friend "thought that [she] should be a figure skater instead of playing soccer, basketball." And yet another respondent talked about a relative commenting in disapproval about her broad shoulders and muscular legs. According to Nakamura, these "body policing" encounters point to the conflicts faced by female athletes as a result of their participation in sports. In other words, the shape of their bodies was considered to be in contradiction to expectations of a "feminine" body (Nakamura, p. 96). Two of Nakamura's female respondents also mentioned that because of their religious beliefs, they felt uncomfortable with the foul language at sporting events. For these females, therefore, parental and social expectations and practices influenced their expectations of and commitment to sports, and ultimately their participation in it.[9]

It is relevant here to discuss the movie *Bend It Like Beckham* (2002), for it suitably illustrates many of Nakamura's research findings, particularly in its exemplification of the struggle faced by girls and women to be recognized as legitimate athletes. The movie is about a young South Asian woman, Jasminder, one of two daughters of Indian-born Sikh parents living in England. Jasminder and her sister Pinky represent the different ways that immigrant parents and their children negotiate among themselves the differences in their ethnic (South Asian) and national (British) cultures (without implying that they are homogeneous). In contrast to her sister Pinky, always elegantly dressed (often in pink) and willing to live up to the social and cultural expectations of a stereotyped South Asian woman, Jasminder's clothes mark her as an athlete; as well, she frequently plays soccer with a group of males in the park, and idolizes David Beckham (a White British male professional soccer player, named by many sports journalists as the most famous athlete in the world). One time when she is playing in the park, Jules, a White British woman, notices Jasminder's soccer skills and invites her to play with their team (which played in the professional women's league). But the dilemma for Jasminder is obtaining permission to play from her parents. And knowing that she would never receive permission from her parents, Jasminder initially turns down the offer from Jules. However peer support leads her to play on the team, hiding it from her parents.

Like the respondents in Nakamura's and other studies, Jasminder's parents see education as the key to success in England. So not surprisingly, when her parents discover that she is playing soccer, wearing shorts, and playing with males, they are outraged and tell Jasminder to quit. In fact, she is told to quit playing soccer several times, but each time she returns to the game and lies to her parents about it (she once tells her parents that she is working at a part-time job). This lie is concocted by Jules and a South Asian male friend, who insist that her parents will not understand the importance of sports. To her parents, Jasminder is breaching fundamental cultural principles and family values; by playing soccer she is interacting with males (her coach and sometimes players), lying about it, and "baring her skin in public"—something that her father says is unbecoming of a young lady her age, and that her mother sees as bringing shame on the family because Jasminder is not acting like a "good" South Asian woman. Her mother expects her to learn to cook in preparation for becoming a good wife. Similarly, and unlike Jules's father, who supports her interest in soccer, Jules's mother discourages her from soccer, fearing that she will never win the attention of potential male partners. Jules's mother purchases non-athletic clothes, hoping to make Jules look "more feminine." This concern about Jules is also about her sexuality. Jules's mother overhears a conversation between Jasminder and Jules—a conversation that she misinterpreted—and becomes suspicious that they are lesbians. In this scenario, *Bend It Like Beckham* illustrates the suspicion, scrutinization, stereotyping, and misconception experienced by female athletes.

The experiences of the character Jasminder, as well as those of Nakamura's respondents, reveal the obstacles—both familial and societal—with which they must struggle in their involvement in sports activities and culture.[10] Moreover, with coaches and teachers giving little attention to their cultural differences and parental expectations, as shown by Simmons (1999), we can expect that for racial minority immigrant athletes, access and opportunities to participate in sports activities in school will be limited. These limitations cannot be interpreted as self-motivated, but rather a product of an inequitable educational system, which includes educators who fail to recognize their own role in perpetuating the inequity. Like Simmons, in her study of the experiences and perceptions of eight junior basketball team members, two coaches, and the principal at Western Collegiate in the Toronto area, Dabovic (2002) found that faculty believed that female athletes have equal opportunities to participate in sports. The female head of the girls' physical and health education pointed out that the school did not do things differently for the girls compared to the boys—for both groups, she said, "it's their interest level that generates teams" (Dabovic, 2002, p. 60). Doing things the same way, then, for these educators constitutes providing an equitable program. Therefore, no consideration is given to the institutional or structural barriers, or the conditions based on gender, that might inhibit athletic opportunities. Indeed, as the principal contends: "And do I want equity, gender equity for my students? Yes. Do I have it? No. Will I get it? Probably not. Will I get closer? I sure hope. And it's the sure hope. Why will we not get it? The society doesn't—it doesn't happen in the real world" (Dabovic, 2002, p. 98). So, the fact that school is the only place for these females to play basketball seems not to make any difference to the resources they are given. All they had were the school's sports teams and their physical education classes. As one athlete commented: "the guys always play basketball on the street ... girls don't ..." Besides, as Dabovic also notes, "There were no intra-murals, no house leagues, and no pick-up games at lunch or after school inside of the school" (p. 62). To most of the respondents, and contrary to the views of the principal and coaches, the school did not treat them fairly, for they did not have the opportunities that the boys had to be involved in tournaments or have the available time and space to play basketball. In addition, one respondent pointed out that they had to wear old uniforms while both the junior and senior boys' teams were given new ones; and unlike the senior boys' basketball team, whose sponsor provided free basketball shoes, the girls had to purchase theirs. In general, Dabovic found that these female basketball players did not have equitable opportunities to play basketball; neither did they have the support and encouragement needed to enable them "to overcome barriers such as financial constraints, lack of confidence," and the undervaluing of their abilities and skills as female athletes (p. 67). "The female athletes," Dabovic writes, "regularly compete in a closed gym ... with no spectators to encourage them, and no announcement made before or after the games; thus providing little opportunities for other students to become interested in or knowledgeable about the achievements or capabilities of the team" (p. 116).

But the inequitable opportunities, and the related lack of encouragement and support from coaches, peers, and principals, which would make possible the realization of their athletic ambitions, are not simply a consequence of gender. Of course, race, ethnicity, class, and immigrant background interact in complex and varying ways to inform and mediate these athletes' interactions with coaches, teachers, and administrators, as well as the educators' expectations of them (and their expectations of themselves). In this respect, it is telling that in a school where, according to the principal, "the heritage of 60–65 percent of the students is from the Indian subcontinent" (Dabovic, 2002, p. 84), the vast majority of the students participating in basketball are Black. Ironically, none of the seven Black/African Canadians or the one Pakistan Canadian[11] who participated in Dabovic's study thought that race had anything to do with their experiences. And, not surprisingly, their coaches and principal did not see gender, race, or ethnicity as mediating or influencing their young women's experiences either. Nevertheless, as Dabovic admits (notwithstanding her hesitation in using race as an organizing concept):

> The structure and racial composition of the team indicates that stereotypes of the wider society are at work here too: the population of this school is not primarily Jamaican-Canadian; it is diverse; yet this basketball team is primarily (Black and) Jamaican-Canadian. This over-representation supports Vertinsky and Captain's (1998) claim that Black women may find themselves streamlined into certain sports such as basketball (p. 119).

Besides, there were occasions when team members received "props" or encouragement, which reflected race-related expectations. Dabovic also noted that not only did the players internalize, and hence operate with, the racialized notion that they should win their game against White team players, so did their "White" coach who, like the players, "found it '*strange*' to lose to a White team." The one South Asian on the team also subscribed to the racialized notion of Black superiority in sports, and basketball in particular. In reflecting on her dilemma of her relationship to sports, she commented that she used to hear from people that she did not "fit in," even with basketball, which she was "really good at."

> I used to like soccer, and they used to say that Italians like playing soccer, and I don't fit into Italians. Or basketball, you needed height and you needed to be Black, and I didn't fit into that either .... And then I started thinking what sports are there that my culture, colour, race, I don't know ... and I couldn't think of any (p. 87).

Unlike their Black male counterparts, these female basketball players did not seek to win athletic scholarships to US universities (as witness to their abilities and skills). In fact, only one of the eight athletes was "actively pursuing a scholarship" (she had a sister at a US university on an athletic scholarship), but they all endeavoured to succeed in their academic work. While these players' interests in academic rather than athletic pursuits is to be applauded, the sad irony is that their interests and aspirations are informed by a lack of information about scholarship opportunities, and a schooling context that supports the aspirations of the male basketball players, but not the females. So while the girls did have some encouragement from their family members—most of them recalled encouragement by family members such as brothers, cousins, aunts, and a few learned about some possibilities in sport sfrom these family members—for the most part, no such information or support were forthcoming from their coaches who, with the exception of one South Asian Canadian and one White male, were all White females. Hence, we can surmise that their lack of support has to do with their lack of recognition and their coaches' and teachers' limited understanding of race-related inequities and discriminatory realities. I concur with Dabovic's conclusion that:

> these women's' potential for achievement have been stunted by unequal social relations, and coaches/educators inadequate knowledge about and regard for their unique needs. To address their situation, then, these young women need to be given greater support in and exposure to athletic programs within an educational context that will enable them to reach their potential (p. 123).

One Black female student athlete who received the necessary support and encouragement from her school, coaches, and parents, was Alicia; she was able to negotiate effectively the gender and race obstacles, and win scholarships and ultimately a place on Canada's national team. What follows is her story.

ACHIEVING THE DREAM: ALICIA'S STORY

Using Alicia as a case example, I seek to make sense of the path her athletic career followed, and her perceptions and understanding of what it meant/means for her to be an athlete. In this respect, a life history approach will not only illuminate the complexities of Alicia's lived experiences, but will also assist in providing a contextual understanding of how historical, political, cultural, societal, institutional, familial, and personal circumstances and events have shaped her life and role as an athlete (Bellaby, 1991; Cole & Knowles, 2001; James, 2002). And following Henry's (1995) lead, I focus on one student athlete in an effort to contribute to our understanding of a life that is affected by structures of racism, classism, sexism, marginality, and alienation. In doing so, I seek to avoid homogenizing Black female athletes into a single dimension, but wish to recognize their diversity, complexity, and hybridity. In this regard, Alicia cannot be said to represent the group.

According to Cole and Knowles, a life history approach enables us to gain insights into the broader human condition by coming to know and understand the experiences of other humans. It is about understanding a situation, profession, condition, or institution through coming to know how individuals walk, talk, live, and work within that particular context. It is about understanding the relationship, the complex interaction, between life and context, self and place. It is about comprehending the complexities of a person's day-to-day decision-making, and the ultimate consequences that play out in that life; this approach enables insights into the broader, collective experience of a group. Individuals' lives can be understood in relation to the context in which they exist (2001, p. 11).

Denzin (1996) points out that the stories people tell in life history interviews are shaped by, and reflective of, the perspective of the teller, which in turn is shaped and structured within a wider socio-political and economic framework. Therefore, all life stories are partial accounts of lived experiences, since the teller is always in flux and the tales he or she chooses to relate are never simply "descriptions" (Monro, 1998; Sparkes, 1995), but rather are interpreted, reinterpreted, and invested with subjective truths and significance. Accordingly, this interpretive account of Alicia is not a static product, but captures the developing process and changing picture of her life as well as the contradictions, ambiguities, and transition that are all part of her lived experiences.

Alicia was interviewed by me and Yasmin Razack (an acquaintance of hers) in the fall of 2002 during her brief visit with her parents, and a few days before she returned to the United States, her home base. The initial open-ended interview was approximately one and one-half hours long, and was audio-taped and transcribed by Yasmin. Follow-up contacts were made via email. (In keeping with the principles of research ethics, at the time of the interview, we obtained permission from Alicia to include her in this project, and we discussed the problem of maintaining her complete anonymity given that she has such a national profile in basketball). I also recognize, as Sparkes (2000, p. 20) suggests, the tension between providing thick description in a biographical study and keeping Alicia's identity anonymous, for I need to provide sufficient detail to both contextualize Alicia's comments and make her recognizable to herself and to others. In what follows, I discuss the role of Alicia's parents and coaches in her educational and athletic (basketball) career, and how she negotiated the interconnected gendered, raced, and classed structures of basketball to become the professional athlete that she is today.

Now 24 years old, Canadian-born Alicia grew up with both her parents and one younger sister in a middle-class suburban neighbourhood in the Toronto area. Originally from the Caribbean, her parents immigrated to Canada over 30 years ago. Both her parents have worked in clerical positions: her mother, now retired, worked at a bank, and her father, with a transit company. Noting that this background—Black immigrant parents with average income—tends to be characteristic of many of the youth who are recruited to play basketball or track and field in school, and who eventually would use sports as a means of earning an athletic scholarship, typically to a US university (see Chapter 3), I asked Alicia if she considered herself as typical or fitting the stereotype of a basketball player. The six-foot-plus Alicia replied:

Am I typical? No, my parents work very hard .... I live in a good neighbourhood. I know if I wanted to go to university here in Canada, I would have been able to do so .... They [parents] gave me the choice—if I wanted to go to the States, it was fine. Or if I wanted to stay here, it would be fine also because we would find ways.

In distancing herself from the stereotype, Alicia tried to show that she is different because her two "hard-working" parents made it possible for her to live and attend high school in "more of an upper-class area," and they provided her with educational options. The implication is that many of her peers did not have such parental support, privileges, and options, for, as she stated, "the girls came from single-parent or lower-class backgrounds." However, while claiming that taking the scholarship route to attaining a post-secondary education was an option or choice for her, Alicia also noted that she welcomed the opportunity to "get a scholarship [since] that would help out my folks where we would not have any bills to pay." So, educational expense was indeed a consideration for Alicia and her parents.[12] This idea of parental support, having options, and making decisions with respect to her involvement in sports were common themes throughout her interview. For instance, in relating how she first got involved in sports, Alicia said:

> Actually, I started playing in the seventh grade, and I remember playing in like a little league .... I think it was the coach of [Maurice] High [School] who saw me play and he was telling me about the program there ... and things that they've done. I guess there was something that I wouldn't have gotten if I went to [Howard High School] ... [which] did not even have a basketball team. So it was a decision that I made, I told my parents, and we decided, you know, maybe I could go this route. So I tried it for a year and liked it. Obviously we did so much more at [the high school]—we travelled, played in tournaments on the weekend, and got a lot of exposure, which was key to getting, you know, being recruited by coaches across the border.

By rights, Alicia should have attended "Howard High School," her neighbour-hood school (as well as being where "all" of her friends went); nevertheless, as she said, that was a "sacrifice" that she willingly made. It is understandable that looking back now, Alicia would say that the decision to attend "Maurice High School" was the better one; it not only complemented the "many sports activities" in which her parents had her registered, but also opened up new possibilities.

In a way, then, like many other Black youth, especially males, it was the sports option rather than the academic option that determined the secondary school that Alicia attended. And the fact that high school coaches would recruit these youth seemed to be of no concern to them or their parents for, as

Alicia pointed out, there was the chance to travel, play in tournaments, and get exposure to university coaches (see Frey, 1994; James, 2003c; Solomon, 1992; Chapters 3 and 5). Being recruited by high school coaches, especially if there are no previous relationships, can be seen as a good test or indication of a sporting potential. Indeed, such recognition helps to reinforce the fact that the athlete has the ability, skill, and potential to become an outstanding player, and in so doing builds his or her confidence. But the idea of recruitment also has a less positive connotation. Hence, when I suggested to Alicia that she was recruited, she struggled with the idea.

Carl: So basically the coach saw you and invited you to come to [Maurice]?

Alicia: The coach saw me and told me that ... he would love to coach me basically.

Carl: You wouldn't say that he recruited you?

Alicia: I wouldn't say that because you can't. I mean really there is no such thing like that in Canada. But, well, no, I'm lying. I know it does happen in a lot of boys' basketball, especially in the Toronto schools. But, ahhhh, recruited? I wouldn't say that term because it really wasn't. He wasn't pushing for it. He really wasn't recruiting. [He] just told me about the situation if I wanted to come play for him. He was just telling what they do—they travel, they play in tournaments, stuff like that, so it really wasn't recruiting. But if you want to call it recruiting then yeah ....

Carl: Okay, and what did your parents say?

Alicia: They've always been behind me—anything that I've done—and, yeah, we talked about it. They liked my coach. Still up to this day they are still in close contact with my high school coach, so it was a good choice that I made.

In this exchange Alicia first disregarded the suggestion that she was recruited, for to agree with my suggestion would be to admit that she participated in something that was against the school board policy. Yet, she recognized that having been recruited was a "good thing" for her. But, more importantly, she emphasized her "choice" in the matter, and that she and her parents together made the decision of which school to attend. Furthermore, her emphasis that it was her "choice," with the support of her parents, to attend "Maurice" High

School (and that she did not do so because a coach "recruited" her) is in keeping with Alicia's belief that she exercises agency throughout her athletic career. In this respect, Alicia was asserting that she was in control of her athletic life, and not the coach. And the fact that her parents "liked" her coach and remained "in close contact" with him over the years indicates that he was not only her coach, but also someone whom her parents have grown to trust and respect. Indeed, this coach gave Alicia and her parents the first recruitment experience.

When I asked Alicia which of the many coaches she credited with getting her to the level of playing for a Division One school, she was decisive in her response: "Well, definitely my high school coach helped me to get in a position to being able to play at the college level, and then my college coach definitely helped me get to where I am now: to be able to play at a professional level." And Alicia was unequivocal in saying that her coach was "like a friend" and not a father figure—a term we often hear athletes, especially males, use to describe their coaches.

> He's been a great coach .... I've been very fortunate. I've heard people saying that father figure thing, but I've had my dad and my mom .... My high school coach ... I guess, like, you spend so much time together as a team, he was like a friend .... He's been there all along if I ever needed him, he was always there. He was one of those people who have been always very supportive, someone who, even up to this day, who calls me and pretty much congratulates me on all my success, and who I can keep in contact with ....

It is certainly interesting how Alicia's high school coach maintained contact with her, congratulating her on her successes and "being there." It is likely that having started Alicia on her career path, her high school coach, like a parent, continued to pay attention to her career journey. After all, it might be said that her success is also his success and a credit to his foresight and coaching skills. Therefore, while Alicia might not see him as a "father figure," he did indeed behave like one.

Alicia was less clear about the role that her high school coach played in her achieving the full athletic scholarship to the US university she attended, but she did suggest that the many tournaments she played while at high school gave her the needed exposure to college and university coaches[13] who would come and watch her play. She added that she also became known through "hearsay." In fact, she suggested that it was such "hearsay"—a team

126

member telling an assistant coach who told the head coach—that got her the scholarship. According to Alicia, it was one of "70 or so" scholarship offers she received. And of the five universities she checked out or visited, it was the one that, as she said:

> I just felt as though I fit in there—met the girls, loved the team, loved the coach, and everything pretty much was there. Everything that I was looking for, I mean, academically, everything was there. I mean they used to be an ivy league school, so they had great academics there, and athletically I was looking forward to help build a team to do well.

When asked what constituted the "fit," Alicia explained that she wanted a university that "was not too far away from home—eight to nine hours' drive—somewhere that had a great academic program—very important, athletically, a coach that I knew would enhance my game. Basically, just getting along with my teammates—over four years, those are your sisters." In suggesting that the reputation of the university was important to her, Alicia, in a way, was gesturing to her own accomplishment and the merit of her education. After all, this was no ordinary university—it was "an ivy league school" she attended. Furthermore, it is possible that Alicia was attempting to underscore the fact (hence, refuting the stereotype or stigma) that for her, university was not merely about playing basketball, but also about getting a quality education and eventually graduating. In making this point, she commented that in university, students were expected to work, and there was a supportive environment to make this happen. She continued: "One thing with a scholarship, you are provided with a tutor and stuff like that, which I think is definitely a benefit. I always said I don't know why athletes don't graduate because they have access to so many resources and so many people that are willing to help."[14]

But not to be missed in Alicia's above comments is the significance she placed on relationships—not only that which she had with her family (see also Lopiano, 1995; Nakamura, 2003) and expected to maintain by being geographically close—but equally important (note that she used words such as "very important" and "basically") were the good relationships that she needed and wished to build with her coach and teammates. As Alicia acknowledged, these were people who, over a four-year period, would become like family members. Seemingly, then, from Alicia's perspective, having a productive or successful athletic (and academic) career depended on group efforts and support—on how well they were able to work, play, and live together—and not only on individual abilities, performance, and hard work. This valuing of relationships appears to be a recognition of the interdependence of team members and of the gendered social and cultural reality of their existence as women. Alicia was well aware that as basketball players, they were playing a sport dominated by males in an institution where they are often marginalized, devalued, and receive less resources and recognition. For instance, after making the connection between the large amount of money that "men's sports bring into the university—especially football and basketball" and the high income of the men who play in the NBA compared to women who play in the WNBA, Alicia went on to say that for female athletes the education "degree is incredibly crucial." And she reasoned that given the time they put into playing basketball, "you [Black women] are not really getting a free education ... with the scholarship because you are working every single day for it. Basically, that is what it comes down to." This "basic" awareness of their place as women within the institution (see also Lenskyj, 2003; Lopiano, 1995)—"it is one thing that I tell people all the time"—was something that Alicia expected would be a by-product of the relationship with her teammates and, in turn, a means of enabling them to effectively negotiate and navigate the inequitable institutional and athletic structures that could limit or enhance their achievements in the sports arena.

Alicia also recalled the tensions and the struggles that female athletes experience "especially at the teenage years." As might be expected, Alicia viewed her roles as athlete and woman in "separate" terms because, as she stated, "I learned you have to be able to separate on-the-court stuff and off-the-court stuff." For Alicia, then, the result has been that "on the court you are [I am] a basketball player ... off the court I try to carry myself as a woman." And she added,

> once we step off the court we like to dress up and go out .... You know that's what we do. Me, myself, I'm probably not that "typical," you know; I like to put on my jeans and my heels and stuff like that when I can. You know, I like dressing as a woman off the court. That's just me. But there are a lot of times that you are so tired and you just find it easier to dress in sweats. So when you see all these guys, especially athletes ..., it really is just so much easier just to throw on a t-shirt and some sweats and some running shoes and just go.

Alicia is making the point here that for males, being an athlete is "so much easier" and more convenient, whereas for her (and others like her), they have to contend with a dual existence or two "selves"—athlete/woman—which do not always easily seem to cohabit the same body at the same time (see also Varpalotai, 1996). This idea was similarly expressed by one of Dabovic's (2002) Black female respondents. Her words were: "I can't be a girl on the court." In the same vein, identifying the masculine character of basketball, another of Dabovic's respondents said, "I love playing guy sports." This understanding and performance of gender by Alicia and others is apparent given that the males who participated in this project made no such distinction (see Chapter 5) nor were they expected to separate their roles (see above, the coaches' comments from Simmons's study). In fact, "off the court" these males took pride in exhibiting their connections to basketball through their clothing, behaviours, and language, which were all part of their racialized masculine basketball culture (see Chapter 2).

We noted that Alicia wanted her Black female peers to understand that a scholarship did not mean that they were "getting a free education." Implicit in her comment is the role of race (like gender) in the access and opportunities they have achieved through sports; that is, winning athletic scholarships and getting to play in the WNBA. Her view was that, rather than operating as a barrier, race operated more as an asset because sports "is a business and people want to win .... And they can surpass that colour barrier." Alicia continued to explain:

> Alicia: It has to do with athletics and if you can play. True athletes predominantly are non-White ... when you look at it. I know athletic people, and I know they have tried to figure it out, and done studies on it .... They even had a movie: *White Men Can't Jump*. I mean, when you think about it, that's just the way that it is portrayed or presented.
>
> Carl: So do you think that Black people are better athletes?
>
> Alicia: You know, maybe it's not that they are better athletes; maybe it's just that the majority of them are lower income. Maybe it's just that they have a better drive. Maybe they have a better heart .... You know, the White man who they are fighting against already got money, so he is not as interested to put out. I don't know .... I really don't know what it is .... Well, it's all about making money, and whoever performs the best will be selected, right?

According to Alicia, then, Blacks are not better players because of genetics, but because they are "true athletes"—the kind of players who, because of their social position based on race and "lower income," see athletics as a means of making money and hence are "driven" to put their efforts and energies into sports. So is it really that "they can surpass that colour barrier"? Or that the colour barrier always remains, and hence minority athletes must develop strategies to negotiate these barriers? Indeed, as Alicia indicates (and correctly so), race matters in Canada, and helps to determine social class position. But believing that meritocracy exists, she also claimed that it is performance and not skin colour that ultimately determines individuals' athletic and financial outcomes. This idea seems quite logical for someone like Alicia who believes that her performance alone was responsible for her athletic scholarships (and later to play in the Olympics and for teams in the WNBA, as well as in Europe and Asia). But there is a contradiction here, for race is not merely a matter of skin colour or a physical attribute that individuals' efforts and ambitions can easily transcend (see Chapter 5 for a further discussion of this point). Race is, more importantly, a social construct, which in Canada not only structures individuals' limits and possibilities, but also operates as a signifier of citizenship or immigrant status (Abdel-Shehid, 2004; James, 2003a; Walcott, 1997). Cognizant of the role that race plays in the Canadian/non-Canadian identification, I asked Alicia how she identified herself: "I am Canadian at heart .... That means, you know, first and foremost, I am Canadian. I played in the Olympics ... [and was] very, very honoured to represent my country." And she later added:

> I do classify myself as part Jamaican because my parents are Jamaicans ....
> But if someone were to ask me the question, I would say Canadian because
> I was born [and] here grew up here. I was raised here in Canada. Jamaican
> is part of my background. I do understand and I know a lot about it. I do
> classify myself as Canadian.

Evidently conversant with the issue of identity, Alicia was quite emphatic in saying that above all else she is Canadian and proudly so, especially taking into account her contributions to the country with which she so strongly identified—"my country."

Today, Alicia (who held the MVP/Most Valuable Player title in high school a number of times, and at one time won a National Black Award for athletics) graduated from university where she majored in women's studies and African-American studies. She thinks that some time in the future she "probably" will go into teaching, but, as she said, "right now, I'm playing ball." She plays on a team in the Women's National Basketball Association (WNBA), and during the off-season, she plays in Asia and Europe on deals secured for her by her agent.

CONCLUSION

The experiences of all student athletes are mediated by a combination of their gender, race, ethnicity, class, immigrant/citizenship status, and other factors. And given the structured gender inequity within society, and by extension within educational and athletic institutions, females do not have the same access and opportunities to educational and athletic opportunities as males. In reality, gender (in addition to the other demographic factors) helps to determine both the form and nature of females' participation and achievements in sports. Furthermore, sports, maintained as part of the male system of hegemony, will continue to be an arena in which females will be marginalized and undervalued. So it is not merely a matter of individual females' choice, abilities, skills, or ambitions that determine their limits or possibilities, but the educational and athletic systems in which they participate, and the supports and encouragements they receive along the way. What are needed, therefore, are support systems that address the needs, interests, and aspirations of females. In addition, we need a critical understanding of how these structures operate to affect females' opportunities, scholarship attainments, and even their professional career destiny. More resources are also needed that will enable female athletes to negotiate the barriers that they face, in particular an education that will help them to question and challenge the dominant ideologies that continue to perpetuate unequal athletic possibilities. Lenskyj (2003) argues that we cannot address the concerns of women within the hegemonic structure of sport that has been traditionally defined by and for men (p. 71). Hence, she says, perhaps the time is ripe for a "women-centred alternative" and a conceptualization of sports within the genre of feminism that will change the way sports are thought of, organized, and played. To do nothing will continue to limit females' participation in sports, for existing practices, as Hanson and Kraus (1999, p. 96) write, "maintain male dominance and separateness, [and also] deprives women of the networks, character development, sources of status, and so on, that men achieve in sport and apply to success elsewhere. In fact, it deprives women of the skills and attitudes that would allow them to compete fairly with men in public life."

NOTES

1. It goes without saying that gender refers to both males and females, and not just females (as is often the assumption). Indeed, gender is the social construction of male and female, whereas sex represents biological differences between males and females (see also Hall et al., 1991; Schempp & Oliver, 2000). That said, my intention here is not so much to draw comparisons between the *gendered* experiences of males and females, but to discuss the experiences and participation of females in sports.

2. Indeed, from their early participation in sports such as hockey, soccer, baseball etc., boys grow to understand that playing sports or being an athlete is a signifier of masculinity. Hence, their participation in it (along with their traits, dress, and behaviours) demonstrates their masculinity, in particular, a "racialized" masculinity, to quote Abdel-Shehid (2004).

3. Sexism is the system of power relations between men and women and in which men, as a social group, are ascribed with more power (and corresponding privileges), which they exercise over women (Hall et al., 1991; Schempp & Oliver, 2000).

4. Coakley & Donnelly, 2004; Dabovic, 2002; Dahlgren, 1988; Fenton et al., 2000; Fejgin, 1994; Frisby & Fenton, 1998; James, 1995; Kerr, 1996; Lopiano, 1996; Nakamura, 2003; Simmons, 1999.

5. Simmons writes: "While I initially paid little attention to the race of the coach as I felt it had little to no bearing on my research, I feel obliged to note here that all of the coaches were White and presumably from a Christian-Judaic background." He went on to say that the significance of this observation became evident later in his work (pp. 26–27).

6. Interestingly, this coach looked for the reason within himself and not at the social conditioning of the girls or the cultural structures within which they must function. I think here of the gendered language like the call to players: "Mark your man."

7. One female coach at another school did find female athletes there had similar ambitions as the boys; hence, noting that "the Black girls do not have realistic dreams" (Simmons, p. 68).

8. See Griffin, 1996; Lenskyj, 2003; Schempp & Oliver, 2000; Talbot, 1993.

9. Nakamura reports that one study found that Asian students preferred sports activities in which interactions were indirect, e.g., volleyball (p. 40).

10. See also Fleming, 1994; Raval, 1989; Talbani & Hasanali, 2000; Tirone & Pedlar, 2000. Raval (1989) makes the point that analysis and explanation of South Asian females' participation in sports should shift from considerations of Asian culture, religion, norms, and values to the racist structures and institutions in society (p. 239).

11. Of the eight respondents (ages 15 and 16 years), six were of Jamaican origin and five were born there, and one was born in Canada; one respondent was of Nigerian origin and was born there. The Pakistan Canadian was born in Canada. Those who were born outside of Canada immigrated with their families and had been living here between four and 12 years (Dabovic, 2002).

12. Alicia said that it was probably around Grades Eleven and Twelve, when she started getting scholarship letters from US universities and colleges, that she and her parents considered the athletic scholarship route to university.

13. Alicia also played on a team that Robert coached—the same coach with whom Amir (in Chapter Five) played. She recalled going to Chicago with his team to play in a tournament.

14. Alicia also noted that even though she had team practice "from 9–12 every single morning" and could not take classes at that time; in the senior years you could work around that time, and probably take classes at times like 8 am and 10 am, especially when practices were at 6 am. Alicia credited her university coach, who was "very high in academics and wants to see you graduate and get your degree; and ... if you were not meeting certain GPA [grade point average], you are not playing, you were not practising. She does stick to that strongly."

5

SET DREAMS, FAILED PLANS, FRUSTRATED TRANSITIONS, AND LESSONS LEARNED

IN OUR DISCUSSION OF THE EDUCATIONAL ASPIRATIONS OF STUDENT ATHLETES (WITH A particular focus on basketball players), we have noted that while many had a deeply held ambition to win athletic scholarships to "play ball" at an American college or university, the ultimate goal was to play professionally. To this end, many student athletes, starting as early as Grade Eight (see Chapter 3), would choose their high school and plan their secondary educational program with this goal in mind. Obviously, there are many whose plans and aspirations are frustrated for any number of reasons. What happens to these student athletes? What happens to the "sport-identified self" that once significantly accounted for their expectations of, interests in, and engagement with school, and informed their aspirations? In what new ways do they think of their schooling, and what new aspirations do they construct? What happens to their "interest" in post-secondary education? In short, what new "life narrative" (Sparkes, 2000) do these student athletes construct in relation to their educational, social, and occupational goals and outcomes after events force them to think of their future differently? In this chapter, I consider these questions via the stories of Amir, Devin, Lori, and Greg, who were unable to secure athletic scholarships or the chance to play their sports professionally in North America—aspirations that had special relevance to their identities. The stories that these student athletes tell of their experiences, aspirations, and outcomes provide insights into how they deal with their forced transitions and disengagement from the athletic and educational pathways around which they had built their future life stories. In this chapter I expose the realities of "unrealized dreams," and what happens to student athletes who, according to Drahota and Eitzen, "lose what has been the focus of their being for most of their lives, the primary source of their identities, the physical prowess, the adulation bordering on worship from others, the money and the prerequisites of fame, the camaraderie with team mates, and the intense 'highs of competition'" (cited in Sparkes, 2000, p. 13).

My interest in examining how student athletes deal with frustrated aspirations and unrealized dreams is related to a number of observations and concerns that have emerged through my years of studying the schooling and educational experiences of students for whom a specific "sport identification" (for example, in the case of Black students it is basketball) played a major role. Sparkes (2000, p. 14) uses the term "athletic identity"[1] to refer to "the degree to which an individual identifies with the athletic role," noting that individuals with a "strong" sense of athletic identity, compared to those with a "weak" sense, were more likely to interpret a given event in terms of athletic implications. There are, of course, both positive and negative consequences associated with having a strong athletic identity for, as Sparkes points out, "it could act as either a 'Hercules' muscles' or an 'Achilles heel.'" Specifically, individuals can benefit from their "development of a salient self-identity or sense of self, positive effects in athletic performance, and a greater likelihood of long-term involvement in exercise behaviours." But there are also potential risks for individuals with a strong athletic identity, who may experience difficulties resulting from changes or alterations to their plans as a result of, for example, not attaining their scholarship goals, or "being deselected or injured, or reaching the end of their playing careers" (Sparkes, 2000, p. 14).

It is important to alert student athletes to these risks—something that I think coaches, educators, and parents too often have neglected to do in their efforts to support and encourage student athletes (see also Jones, 2000). In this regard, then, we are likely failing student athletes, many of whom are of working-class, minority, and immigrant backgrounds, because we have not helped to prepare them for some of the outcomes. This is especially true of those who invest all their energies into one sport, clinging to the belief and dream that they will make it to the big leagues through hard work, determination, skills, and exposure to scouts. I suspect this failure to alert student athletes to their potential "Achilles heel" reflects, in part, the deeply held liberal notion that "if someone wants something bad enough and works hard to attain it, then she or he will succeed." Persuaded by this meritocratic belief, especially presented with a number of "successful athletes" (of course, the ones who don't make it are certainly not brought to schools to act as a role model), many student athletes set out on their athletic pathways only to realize that their dream is unachievable. The fact is, making it in sports does not rely solely on individual efforts. The same structures of classism, racism, and sexism, which are likely responsible for their over-reliances on sports as a means of gaining social mobility, also operate as barriers to the very goals they seek. In this chapter, therefore, we use the experiences of four student athletes to show how the system of stratification and inequity operates to influence their outcomes. In other words, to understand the experiences and outcomes of Amir, Devin, Lori, and Greg, and their storied selves, we must take into account the larger context of economic, political, educational, athletic, social, and cultural structures within which they, their parents, coaches, educators, and role models construct their aspirations.

In the fashion of Sparkes (2000), I examine the complex ways in which a strong athletic identity has acted as an Achilles heel, shaping individuals' reactions to disruptions of their athletic paths. It also affects the consequences of their reactions, the loss of their "successful" athletic selves, and finally a "heightened reflexivity and awareness of previously taken-for-granted aspects" of the "selves" that they had ignored (Sparkes 2000, p. 15). I use the stories that individuals construct to retain their coached confidence, perpetual optimism, and constructed identities. These identities are not constrained/limited by disruptions, but in the restorative process, they may come to see possibilities for their lives with and without athletics. Following the profiles of the four study participants, I discuss their stories, and conclude with some implications for student athletes, coaches, teachers, principals, educators, youth workers, and community members. I hope these stories may serve as examples to others who find themselves in similar situations.

THE PARTICIPANTS

Yasmin Razack and I interviewed all four participants at the university.[2] Known to one of us, they were all asked, and consented, to participate in the study because of their reputation interests, aspirations, involvement, achievements, and athletic careers.

137

Greg was particularly asked because, compared to the other interviewees, he had a fairly well-established athletic career with a number of notable achievements, but had sustained an injury and, at the time of the interview, was working on an alternative career path. It was during the interviews with the others that their "frustrated aspirations" became clear, and this led us to spend much time discussing their disengagement from their athletic ambitions and their options. In sharing their stories and experiences with athletics, participants provided insights into their subjective realities as individuals and their interrelationship with the institutional and systemic structures with which they interacted (Bertaux, 1981; Denzin, 1989). Their conversations reveal a complex understanding of their expectations of high school and university, their sports identification, their athletic aspirations, their awareness of the opportunity structures and access routes, and what it might take to attain their goals. In the interviews, we engaged in a process that enabled us to gain an understanding of these student athletes' conditions and situations, and the contexts in which they operated and constructed their aspirations. It was a process through which we tried to understand the complex interactions and relationships between each participant's life and context, self and place, and attempted to comprehend the complexities of her/his decision-making and the consequences of those decisions (Cole & Knowles, 2001). I would describe the interviews as conversations in which we all actively, when and where appropriate, shared information about, and perspectives on, a range of key issues. Most significant was some of the participants' interest in obtaining my perspective, suggestions, and support on issues related to educational and career options (particularly related to my role as a university teacher) as they struggled with "what to do" if and when their alternative plans did not materialize. Not only did our "active listening" (Wolcott, 1995) help to sustain the conversations and provide rich interview information, it also gave participants the opportunity for dialogue on an important topic in a way that they had rarely and, in some cases, never had before. Further, the conversations set up a rapport with two participants, whereby they came to see me months later to discuss career options and entrance to university.

As noted in Chapter 4, an ethical challenge here is how to fully present the stories of participants—specifically two of them—and at the same time protect their identities, knowing that their reputations and particular achievements were already in the public domain (Sparkes, 2000, also talks to this challenge).

For this reason, they were asked how they felt about the publication of their stories. They all agreed that it was "okay," and even suggested that I could use their names (they are nevertheless all pseudonyms).

Amir

Eighteen-year-old Amir was in his final year of high school when we met after school for the interview in my office at the university (November 2002). The six-foot-tall, smiling young man with a low-cut haircut entered the office dressed in new baggy jeans, an oversized "Phat Farm" shirt, and K-Swiss sneakers. Canadian-born Amir, who identifies himself as a "South Asian," grew up with his parents and two younger brothers in Toronto in a largely immigrant, ethnically diverse, working-class community northwest of Toronto. His parents moved into a middle-class, ethnically diverse community during his late adolescence. He said that his interest in basketball developed when he was a young boy, but at around eight years, when as a "brown kid" he tried to play with his mostly African-Canadian neighbourhood peers, "they would never let me play." It was not until Grade Nine that he:

> got my first chance ... I got to play for my high school .... The team wasn't really good at the time, it was like crap ... but I got my chance .... I got a feel for what the game is and I started to have more and more fun with it ... and I progressed as fast as I could.

His maternal grandfather encouraged Amir's interest in playing basketball because of his height.

Amir attended a racially diverse high school in Toronto, which was about a two-hour bus ride from his home. He was one of about 60 Grade Nine students who entered the school upon the recommendation of teachers after passing the entrance examination. Although the school was a considerable distance from his home, it was a school that his parents wanted him to attend because of the science-oriented, "enriched" program. Equally important was the fact, as he put it:

> My mom didn't want me to go to the schools around my house because the guys that I was growing [up] with at my old school, I was always getting into trouble or stuff like that. The [neighbourhood] school itself didn't really have a good reputation .... I saw it as a good escape for me.

Amir reported that he had been doing "really good" throughout his high school years. "My marks," he said, "were really good. I didn't even have to study. I was just naturally good .... And that was the way I was right up to Grade Eleven and now Twelve."

In high school, Amir also managed to successfully combine his academic and athletic interests. In fact, throughout his high school years, he played on the school's racially diverse basketball team, which was coached by a Black volunteer. But while expressing appreciation for the chance that the coach gave him to play on the school team—"He gave me my chance. I am really grateful for that"—Amir went on to say:

> But he [the coach] did play favourites to the Black players on the team. I knew that I had to be extra good, faster, just to prove myself more than the Black players on the team because I was not Black .... So me and him don't really get along .... He wanted me to play the game a certain way that I did not want to .... He was always giving preference to Vernon and the other players. He wanted me to play positions that I did not want to play.

Amir wanted to play positions that would utilize his strengths. Vernon was also Amir's best friend; and while they were not in the same program at school, they "played together, had a lot of similarities [and] fed off each other." In fact, after playing together for a time, Vernon would "act" as Amir's *sponsor*, and helped him to develop his basketball skills. Amir joked that at first he was playing in Vernon's shadow, and was "kinda known as Vernon's tagalong." This close relationship lasted for a time while, as Amir said, "I was trying to construct my own identity as a player. After a while we did part our separate ways—I mean in basketball. We are still best friends, but I needed for people to take me seriously." Amir described Vernon as "my boy" who has "a natural athletic talent to play basketball."

It was Vernon who introduced Amir to a weekly basketball camp run by Robert, whom Amir credited with many of his accomplishments:

> I owe who I am as a person to Robert. He taught me values about life and all that and [the school] basketball coach was the one [who] taught me a lot about the game of basketball: how to master my skills in basketball .... Robert, for real, became a father figure because, well, because my father and me don't really get along. Basically, I consulted him [Robert] with every major decision—where I wanted to go to school. He was [the] one who

really pushed me to pursue getting a scholarship to the States. He took me on tournaments to the States to give me exposure. I already wrote my SATs, so, I mean, he gave me the confidence that I could do it.

Later, in a follow-up conversation with Yasmin, Amir's disappointment and anger was evident when he spoke of some of the ways in which Robert had dealt with him in recent times. He suggested that Robert had made many "false promises" to him related to the possibility of attaining athletic scholarships to American universities. Amir perceived that Robert basically saw him as an "academic" because whenever Robert introduced him, even at basketball events, Robert referred to him as "very smart or highly intelligent instead of a good basketball player." Amir felt that Robert expected him to take an academic, rather than an athletic, route to university, and on this basis emphasized Amir's ability to attend a US Division One school on an academic scholarship rather than on an athletic scholarship. Amir preferred to be known as a good basketball player, rather than for his good academic average.

But Amir's commitment to basketball was questioned by his parents and some of his peers. He said that he often fought with his mother (the parent with whom he talked and was closer to) over his involvement in basketball. A main source of the fights was his long days and time away from home—something that, for his mother, was not a sign of a "good kid." In fact, Amir's days usually began by going to the YMCA "to work out in the gym" before going to school, and after school he "would play ball for four to five hours [and] ended up coming home around 11 at night." This is something that he had done "for the past three years or so." For his mother, who had been to only one of his basketball games, this kind of commitment was incomprehensible. Regarding his academic work, Amir said that his mother had not seen any of his grades since Grade Nine. Like his mother, Amir's South Asian peers, whom he described as "nerds," also questioned his strong affiliation with basketball and his association with Black friends and "Black culture" (it is likely that his preferred music—rap, hip-hop, R and B, and reggae—is a factor here). He claimed they were antagonistic toward him and would criticize his dress—"baggy clothes, not the preppy stuff that they wear"—and felt that they saw him as "thinking that he was better than them."

When asked what he intended to do after high school, Amir responded by saying: "Well, my ideal intention is to get a scholarship, either academic or athletic, somewhere in the States, right .... If that doesn't work out ... my alternative is to, like, go into any university—a Canadian university still play ... basketball—and focus more on my studies." But while it might seem here that Amir was beginning to think he might not receive an athletic scholarship, for the most part, his discussion of his post-high school ambition reflected otherwise. For instance, during the interview, Amir (an A-student) insisted that he was going to obtain an athletic scholarship to an American university; hence, he had no interest in applying to Canadian universities, whose application deadlines were fast approaching. He expressed confidence that his athletic skill and ability would earn the attention of large American colleges and universities. He was motivated to obtain an athletic scholarship because he did not want to go into debt for his university education, nor did he want to ask his parents, specifically his mother, for the money, given how much support she had already given him. In addition, all of his close friends (mostly basketball players) had similar aspirations to win athletic scholarships to US universities and colleges.[3] And his confidence and optimism were sustained. He recalled that the coach from one of these universities had spoken to him at a tournament, asking him about his plans, and saying to him that he "was a very good shooter." But as the end of the school year approached, after taking the SAT examination and scoring well, and not having heard from any US universities or colleges (and convinced that Robert would not help him attain his goal), Amir began writing to US coaches himself. His efforts did not produce that scholarship letter he so desperately expected; instead he received an invitation (with an offer of money for tuition and basketball wear) to join the basketball team of a local community college. He refused the offer, choosing instead to attend a Toronto university that was near his home.

By the summer of 2003, Amir felt that his skills would eventually lead him to the NBA or playing on a national team overseas. To this end, he continued to play basketball in an effort to maintain his skills. He said that he did not want his hard work to go to waste. By the time of writing (November, 2003), he was registered in a social science business program, but was unsure if he would continue the program, thinking instead that he might major in business administration or kinesiology. He was not working, but hoped to find a job to pay his way through school. He suggested that his uncertainty about his major was because he "needs time. I was young and immature and didn't know what I was getting into." His optimistic view of one day playing on a US university or college had waned. He used the word "realistic" in saying that his dream was "becoming less and less reachable." So while he continued to play recreationally and did all the drills, he did not have the necessary support to pursue the dream of a scholarship and/or playing in the NBA.

Lori

Lori, as she described herself, is "a White middle-class blond female who plays basketball." At the time of the interview (December, 2002), the five-foot-seven, 27-year-old former varsity basketball player worked as an elementary teacher at a school north of Toronto, where she also coached basketball. As well, she was an assistant coach at a post-secondary institution in Toronto. She grew up with her parents and an older sister in a small town west of Toronto. She was introduced to basketball at a "very young age" by her father, a former member of one of Canada's national basketball teams. Recognized for her potential and talent in elementary school, Lori played basketball and other sports with male peers who were often older. Known for her athletic skills (which, to an extent, had been honed by the sports camps), she was recruited by the two high school coaches in her town. But rather than attending the "big powerhouse high school where the sports were really good and everybody was really good" (she noted that "a lot of people went on to win [athletic] scholarships"), unlike her friends, and with the support of her parents, Lori chose to attend the school with the second-rate basketball team. The reason was as follows:

Lori: The coach from the high school that I went to was nicer .... I liked him and I just fell in love with him, and what he stood for and everything that he said to me. And he convinced me to go to the high school that I went to even though it wasn't that good, and we never did as well—we were always second best ....

Carl: Any other reasons why you chose to attend a high school that your friends were not going to and was second best?

Lori: Well, the first reason that came to my mind as you were asking that .... Selfishly, knowing that I could go to the second, the other high school where ... there was a lot of good athletes there. But I knew if I went to that high school I would be one of the better players, and I would start right away, and he was really excited about me, and the other high school wasn't.

143

As predicted, in high school, notwithstanding her low grades and the fact that her "teachers treated her poorly because she was in sports," Lori easily got a chance to play on the senior basketball team, and had the opportunity to travel "to all different parts of Canada and even the United States." It was then that she started to think about playing basketball "at a higher level," specifically "university and on the national team and the Olympics." As with her choice of high school, Lori's choice of university was influenced by the fact that the particular university coach "cared" enough to come to see her play at her high school. He was one of three university coaches whom her assistant high school coach had contacted and invited to her games. And even though most of her friends had chosen to attend the university nearest their town, the interest shown by the university coach (of whom she said: "I loved him from the first day I met him"), and the fact that this was the only university that did not have a math requirement, were significant enough to make Lori choose this university. Given her talent, and support from her coach and parents, I asked Lori if she ever thought of pursuing an athletic scholarship to a US university. She indicated that she was indeed recruited "heavily in Grade Eleven and Twelve" by US universities, and while she was "excited" about the offers she received, she nevertheless turned them down even though in her town, as in other areas, winning an athletic scholarship was "a big thing," especially among "all the good basketball players." There was also the idea that "if you're any good you get a scholarship. That's just what you feel like when you are in high school." Demonstrating the same pragmatic reasoning as in her decision about high school, she added:

> I really wanted to play in Canada .... I wanted to make the national team so bad. So I thought if I stayed in Canada I would be more well known in Canada, and I would make more connections than I did, and ... I would .... I just I would have a better chance .... I just didn't think it was a big deal because I didn't need to be on a scholarship—my parents supported me—so I didn't need the money. I was also afraid if I went over there I would just get shoved under the mat. I wanted to be valued, I wanted to go for what I was worth ....

Lori's aspiration to play on a national team is related to her dad's aspiration for her and possibly his vicarious experiences in her career ambitions. In fact, as Lori admitted,

I think my dad really wanted me to do it because he knew it would be great experience because he had gone there .... Because in playing basketball he also tried out for the Olympic team and played at a very high level, and got to travel the world, and it's just a really good experience .... 'cause then you meet people ....

So with the support and encouragement of her parents and coaches, Lori went through university, majoring in kinesiology and health science (and taking a "slightly lesser course load so that I could stay an extra year and play basketball"). While at university, she played on the varsity basketball team (a team that won a silver medal in the Canadian Women's Championship), went to All-Canada Nike tournaments where the majority of the players were Black; and to supplement her practice and hone her skills, she played with some Black males at a community recreational centre.

Lori:　　It was all Black and I was the only girl—I was the only White person there—and that was really hard because they just hated me coming more than anything. If I played well, they hated that even more. Some of them wouldn't even guard me and I would score even more, and then they would hate me even more. People would make fun of me .... They just made me feel like an outsider. I had one friend that brought me there; he was a Black male and one of the best players there, so he would stick up for me. And then by the third or fourth year of me playing every summer, I started knowing people's names, and once they got to know me, they liked me. I wasn't trying to compete with them or take anything away, I just wanted to get better for me ....

Carl:　　So why did you go? Why did you put up with such treatment from these Black men, ballers? Did you feel you were intruding?

Lori:　　'Cause I knew I could play basketball. 'Cause I didn't look at it like I was intruding. I just wanted to make the national team, and I thought if I went to play at this centre ... there is nowhere else that would make me better that I could go. I was in a women's league and it was completely different and I just thought if I go here where everyone could block my shot, I'd have to get better .... It was a challenge to fit in and be accepted. It took me three years, and their skills were a challenge. I could never be better than

145

them. I think maybe I was better than a couple, but the majority
was better than me.

Also during her university years, Lori contacted the national basketball coach
by email, requesting a chance to try out for the team. In not receiving a timely
response, she continued to contact the coach, asking, "What do I need to do
to make this team?" Lori also went to observe a tryout. Finally, almost three
years after she initially contacted the national coach, she was invited to a
tryout out west, to which she had to pay her airfare. In reflecting on this very
important opportunity—the opportunity for which she had lived and worked
until then—Lori said, disappointment reflected in her voice, "I don't think
anyone really cared that I was there. I didn't even have my name written
down on a piece of paper." So, after all her concerted efforts, and what could
be termed a successful basketball career at university (she received numerous
MVP—most valuable player—awards and scholarships), Lori, who admits
to listening "to Black music"—that is, "hip-hop, reggae, and R and B"[4]—has
not, and likely never will, attain her dream of representing Canada one day at
the Olympics. This is a reality she acknowledges that she has accepted, and
she has "no regrets" for having put the amount of effort, energy, and time into
basketball. Today (Winter, 2003), Lori is teaching in the Middle East with no
set plans for returning to Canada.

DEVIN

As far back as Devin can remember, he "was always playing sports ... soccer,
baseball, hockey," and, as he said, he "picked them up pretty well." But it was
basketball in which he "excelled" the most, and the sport to which his mother
"introduced" him at about age 11 when she bought him his first basketball.[5] It
was also the sport that was popular among the youth of his neighbourhood.

When asked why not hockey since he "skated well," Devin, now 25 years
old (November, 2002), replied:

> I never really got the opportunity to play ... at a very high level. To play
> hockey costs a lot of money and we were not in any situation for me to pursue
> that .... I think that basketball was a financial choice to even baseball. I never
> had my own baseball glove. I probably would have been a better baseball
> player than anything. I just couldn't afford a baseball glove or a baseball bat.

> Anytime I wanted to play, I would have to go call my friend and borrow his glove, and in my area I was probably the best baseball player .... I got a chance to play in the Skydome, 'cause I made this rookie ball team. I just couldn't afford my own glove; those cost about fifty bucks at the time; and basketball is just a ball—you need a hoop and yourself and that's all you ever need.

The fact that a hoop was just outside his house was particularly convenient for Devin, who, at age 13, would go onto the court with his basketball to escape from his house during the difficult period of his parents' separation. Thereafter, Canadian-born Devin, the second of six children, lived with his immigrant mother and siblings in a working-class neighbourhood in the west end of Toronto, where the people were mostly racial minorities and immigrants. Of Southeast Asian (SEA) background, he recalled that "most of his friends were Black" and like them, he "gravitated toward basketball around the time that Michael Jordon was just emerging and everyone was mimicking his commercials: 'Be like Mike.'" Not having a television to see the commercial, Devin "modelled his game after the guys he grew up with because he could relate to them" and not to "anyone in the NBA because they didn't look like me." He reasoned, "maybe I was blind, like they were no ... [SEA] families or anything like that. I didn't even consider myself to be Asian at the time." And he suggested that his "colour-blindness" might be related to the fact that he and his friends "were all in the same situation."

> I'm not even sure how they saw me. They didn't see me any better or worse .... We were all in the same situation, I mean, my family, after my dad left, grew up on welfare. I mean, we were financially disadvantaged .... They understood my problems and they never judged me because I think they felt like they were in the same situation. I was always welcome to play with them because I could play.

This strong bond between Devin and his friend also influenced his choice of high school. (There was no input from his mother.) Rather than attending the Catholic high school that was directly across from his house, Devin and his friends went to the public high school that was a short walk away.[6] Of course, the opportunity to play basketball was an important motivation. In fact, by the time they entered high school, Devin and his friends were on the basketball team at the neighbourhood community centre, which had won about three championships. So the idea then was to bring their "good basketball" team to the high school where they would continue to "stick together ... and start the dynasty there." But things did not work out quite as Devin and his friends had planned. One reason was that they did not find their teachers supportive.

> I think the teachers in that school did not care about the students at all. They were there to get the pay cheques, and they would say: "We're here to get pay cheques. If you want to learn, fine. If not, don't ruin it for everybody else. We're going to teach; we're going to get paid." So if you didn't get 60, they'd be happy to make sure that you didn't play. Yeah, they really didn't support your ambition in terms of your athletic ambition ....

While on the surface, this idea of attending a particular school in order to play basketball might seem absurd, Devin made this argument: "looking back on it now, the basketball kept us out of trouble, kept us in school for a reason. We weren't going to school for school, we really weren't, but it kept us there, and we did work because if you didn't have a 60 average, you couldn't play. Maybe we were in school for all the wrong reasons, but at least we were there ...."

While in high school, Devin's association with his friends and basketball provided him "status, recognition, and ensured that he was not easily forgotten." "I think," he said, "that might have driven me. Maybe I'm driven to not to want to stand out, and that was just something I knew I could succeed in and I took that route." But as he indicated in the following comment, because of his success in basketball, he was able to enter spaces in school colonized by Black students (who also dominated the basketball team); however, "fitting in" was still a struggle for him, particularly in terms of identity.

> But I never ever felt like I fit in anywhere in that school .... As I grew older I knew that, okay, I wasn't Black, I'm [SEA]; I am not White .... But there is no one else like me that I could ... just associate it, or consider myself to be a part of. So I struggled with that a bit—not having an identity that I could call my own. So I kinda created my identity—take pieces from different cultures that I like. And, you know, being able to cross cultural barriers and just jump back and forth, I felt like I could do that pretty easily.

This identity struggle, plus a combination of wanting to escape the "trouble-maker" reputation of his older brother who was attending the same school,[7] lacking support from his mother, and deciding that this high school did not provide a "positive environment for learning" (in his view, the teachers behaved like they "had given up"), Devin decided to change high schools, going instead where he would receive support for his "educational and athletic ambition." To this end, in Grade Eleven, he left home[8] and moved with a friend to a Catholic high school in the eastern part of the city—a considerable distance from his home.

At his new school, Devin did get to play on the basketball team and gained the confidence and full support of the coach. After one year, he moved from his friend's place to the home of a Southeast Asian immigrant couple and their son. He was invited to live with them by the man whom he had met at the school. All along, Devin was fully focussed on his dream of winning a basketball scholarship to the United States—an aspiration shared by his three friends. And, like him, his three friends also changed schools:

> We all just knew that we had to go if we wanted to fulfill our dreams. We all had dreams of our own. We all had dreams of going to the States and getting scholarships, and we knew that it wasn't going to happen there .... Yeah, we all had to find places to go. I really, really wanted to play basketball. I didn't see myself doing anything else. We ["the dynasty"] all were just really good at basketball. We always made the city all-star team; everybody recognized us as the city's best players. We looked in the mirror and we thought we were the best. I don't think any of us ever had any doubt that we were going down south.

Despite his efforts, however, he did not win a scholarship in his final year in high school: the teachers went on a work-to-rule that lasted throughout the basketball season, so Devin never got "a chance to go the States" (thereby missing out on the needed exposure to US scouts). It was not until Christmas of that year, as Devin said, that it dawned on him that he would never get a scholarship. But he was so determined to go to the US that he had not previously considered applying to Canadian universities:

Devin: One day I was at school and someone asked me if I was going to apply to a Canadian university. I was like "what?" They have universities in Canada? I had no idea of the names of the colleges or universities in Canada. I knew there were Duke, North Carolina, and Wake Forest in the US .... I knew there was Humber College because it was in [the west end], but I just thought it was another high school. That's it. I'd never been on a Canadian university campus; I never associated with anyone that attended a university here.

Carl: You never knew the names of Canadian universities?

Devin: No, I just knew those in America, and I was going to get a scholarship to go to a university down there. I never talked about anything else. Anyways, so at this point I didn't have any scholarship offers. I did have the grades to get in to any university of my choice—might as well just apply as a backup plan ....

Devin eventually applied to, and was accepted at, a university in the Toronto area. He came to know about the university and its program through his high school coach, a friend, and girlfriend who encouraged and supported his efforts, and told him about Ontario Student Assistance Program (OSAP). At university, he played on the basketball team, and at one time earned the National Rookie of the Year Award. This win, as he said, was "a major big deal" for members of his ethnic community to which he felt no connection—"I never looked at them as being part of my culture. I mean, I didn't grow up with them"—and whose members he described as "short and unathletic." As a result of this award, six-foot Devin gained a recognition that translated into opportunities to play for a modest sum of money in parts of Asia, which he did for two seasons, returning to university in the winters to continue his studies and rejoin the university team. But he was unable to play for an entire season because of his seriously injured arm. Devin described this as a difficult and depressing time for him.

At the time of the interview (November, 2002), he was in his final year of his four-year degree in kinesiology, and was working as an assistant manager at a sports clothing store, which, according to Devin, "pays the bills." Also at that time he was awaiting his ticket to fly overseas to play on the country's basketball team as he usually did. Since then, he received the ticket, went overseas, and returned home within a month because things did not "work out."

Obviously, this experience does not meet Devon's earlier aspirations; he had had good grades and, as he claimed, was just as good as the other members of the basketball "dynasty." These basketball players attended a public school and eventually won scholarships to American universities. In expressing his disappointments and "resentment," Devin remarked:

> Schoolwork was never really difficult for me. I considered schoolwork to be an easy part of life. I thought the harder things in life were where is my next meal going to come from, where is the money going to come from, how am I going to support myself? Those were the things I thought about in high school. And when I came here [university] nobody around me came here with my situation, no one around me came where I came from; everyone would always ask, where are you from? What do you do? What do your parents do? My dad ... well, I haven't had any contact with him for years, months ... and my mom is on welfare ...

And talking directly of the efforts he had put into basketball, he said:

> It's like you give so much to this sport. You dedicate so much time and energy, you sacrifice so much, and what does it give you back? Nothing! I feel as though everyone liked me because I was good at basketball. All of my friends growing up liked me because I could play basketball. All my friends in university were my friends through basketball. I feel my girlfriend was with me because of basketball, and now it doesn't exist anymore. I feel as though I am going through an identity crisis because I am not playing the game anymore.

Since his return to Toronto, Devin has called me to follow up on some of the points I made to him during the interview. Then I had asked him if he ever considered becoming a high school teacher, especially given his subject area. While he did not enthusiastically welcome the suggestion, he did ask in detail about the possibilities of getting into the faculty of education (where I taught) and what it might take to get a teaching job. Today (Winter, 2003), while working, doing volunteer teaching, coaching at a high school in Toronto, and taking some additional university courses, Devin is in the process of applying to a faculty of education in hopes of teaching high school. In a recent email to me, he wrote: "I am committed and excited about this new endeavour. I will take with me all my past experiences and lessons I've learned, which will make me an excellent teacher" (November 5, 2003).

151

GREG

I first was introduced to Greg over the phone when he called me at my office to inquire about applying to the faculty, following a suggestion from another student. Shortly thereafter (Fall, 2001), Greg came to see me. At six-foot-five, clean shaven, well dressed (wearing a leather coat), and congenial in manner, he presented as someone who would make an excellent teacher, especially in physical education, where there are very few Black teachers. During this meeting we talked about his interests in teaching and about his basketball career, which was on hold because of a recent injury. He also brought with him his university transcripts and his portfolio with all his certificates, awards, and commendations, as well as newspaper articles in which he was featured—many about his winning the national league's slam-dunk championship. At the time of the interview (October, 2002), Greg was in a teacher-education program in one of Toronto's universities.

Born in Jamaica, 29-year-old Greg was raised there by his maternal grandparents until age 13 when he joined his mother, who had immigrated to Toronto eight years earlier. He initially lived in downtown Toronto with his maternal aunt and two cousins because his mother lived with the suburban family with whom she was working. Greg, who had been attending high school in Jamaica, struggled to (and finally did) enter Hampton Collegiate, an academically oriented school instead of the "vocationally oriented" school to which he was being directed by school personnel. His mother's struggle with school personnel also kept him from being put back to Grade Eight. Within a year, Greg moved to live with his mother, who by then had rented a bachelor basement apartment in the northwest area of downtown Toronto. This meant that Greg had to change schools, but he continued to get "into trouble primarily because I was dealing with the transition." In fact, in the process of adjusting to his new living situation—his mother (whom he had not seen during the eight years he remained in Jamaica), his schooling context, the "lonely experience," "huge culture shock" and "minority" status (at Hampton, he was referred to as "the little Black guy") in Toronto—Greg found "refuge" in basketball, a sport at which he admits that he was not initially very good, but that came easily as he had high jump skills learned in Jamaica.

So important was basketball to his life that Greg sought every opportunity to play. In the absence of access to gymnasium space in the area, at Elliot, his new school (where, he said, the teachers rushed home at 3:30), and even at the community centre in the nearby neighbourhood,[9] he would break into the school gymnasium with his peers and play. Greg explained his actions by saying that playing after school, when no one was around, alleviated his stress.

> It became a release .... At that time my mom and I ... we were having trouble getting along .... Remember, I hadn't seen her since I was five. I had become very independent from living in Kingston and going through high school—was by myself—and my mom was telling me what to do all the time. Even though it is my beloved mother, it's difficult .... I'm sure it must have been difficult for her too. It wasn't like the little White kids that are used to being babied, that she was used to taking care of. So it was really tough on both of us. And I think basketball started out as total refuge .... It was a total getaway.

For Greg, playing basketball became the means by which he coped with his transitions in life—being a new immigrant in Canada, and during a suspension from Elliot High School on an assault charge (which was eventually dismissed). According to Greg, during the long months of suspension, he fell "in love with basketball even more." He occupied his time by playing outdoors and at the parks and recreation centre where his cousin worked. It was this cousin who advised him not to return to Elliot High School after his suspension from the school. For this reason, Greg went to live with his cousin in the downtown area, where he attended Trail High School, and after school played at the community centre. But Trail, Greg said:

> wasn't very good in basketball. It would not make me fulfill my goal of obtaining a [sports] scholarship. So I transferred over to [Kane High School where] instead of beating [Trail] by 40, we started beating them by 60. We went to OFSAA [Ontario Federation of School Athletic Association], that kind of thing.

But Greg spent only one semester at Kane because he moved again to live with his mother, who was now living in an apartment north of the city. The neighbourhood school that Greg was expected to attend did not have a basketball team, so, based on his "reputation" within the Toronto high school basketball community, he was recruited by friends and at least three basketball coaches of schools in the area. He eventually chose to attend Glen High School, which was not only outside of his neighbourhood, but was in another school district. And in order to legitimately demonstrate that he did live in the school district, Greg moved in with his friend Dave's family,[10] "a Jewish family of five children" (a situation he describes as "great—they had a basketball court in their driveway"). He added that Dave's "father would say, Greg, you're good player. You go and play with Dave. Go study with Dave."

Glen High School was thought to be a very good school since, as Greg said, it had "so many more program around—not only programs but a caring coach, one of the more influential people in my life. His name is [Frank Moss] ... and we immediately became friends." By way of illustrating the ways in which Frank was a more caring and respectful coach than the coach at his former high school, Greg noted that he had problems with his coach at Kane:

> because I had to work after school and I wasn't from the background of some of the other guys .... He [Kane's coach] didn't want anyone to have after-school jobs. He was not really understanding and he wanted full dedication, which I could not do. I had a part-time care-taking job [at three different schools]. I used to clean up quickly so I could play in their gym after I was finished.

In continuing to comment on the important role that Frank played in his life, Greg continued:

> I am telling you the truth .... this guy was the closest thing I had at the time to a father figure because he expressed a special interest in me. He went over and above for me ..., maybe it's because he realized what I was lacking in my life at the time, what I needed, and what basketball meant to me; I had goals and he knew about these goals. And I just had this burning passion in myself that I was going to make it .... Outside [of my cousin] and my family, [Frank was the] first person that was part of the institution, the system that could influence me; that saw it [interest] and nurtured it and helped me. He knew that I set goals for myself .... Last Friday, I went back to [Glen] and first thing that I did was go to his office and was, like [Frank], what's up? [Greg slapped his hands together to form a friendship hug and handshake]. That's the relationship. So I mean without saying more, he was obviously influential. This guy was the first person to listen, which is total opposite to [Mr. Murray at Kane] because he encouraged me to get a job. He would

make practice shorter so that we could travel to our job. Kane really pushed ball, it was everything. They were, like, don't work because you have to play ball; this is important to practise .... My point is that those guys that stayed at Kane did not get the networking skills that someone like me got. I was a hustler from day one .... Every kid needs someone with credibility to tell you that you could do it.

Greg later added that Frank not only recognized his ability, but:

he was the first person that started telling everybody to give this guy the ball; starting drawing plays for me, so it was a huge boost of confidence. Once we had that kind of trust—and I saw that we were on the same wavelength—he was looking out for me. He was like: [Greg] you have to pull your grades up if you want to go anywhere.

In seeking to ascertain the role that his mother was playing in his life as he settled into life in Canada and pursued his athletic goal through school, I asked: "Where was your mom in all this? What was she doing? What was she saying to you?"

Greg: Making the bread. She was the key breadwinner for the family— making sure we had clothes and shoes. I know I spoke earlier about us not getting along; part of why we did not get along is because she was trying to survive, so she couldn't make it to every game. She made it to more games than the average—than any Black parent. Like my friend Dave, the White kid, had his parents there every game, cheering: "Hey Dave, way to go! Get the next one!" You know what I mean? I didn't, per say, have that. I mean my dad was in Jamaica and the only time he got involved was key decisions. When I say key decisions, like, when my mom was gone for eight years, I saw him once.

In the absence of his father and given the limitations of his mother, Greg came to rely on the support that he was receiving from Frank and Dave's family. In fact, Greg had become so much a part of Dave's family that when Dave was going away to basketball camp for a month in the US the following summer, Dave's father invited Greg to join Dave. And recognizing that Greg's mother could not afford the $400 weekly fees, Dave's father made an arrangement with the camp whereby Greg was allowed to attend the camp and work as a bus boy, which meant, as Greg explained:

> Everyone would wake up for breakfast at eight. I'd wake up at six and help them prepare breakfast, set the table, clean up and whatever. Let's just say that .... I worked in the kitchen, and I was, like, picking up paper, everything—bottles. That was my job. It was tough 'cause I had a lot of pressure, you know, and here are these little White boys throwing stuff on the ground, hitting me with spaghetti balls: "Here's a mess, clean that up!" You know what I mean? [They were] rude kids .... It was an experience that I loved because I was able to play ball against kids that were heading places—playing for the scouts, in front of scouts. Hundreds of scouts just watching the kids play ball. Compared to some of the guys that I played with up here, they were headed to big universities because they had exposure, and they had opportunity with the programs. While at the camp, I really learned how to deal with things. If I were to lose the opportunity, [it would be] if I beat someone up [or] if I was to not wake up. It was breach of contract so to speak, so I did what I had to do. It was real responsibility. Where I got my revenge was on the court .... I was playing, [I was] motivated. I was there for weeks. I made the top 20 every week. One week I was MVP; another week I got the hardest working camper award .... One week I got the sportsmanship award. Each week I got something that was so encouraging. One of the main things I got was exposure.

The camp provided a welcomed opportunity for Greg, since he really did not want to return to Glen High School; for despite the fact that during his year at Glen he had the strong support of his coach and his peers, and did go on to win the district's player of the year award, he felt that there was still "something missing":

> the competition wasn't as good as it was at Kane, and I had one year left for high school and, you know, I didn't think I was going to get the exposure ..., my grades throughout this process was very bad. I had 50s. If I got a 60, it was a big deal.[11]

So the camp offered Greg the break he was looking for—to be in the United States since "in Canada there is definitely no opportunity to get on the big stage and get into professional basketball." This is why his experience at the camp was an important turning point for Greg. It was there that he was recruited by a number of university scouts, including some from Division One universities, but because of "bad grades" and incomplete high school credits, he never received "a letter from any of the schools." (He also said that he had not taken the SAT; in fact, he had never heard of SAT.) Given his educational needs, therefore, one coach directed Greg to a "prep school" (population about 300) in the western US that catered to student athletes demonstrating athletic ability. Greg quoted the university coach saying to the prep school coach: "You gotta come up and see this kid. He's raw. He's gotta lot of skills, but put some time into him. He will be a good player. He could win you the state championship." Based on his impressive skills, abilities, and (allegedly) such a glowing assessment, Greg received a scholarship and attended the prep school. Being a Canadian and one of a few people on scholarship, he felt a pressure to perform. He did perform, and in the process learned "discipline, time management, and to balance academics and basketball." "It was," as Greg said, "the beginning of true academic success. Since then I maintained a good academic average."

Greg reported that while at the prep school, he received much exposure and calls from various university and college coaches "promising him the world if he attended their school." He went on five recruiting trips and afterwards decided to accept a scholarship offer from a college in Maryland. But at that university:

> I began to realize what I thought was a dream was a joke. I was pretty much told to take philosophy because that coach would be lenient with basketball players. "Take Mr. J's class because he loves basketball." Although I had planned to take all of these courses, it never worked out that way. They pretty much had it all planned out for me and I had no power to change it. They made me take philosophy and I never went. And when I did, I would end up [he made a snoring sound to represent him sleeping]. I resented that school because that is not what they told me when I went there. So I ended up getting bad grades my first year because I was not doing what I wanted to in basketball. I wanted out of there .... I hated it. It was a really humbling experience for me. The coach was intense.

So after only one year of "butting heads" with the coach (not having received the playing time he was promised), and feeling that he had the ability to compete with his teammates, Greg "left and went to a junior ... college" in Texas on a one-year scholarship. Things were no better at this second college. In fact, Greg complained of having to deal with racism and a coach who was "a very negative person." He went on to say that the college was a "joke" because he was enrolled in courses such as karate and sewing. Greg also explained that the junior colleges he attended are known as "university prep schools," which were part of the "farm system" designed for student athletes who intended to go to larger universities in the NCAA.

The following year, Greg was recruited to, and attended, a Florida university where he played for the team. He had intended to major in physical education, but because of the little support he received, the variety of courses he took enabled him to obtain a degree in sociology with a minor in "exercise science." Notwithstanding the inconsistencies in his attendance at classes (which was reflected in his grades), Greg felt quite satisfied that he was able to get an education—thanks in part to some tutoring—that has worked for him so far. However, in reflecting on his academic experience, Greg wrote to me, saying:

> I was not pleased with the academic support. I felt that they provided tutors with the intention of keeping you eligible to play. It was difficult to combine studying with basketball. Obviously one suffered for the other at times. I am very proud of the fact that I am one of a very few who graduated especially on time. It took a lot of dedication and determination. I had to be *disciplined* [his emphasis]. If I had to do it all over, I would be more careful in selecting what university I attend. I would make sure that they had the major I wanted and that other members of my team were majoring in the same thing. This way I would know that my classes won't interfere with practice times (December 26, 2003).

It was also in this university that he experienced the fragility of life. During a warm-up session in one of his first basketball practices at the university, his roommate and friend collapsed and died of a heart attack. Greg explained how the psychological impact of this incident has remained with him. After graduating from university without being drafted to the NBA, Greg went on to play basketball for teams in the national leagues of two European countries. This opportunity came when he participated in the 1999 NBA summer league— "playing against every NBA team, giving them the opportunity" to see him.

But it was while participating in the free agent camp "with no guarantees" that he was offered and "immediately" accepted an opportunity to play in Europe. He reasoned that "a bird in the hand is worth more than many in the wild." In the off-seasons Greg returned to Toronto where he ran basketball camps that are now part of the youth organization he founded in 2001. This was also the year that Greg reinjured his knee (first injured in the 1999 season), and so was unable to continue playing. Unsure of the long-term effects of the injury on his future playing, Greg took up teaching as an alternative career—a career that was also inspired by his coach Frank:

> I think one main reason why I wanted to teach—like teach physical education—was because I know that no teacher of any other subject could reach me the way Frank did because they wouldn't have had my attention. Frank had the key because he had the key to the gym, and he had the basketball, and he had the key to me getting to my goal because he was the coach of the basketball team, so he pretty much had the key to my future.

Greg later added that becoming a teacher was also a way "to give back to his community" (see James, 2000: "Returning the Dues"). Greg also credited the financial and athletic successes that he enjoys today (a nice expensive car, a condominium in the city) to his hard work and hustling.

> It took me taking a plane down there [to the US] using my own money to go for those tryouts. It took me going to camp working as a bus boy, cleaning up crap, stuff that most of those guys [his basketball peers] would not do. Sometimes it is not just ability to play to make it or get an athletic scholarship.[12] Hunger, work, determination, and just a passion, and burning desire, and, of course, encouragement like having someone telling you [that] you can do it is a huge thing.

While in the teacher education program, Greg, who had refused to accept the earlier diagnosis that his injury could not be corrected enough for him to play basketball again, sought other medical advice. Based on this advice, he underwent the third surgery (all paid for by his insurance) of his basketball career. He has recovered, and this ended four years of "playing in pain". Today, with his teaching degree, he is again playing in Europe on "one of the top leagues in the world outside of the NBA." He went on to say: "I have faith that my body will be fine with God's help."

DISCUSSION

Recall that our interest in this chapter is to examine the experiences and achievements of "athletic-identified" students for whom sport was once their "Hercules muscles" and, in some ways, later became their "Achilles heel." For all four athletes, the schools they chose to attend, the friends with whom they associated, the people with whom they cultivated and maintained relationships (i.e., teachers, coaches, relatives, significant others), their dress, their music, their educational and career aspirations, and their extracurricular, summer, and community activities were focussed around basketball—their "Hercules muscles." Their stories reveal that basketball was so central to their existence that they sacrificed both a certain multidimensionality of self, as well as broader educational and career opportunities. This is understandable since through basketball all four of them in their high school years experienced glory, fame, recognition, and celebrity. This recalls Adler and Adler's (1989) description of the elite athlete as the "gloried self," which characteristically "is a greedy, intoxicating and riveting self, that seeks to ascend in importance and to cast aside other self-dimensions as it grows" (cited in Sparkes, 2000, p. 24). So basketball was not merely an athletic activity in which these four students participated, it was a subculture: this included a value system, an educational and career path, a form of dress, verbal and non-verbal language, in short, a "way of being" (see also Abdel-Shehid, 2003).

But in stratified societies like the United States and Canada, where what you look like and "where you're from" matter, the "way of being" or cultural identification (ascribed or taken) is simultaneously tied to class, race, citizenship/immigrant status, gender, and residency (i.e., rural, urban, suburban, "inner city" neighbourhood). Hence, as we observe in all four cases, race and class were incorporated into constructed "basketball" identities. Most notable are the ways in which Amir, Lori, and Devin identify with "blackness," or were identified as Black. Devin reported that at times basketball players and fans alike would say that he was "Black" or "half-Black." For their part, not only did Amir, Lori, and Devin mostly "hang with," and "dress like" their Black basketball peers, they also admitted, as Lori did, to listening "to Black music ... hip-hop, reggae, and R and B." Even more telling is the fact that Amir and Devin went as far as distancing themselves from their ethnic group peers whom Amir and Devin saw as "unathletic," and therefore had little in common with them. As Devin said, "I never looked at them as being part of my culture. I mean, I didn't grow up with them." What was behind Amir's and

Devin's distancing of themselves from their peers of similar ethnic origins? Was it necessary for them to have done so?

The fact that Amir and Devin distanced themselves from their South Asian and Southeast Asian peers respectively, and/or visa versa, is likely related to the subculture of basketball with its links to a given racialialized group. Hence, it would appear that through their socialization into basketball, a "Black referenced identity" emerged, which became socially, psychologically, and culturally central in their "constellation of identities" (Sparkes, 2000), and with which they needed to identify to follow their aspiration in a sport dominated by Black student athletes. This would account for the fact that all three of them had to have "sponsors" (Devin referred to them as his mentors)—Black student athletes who excelled at basketball, and were able to vouch for or legitimize their basketball capabilities, abilities, and skills. Amir had Vernon, whom he endearingly referred to as his "boy" with "a natural athletic talent to play basketball." For Lori it was a Black male friend, "one of the best players" in the group who "would stick up" for her. And for Devin, it was his Black high school friends through whom he gained status, recognition, and the chance to enter school spaces that were colonized by Black students. But "fitting in" and getting the recognition they sought was not without struggles—they had to prove themselves in a context where, in some cases, they were the only ones who were not Black. But so important was basketball to their life stories that they were willing to persevere with the challenges of "outsider" status until they gained acceptance (not only on the basketball court but also through music and social activities). As Lori said, there is nowhere else that they could go that would make them better players. Is the idea here that the best basketball players are Black and hence the best people with whom to develop the necessary skills and competence? Can we see a process of racialization at work here? Evidently, the ubiquitous and persuasive racialized script has informed the perceptions, practices, and interactions of these players as it does fans and people in general.

So too does the same racialized script frame Greg's experiences in basketball. As we have observed, Greg did not need sponsors; even as a young immigrant to Toronto with little prior basketball experience, he felt confident enough that he would be able to build on his jumping ability and excel in basketball. And skill and ability aside, his smooth movements between schools (as many as five secondary schools in Toronto in a four-year period), and his almost instant chance to play on the basketball teams of his respective schools, make it seem that it was taken for granted that he would "fit in" and become an important team member. Greg could not recall being questioned at any time during his high school basketball career about his basketball ability, not even when he was new to the country, or when he was first trying out for the basketball team. It is possible that Greg benefited from the racialized script of the coaches for, as Amir observed in his failed attempts to get his coaches to recognize him as one of their top basketball players, coaches "play favourites to the Black players" (see Jones, 2000; Armour, 2000). Further, in such a context where he never had to confront questions of his Black or basketball identity, Greg likely developed a gloried self, which led him (more than the other three participants) to limit his attention to other educational, occupational, and social identities, roles, and activities. So, while like Lori, Amir, and Devin, Greg had put an extraordinary amount of time and energy into basketball, he appears to have done so with a confidence (his identity was never questioned or scrutinized—he was a Black basketball player) that he would attain his athletic scholarship ambition. Indeed, a significant number of Canadian players who win US scholarships—those who supposedly "beat the odds" through hard work, determination, and commitment—are Black. Many are from the Greater Toronto Area (GTA), making Toronto, as the *Toronto Star* headline (Clarkson, November 26, 2003, p. C2) reads, "a hotbed for hoops" because, as the headline continues, "High school stars reap rewards of US scholarships." While such evidence might have reassured Greg, it is also likely that it made it difficult, compared to the other participants, for him to re-story his life without sport (hence his seeking another doctor to operate on his knee and his return to Europe to play after his teacher education).

This belief that hard work, determination, and commitment will translate into the achievement of the kinds of goals to which Amir, Devin, and Greg aspired reflects the deeply held meritocratic value of equality of opportunity into which they had been socialized, especially as working-class (as well as first/second-generation minority) males who sought to attain upward social mobility.[13] This relationship between the sport of basketball and working-class status was repeatedly mentioned in Devin's reference to basketball, particularly with reference to affordability—"a financial choice to even baseball." Furthermore, all three males suggested that their scholarship aspirations were also motivated by the chance to receive a university education without placing a financial burden on their parents or getting into debt themselves. In this regard, Lori, whose aspiration was to eventually play on the Canadian Olympic team (trying to attain her own and her father's dream) is an exception, for her parents could afford to send her to university. But she too held the notion that, on the basis of merit, she would attain her basketball ambition. The belief in merit here is not merely a characteristic related to the social class background of these basketball players, but is also a part of their athletic-centred values. Indeed, the narratives of all four athletes indicate that economic and class-related influences have both constrained and enabled their ability to achieve via basketball (see Armour, 2000, p. 73).[14]

Interestingly, Amir, Devin, and Greg did not indicate that their "real" aspiration was to play in the NBA (Amir did, although in a joking manner). In fact, their language was always about winning athletic scholarships to play on a university or college team. The place of education in their story reflects how education is often posited as the means by which upward social mobility can be achieved in Canadian and other stratified societies. It seems logical, therefore, that Amir, Devin, and Greg would narrate their enthusiasm for basketball in terms of how it motivated them to attend school, obtain a high school education, and opened up avenues in which they could negotiate the athletic scholarship networks. In doing so, they were eventually able to obtain the support and blessing of their parents (though at times passive—their parents hardly went to see them play) who, like them and other significant adults in their lives, believed that their skills, ability, and hard work would translate into a university education.[15] It makes sense that Devin and Greg would go from school to school, and choose to attend a school that they felt would provide them the opportunities to play on a good competitive basketball team with supportive players. To this end, it was important for these three scholarship aspirants to pragmatically work with coaches who could facilitate their wishes, assist in their empowerment, and help them to stand out. The coaches, then, were expected to function as conduits to the final goal of securing scholarships.

The stories that all three participants told about their efforts to excel at basketball and win US scholarships might on the surface appear irrational, problematic, and ultimately detrimental, but they are all in keeping with the centrality of basketball to their life goals. For instance, Greg's breaking into his school for the chance to play basketball, Devin's and Lori's willingness to tolerate feeling "like outsiders" among Black players, and Amir's long hours away from home (and fights with his mother) all represent their understanding that achieving their life goals necessarily requires these extraordinary efforts. Roger Saul describes these efforts as an "obsession":

I remember that when I was a teenager like Amir, I was also obsessed with the idea of "going south" (for baseball), to the point that I remember writing to my aunt who lived in the US and asking her if I could stay with her to finish high school. However, I was always encouraged to have a "backup plan" in case my dream didn't work out. I never did think about that backup plan, though, because it always felt like doing that would be admitting defeat or confirming that I may have doubts about my abilities. In the sense that we are always told to "believe in ourselves" and "not to let anything get in the way of our dreams," a backup plan seems out of place, doesn't it? Fortunately for Amir, he had good grades to fall back on (as did I, among other advantages). But it makes you wonder about kids who don't have those and other advantages, and who put all of their stock into their athletic identities (Personal communication, November 10, 2003).

I have often wondered about student athletes not having "a backup plan" (in fact, I often advise student athletes to develop one). But, as Saul suggests, one of the consequences of such advice is the possibility of undermining the efforts, expectations, and confidence—confidence in the fact that they were mature enough to read their situation and make rewarding decisions. It is understandable, therefore, that none of the four participants in this study had a backup plan. In the case of the three males, only Greg, at the time of the interview, did have a backup plan—becoming a qualified teacher. That Greg was working on his backup plan was not only precipitated by his injury and four years of "playing with pain," but conceivably also because he felt he had attained his goals. As for Devin, he felt that he was on his way to achieving his athletic dreams. Specifically, at the time of the interview, he was waiting to hear from his agent about his contract to play basketball in Southeast Asia—in the country from where his parents immigrated. Consequently, Devin was reluctant to think of any alternative to a basketball career. And while during the interview he sincerely reflected on my ideas about teaching as a career option (I was careful not to say "alternative"), it was not until he returned from Asia, when his plans did not materialize, that he was able to think about teaching as an alternative career. Similarly, Amir, during the initial interview, was unwilling to consider anything other than his athletic career. He was adamant that he would attain a scholarship. This did not happen, nor did his written introduction letters to US universities and colleges yield the desired results. That it took a while—actually, some three months into his first semester in university—for Amir to let go of his dream of achieving the athletic scholarship to a US university can be explained by the culture of optimism, confidence, commitment, and merit into which he, like the others, had been socialized.

This socialization is also reflected in the determination of Amir and Devin, who were both doing very well academically, to get to university on the basis of their academic achievements. Their all-consuming athletic identity even trumped their academic identity. They gave little significance to their academic capabilities and achievements or even thought of their academic work as enabling them (as a backup plan) to pursue post-secondary education. So we see Amir resenting the fact that his coach, Robert, expected him to take an academic rather than an athletic route to university in the United States. This conceptualization of procuring a post-secondary education in the US through basketball begs the questions, as Roger Saul asks:

> Is the real goal of the athletic scholarship really to obtain a free education, as so many student athletes seem to say? Or is obtaining a scholarship really just an affirmation of athletic talent that strengthens "athletic identity" and allows athletes to keep dreaming and working toward the real (or should I say unreal) goal of professional status? (Personal communication, November 10, 2003).

Apparently, for Amir, Devin, and Greg, the idea of winning an athletic scholarship is not merely about financing their university education, but also about the gloried self and public recognition. This is illustrated by their disinterest in exploring scholarship opportunities (albeit small compared to US institutions) to universities in Canada. Also in evidence here is the extent to which their faith in and reliance on their athletic abilities and skills (instead of academic competence) was the expected route to university. And they believed that their bodies—despite the fact that all three males had had serious injuries—would remain disciplined and unproblematic.

It is not surprising that only Greg talked with me about his injury during the interview, probably because this was public information that I knew about already. But he did not say much; hence, I did not know of the seriousness of the injury. All I knew then was that he was injured while playing in Europe and he was home looking at other career possibilities. I only understood about the seriousness of Greg's injury through follow-up communications. But as he expressed in a recent (December, 2003) email communication, "I have faith

165

that my body will be fine with God's help." It was in a follow-up conversation with Amir after he had read an earlier version of this chapter that he said to me that there was something else he did not tell me during the interview. He said that while in Grade Eleven, he suffered a knee injury while playing on a team coached by Robert, and could not walk for a time, and only Robert, his friend Vernon, and his mother knew. But they did not know about the seriousness of the injury (he said that "You never tell coaches these things"), and that at times he was in "a lot of pain," which he "eventually got used to." Amir said that he has been to several doctors, but none of the medical attention he has received to date has really helped. He admits that the injury had set him back; nevertheless, he still believes that he will be able to continue playing basketball at his accustomed level. He continued: "I know it sounds stupid, and you can't comprehend." Amir is scheduled to have an MRI this winter. When I asked Amir why he did not tell me during the interview, he said that he did not want "that information to get out" because he was still awaiting his scholarship offer. It was after hearing Amir's story that I asked Devin if he was ever injured. He explained that he had a right shoulder injury for which he had surgery and a recuperation period of eight months. While recovering from the injury, Devin learned to use his left hand, and today he uses both hands. But as he said: "I lost some flexibility and haven't been the same since. My shooting is not as good." When asked why he still pursued basketball and went overseas with the intention of playing, Devin replied: "Realistically, I was going for broke. It was sheer will and determination. My will was carrying me."

What comes through in these males' responses to their injuries is their unwillingness to admit to the limitations of their bodies, and the fact that they could no longer take their bodies for granted. Their traumatizing experiences caused by their injuries, as Sparkes (2000) says, shattered their world views, throwing them into varying states of disbelief and despondency. Hence, the stories that Amir, Devin, and Greg told were about their "restored selves," following the belief that their faith, determination, strong will, endurance, and resilience had enabled them to recapture the past. This construction of their valued *selves* and personal identities in terms of the irretrievable past is referred to as an "entrenched self" that, according to Charmaz (1987),

> represents patterns of action, conviction, and habit built up over the years. These unchanged patterns had been a source of self-respect before illness. After illness, resuming these patterns becomes the person's major objective ...

restoring an entrenched self also has the imagery of a "comeback" (cited in Sparkes, 2000, p. 26).

What is not clear, however, is how much these athletes' current performance measure up to their past expectations. Knowing this would enable us to ascertain the extent to which their athletic identities are a reflection of their prolonged preoccupation with the self-conception situated in the past and their related heightened identity dilemmas (Sparkes, 2000, p. 26).

CONCLUSION

These students' stories reveal how their overarching identities limited other identities, such as race, ethnicity, and academic, all relegated to subordinate status. As such, their athletic identities operated as their "Hercules' muscles," helping them to navigate both high school and university. Further, through basketball, they came to understand and appreciate the value of social relationships and networks, necessary for their career aspirations. In this regard, we see them placing considerable reliance on their relationships with coaches (and other adults, as in the cases of Devin and Greg). They expected their coaches to create conditions that would give them exposure. With the support and encouragement of coaches, parents, and peers came recognition, adulation, respect, confidence, and empowerment—in essence, their gloried selves. These selves, built on their athletic identities, have been nurtured by their belief in the merit system, which holds that regardless of their social class backgrounds, given their abilities, talent, and competencies, they will attain their athletic ambitions. Consequently, they all held out for that to happen, in spite of knowing about the limitations of their bodies due to injuries.

But the reality is that inequality exists and race, social class, gender, and citizenship do matter in Canadian society. In such a context, their athletic identities—their Hercules' muscles—in many instances have also operated as their Achilles heels. Their overarching athletic identities, and the corresponding pursuance of their seemingly unrealistic basketball dreams, provided little space for other identities, skills, and aspirations to develop. So when Amir and Devin failed to win the athletic scholarships they so desperately sought, and Lori did not get the chance to play on Canada's Olympic team, and Greg was faced with the possibility of a shortened basketball career due to injury, they were confronted with a challenge to their perceptions of their futures.

Consequently, we see them attempting to shift from their athletic identity and call upon their other abilities and talents to which they had previously ascribed little significance. But having been encouraged by their coaches, educators, media, parents, and significant others to "work hard," to "commit fully to the sport," and to "not let go of their dreams," it does not seem so strange that they would be reluctant to let go of their basketball dreams. However, as Sparkes (2000), citing Adler and Adler, writes: "The longer the gloried athletic self served as their master status, the harder the athletes found it to conceive of any other identity for themselves" (p. 25). It is not surprising, then, that Greg, who had enjoyed the benefits of basketball for a longer time, would seek to maintain his athletic identity as long as he could. But to conclude that his seeming hesitation to re-story his life independent of athletics is a reflection of his longer time playing would be misleading. For whatever the *re-story* or "restitution narrative" (Frank cited in Sparkes, 2000, p. 27) of Greg, as well as of Amir, Lori, and Devin, they will inevitably draw on the very sources—that is, athletics—on which they have been fixated for years.

It is fair to suggest that the stories or restitution narratives that Amir, Lori, Devin, and Greg have shared are constructs related to a period of their transitions, shifting identities, and the unresolved loss of a fantasized career goal. Their stories about their lives are now reconstructed to enhance their present and past situations, relationships, needs, and aspirations. These time-bound "partial" narratives of self provide glimpses into the complex and layered athletic identities—mediated by race, ethnicity, class, gender, and academic attainment—of these four student athletes. And while the strong athletic identity of all four participants acted as an Achilles heel, there are nevertheless variations in the resulting identity shifts and changes in their career goals. These variations seem to indicate that race, gender, class, age, and ethnic identification, academic attainment, and career aspirations (to earn a scholarship or play on the Olympic team) likely operated to inform the level of athletic identity, which in turn affected participants' degree of acceptance of life without basketball. Lori, who had more modest aspirations, seemed to have given up on basketball much sooner than the males. It is likely that as a female, Lori's level of identification with basketball was not as strong as the males. As for the males, Amir, who was quite successful academically and had fewer years of experience and investment in basketball, demonstrated (at least for now) that he was able to get into his academic work at university and not play on a basketball team. The same cannot be said for Devin, who, like Amir, had to resort to completing his university education in Toronto, but even here, he quickly became part of the university team, and went on to play overseas, as Greg did when he too finished university. Undoubtedly, gender plays a role in these males' strong athletic identification, and so, too, is their racial identification in terms of the racialized link of body to sport and their social class background as it relates to the idea of basketball being "a way up and out." From what we have seen of the participants, the failure to realize their athletic ambitions propelled them to recognize their other identities, which ironically may just be a benefit in the long term. It appears, therefore, that as the earlier student athletes are brought by significant people in their lives to realize and appreciate the precarious nature of their basketball ambitions, their unrealized athletic dreams and failed plans will be very valued lessons learned.

NOTES

1. In elaborating on the notion of "athletic identity," Sparkes references B. Brewer, J. Van Raalte, and D. Linder (1993), as well as S. Wiechman and J. Williams (1997).

2. The two-hour open-ended interviews with each participant were audio-taped and transcribed by Yasmin following our discussions of key issues and themes that emerged in the interviews. I also received permission from the participants to use information obtained in our follow-up conversations and email exchanges. In the process of writing the profiles, I contacted participants in person and via email to clarify queries and questions that emerged, as well as for updates. In the tradition of conducting "respectful research" (Tilley, 1998; 2003), all of the participants received a copy of the chapter for their comments after it was completed.

3. Recently, Vernon became a member of the Canadian national team. He also received a full athletic scholarship to a Division One school in the United States. In a follow-up (Fall, 2003) conversation with Amir after this news was out, he expressed happiness over his friend's achievement; and at the same time recalled how much he missed out on the same level of support and attention from the coaches that they gave to Vernon, whose athletic skills and abilities, as Amir claimed, were the same as his.

4. She stated that she liked this music—"everything except for hard rock." When asked why, she stated, "I do think that, in all honesty, is something basketball influences."

5. Devin also noted that his mother used to play basketball in her birth country where the sport was "pretty big."

6. Devin also noted that cost was one of the factors that influenced their decision to attend high school in the area. As he said: "I don't think people could afford to go out of the area—you know, pay for bus fare and, uh, the meals. That just didn't happen."

7. Devin said that teachers compared him to his brother. In one case, he was "kicked out of a class" because the teacher did not want him there. He assumed the reason for this to be the reputation of his brother with that particular teacher.

8. When asked how his mother reacted, Devin said that he was already supporting himself and she knew that he "was doing well in school and in basketball, and hence was comfortable with his move." Besides, he said, "I have not received a penny from my mom since I was 16 years [old]. I just knew there was no way that she could support me. She was just too busy trying to raise my younger brothers and sisters ...."

9. Greg said that at that time, a significant number of Black youth lived in the nearby neighbourhood and had a similar interest in basketball, but it "was very intimidating for a kid that did not live there."

10. Greg had met this friend, Dave, when they played on the Ontario basketball team.

11. This poor showing in his academic work was a result of, as Greg explained, poor time management, "miscommunication with his mother," and the fact that she was "on his case." "Too much," he admitted, "was going on in my life."

12. Greg also stated that obtaining an athletic scholarship is overrated, but admits it was one of the best experiences of his life. He now helps other students with the same dream to attain the very same goals he did while growing up.

13. Citing Sage, Armour (2000) makes the point that "although the precise nature of the class categories might be debatable, it is undeniable that in America, as elsewhere, 'social class is one of the most pervasive variables determining life chances ... and patterns of social interaction'" (p. 71). And noting that the fantasy of achieving social mobility through sport is a false myth, she adds that "a significant, measurable rise in social class of a large number of athletes is more illusionary than real. What is less clear is how the myths about mobility through sport are perpetuated" (p. 75).

14. It is tempting to make an association between class background and basketball participation. But, as Armour (2000) notes, while it might be possible to associate sports with people who are at the extreme ends of the social stratification system (e.g., basketball as the sport in which working-class people like Devin and Greg would participate), doing so would be simplistic. Indeed, Lori's identification with and interest in basketball alerts us to the complexity of such an association.

15. It is fair to suggest that their parents and significant others also believed that because of meritocracy, these youth would attain their athletic goals.

TEACHING ATHLETES/COACHING STUDENTS: ON THE ROLE OF COACHES

If coaching is to be viewed as a culturally contested site of social practices characterized by a series of power relations that shape individual identities within the wider society, the social and educational responsibilities of practitioners need to be highlighted. Acceptance of such a position, both in relation to the nature of coaching and of the role of the coach within it, would enable practitioners to recognize the liberating and constraining influences upon them, thus progressing to improved practices (Jones, 2000, p. 38).

Educators, parents, and coaches must be aware of the fact that, by instilling notions of competition and team membership unproblematically, without balancing their lessons with words of caution and tolerance, they may be planting the seeds of human suffering, hatred, and prejudice in the minds of children (Fernández-Balboa, 2000, p. 138).

I HAVE MADE MANY REFERENCES TO THE ROLE, ACTIVITIES, AND PRACTICES OF coaches and their relationships to student athletes. In this chapter, drawing on literature, media information, and accounts of participants in this project, I focus on the role and practices of coaches, including considering the relationship they have with students, and on students' outlook on their academic/athletic career. In particular, my interest here is to consider how coaches (most of whom are White) recruit, socialize, train, educate, facilitate, and support student athletes in their sporting interests and aspirations in a multicultural context, and how student athletes perceive of coaches' interactions and roles in their lives. By "multicultural" schooling context, I mean the presumption that Canadian schools provide programs that are sensitive to, and respectful of, cultural differences, and that students have opportunities to develop pride in their cultural heritage and to build positive self-images.

Within the multicultural schooling context, and persuaded by the principles of multiculturalism, coaches, like their other education colleagues, claim to be sensitive to their students' cultural backgrounds and social class; they claim to carry out their tasks and responsibilities while treating all students equally (see Chapter 4). In this regard, coaches tend to see themselves as coaching undifferentiated groups of athletes (sometimes students), thus pretending to be *blind* to the students' cultural differences. The contradiction here is evident. The question might then be, how can coaches claim to acknowledge the cultural backgrounds of students and not treat them differently, recognizing their differences in needs, interests, expectations, and aspirations? In response, coaches, from the perspective of their "sports ethic," would contend that the needs, interests, and expectations of student athletes are related to their personal qualities and choices rather than to characteristics such as ethnicity, race, gender, and social class. And they often believe that because they come to the coaching process without preconceived ideas about students and their athletic abilities and skills, they treat athletes fairly and equitably (see Dabovic, 2000; Simmons, 1999). So coaches would argue that the judgements they make about athletes, such as who to cut or who to play, are based on the *merits* of the "on-the-field/on-the-court" performance of the athletes. The fact is, the male-centred "coaching ethic" by which coaches tend to operate, is premised on the myths of meritocracy and egalitarianism that contribute to the notion that sports are a "great equalizer" and an activity to which all students have access irrespective of their colour, race, gender, sex, class, ethnicity, and language. Within such sports culture, then, it can be expected that in their roles as mentors and role models to sport-identified athletes, coaches would pass on this taken-for-granted existence of meritocracy (see Chapter 5).

In the discussion that follows, I contest the notion of undifferentiated, purportedly equal opportunity and treatment of marginalized student athletes. For athletic activities are not implemented in a neutral school context; rather, that context is structured by the cultural hegemony that exists in academic and athletic programs, which privilege particular activities that often reflect the values, priorities, and interests of students belonging to the dominant cultural group. Coaching, therefore, does not take place in a vacuum; it is a process that is informed by the hegemonic structures of the school and of society, and characterized by complex power dynamics and relationships among coaches and athletes based on the realities of their socially lived experiences.[1]

Therefore, if coaches are to truly maximize the potential of their athletes, they must come to an understanding of their own socio-cultural backgrounds, the ideas and values they hold about their work, the lived experiences of the student athletes, and "the problematic nature of the social bonds that tie coaches to athlete and athlete to athlete" (Jones, 2000, p. 36). Issues of class, race, and gender should be reflected in coaching pedagogy; both students and coaches must be critically aware of the structures within the school system. On this basis, I examine the comments of six coaches. Yasmin and I had conversations with three of these (two males and one female), and three other school coaches were interviewed separately (two males and one female). With the exception of the assistant coach, who was a high school student at the time, they had all been coaching for over 10 years. The discussion is organized around themes that emerged from our conversations. Before proceeding to my discussion, I will briefly re-examine some of the student respondents' comments on their coaches.

STUDENT ATHLETES' PERSPECTIVES OF COACHES— FRIENDS, FATHER FIGURES, AND SPONSORS

A major theme in the stories of all the respondents is the role of the coaches in their lives. In a few cases (Alicia, Greg, Kevin) coaches recruited them, contrary to the education board policy. For these student athletes (e.g., Saeed), their choice of high school was based largely on the influence of the basketball coaches. But for the most part, their coaches nurtured them through high school, provided them playing opportunities and exposure to university coaches, and assisted them in their efforts to enter a Canadian university. For example, Lori and Devin talked of the contact that their high school coaches made with the university coach. But most importantly, in the cases of Alicia and Greg, their coaches encouraged them in their aspirations to attain athletic scholarships to US universities and colleges. According to Alicia, "Well, definitely my high school coach helped me to get in a position of being able to play at the college level." But Greg's comment even better captures the significance of this role (quoted in Chapter 5):

> ... I am telling you the truth ... this guy was the closest thing I had at the time to a father figure because he expressed a special interest in me. He went over and above for me ..., maybe it's because he realized what I was lacking in my life at the time, what I needed, and what basketball meant to me, and I had goals and he knew about these goals. Outside [of my cousin] and my family, [Frank was the] first person that was part of the institution, the system that could influence me; that saw it [interest] and nurtured it, and helped me .... Last Friday, I went back to [Glen] and first thing that I did was go to his office and was, like [Frank], what's up? [Greg slapped two hands together to form a friendship hug and handshake]—that's the relationship. Every kid needs someone with credibility to tell you that you could do it .... He was the first person that started telling everybody to give this guy the ball, starting drawing plays for me, so it was a huge boost of confidence. Once we had that kind of trust—and I saw that we were on the same wavelength; he was looking out for me. He was, like, "Greg, you have to pull your grades up if you want to go anywhere."

For Greg, Frank was "a father figure," and so too was Robert for Amir. This is an indication of how much these educators were not only teacher-coaches, but functioned as some of their most important family members, socializing them into their "values," helping them to pursue their athletic aspirations, and helping them to make major decisions. As Amir said (quoted in Chapter 5),

> I owe who I am as a person to Robert. He taught me values about life and all that and [the school] basketball coach was the one [who] taught me a lot about the game of basketball: how to master my skills in basketball .... Robert for real, became a father figure because, well, because my father and me don't really get along. Basically, I consulted him [Robert] with every major decision—where I wanted to go to school. He was one who really pushed me to pursue getting a scholarship to the States. He took me on tournaments to the States to give me exposure. I already wrote my SATs, so I mean he gave me the confidence that I could do it.

It is noteworthy that it was the males who referred to their coaches as "father figures." In contrast, Alicia and Lori referred to their coaches as "friends," thus, indicating that they did not think of their relationships with their coaches in such familial terms. Nevertheless, they communicated the idea that they had and continue to have very close relationships with their coaches—they talked of "loving" their coaches. Alicia, for example, also noted that her coach became a "family friend" who remained in touch with her and her parents. As she commented:

> He's been there all along. If I ever needed him, he was always there. He was one of those people who have been always very supportive, someone who, even up to this day, who calls me and pretty much congratulates me on all my success, and who I can keep in contact with ... (quoted in Chapter 4).

Keeping in contact with their former athletes seems to help sustain and possibly strengthen the relationships among coaches and athletes. This would explain the longevity in the relationships of Lori, Alicia, and Greg with their coaches. But it is likely that Alicia's coach, for example, did not call her as a mere "friend" to congratulate her on successes, but as someone who, like a "father," recalls nurturing her to become the person that she is today. So, while unlike the males, Alicia's or Lori's coaches were not "father figures," nevertheless, their coaches remained in touch like "fathers" and likely thought of the athlete's successes in terms of their own dedicated coaching.

While it is possible that constructing "father figures" reflects the absence of fathers in these male athletes' lives (Frey, 1994), it is highly likely that their guidance and the conditions that the coaches provided for the learning, bonding, and development of their masculine selves and societal expectations have also resonated with these marginalized students. Furthermore, it is commendable that in operating as friends, father figures, and supporters, coaches provided the guidance and assistance to these young people that enabled them to realize their aspirations. But what was especially evident in the guidance given was the considerable indulgence in and support for their athletic interests and aspirations, sometimes at the expense of their academic work. Most often, they were encouraged to work hard in their sport, aspire for athletic scholarships at US universities, and remain confident that their aspirations were achievable. Student athletes for whom this formula had worked were often used as examples by coaches and students alike, even during the high school "recruiting process,"[2] to support the idea of the coach's ability to produce successful athletes (Gerdy, 1997). Understandably, student athletes like Greg used such evidence to formulate their aspirations and in so doing, attended a particular school (or in the case of Amir, joined Robert's community team), where they came to depend on the coaches. It is not surprising, then, that their coaches became quite instrumental in these students' lives, since they were perceived to hold the "key" to the achievement.

The strong relationships between these student athletes and their coaches might also be due to the fact that, unlike other teachers who more often treated students equally, their coaches did distinguish between athletes and "just" students—a differentiation in which (among other factors), race, ethnicity, gender, and class reflects how the respective ethno-racial groups are socially constructed. In this regard, differentiation can have a negative effect on the student athlete. For instance, as Amir explained in the interview, neither his high school nor community coach (Robert) provided him with the support that he expected; rather, they saw him as an "academic more than an athletic—someone who would be able to win an academic scholarship." Having failed to win an athletic scholarship to a US university or college contributed to Amir's claim that his coaches showed favouritism (preferring his friend Vernon). Although he was not explicit, Amir (a South Asian) did allude to the idea that race was part of the reason why his coaches (both high school and community) did not perceive him to be an athlete (see Greenfield, 2002),[3] but a student who had an interest in sports and was doing well in it. Indeed, in a racially and/or ethnically mixed athletic team situation, there are likely to be questions about racialization or stereotyping, especially when race and/or ethnicity (though subtly used) are used to differentiate "athletes" from "students," forming the basis on which coaches make their assessment of the abilities and provide support and encouragement. It is certainly conceivable that Vernon, an African Canadian, might have been thought to be the "better" of the two players, for as Kai James (2000) revealed in a letter to his White friend Alex, he "remembers the track coach coming into my Grade Nine gym class and asking all the Black students if they would be participating in the track meet" (p. 54; see also Introduction and Chapter 2).

In Chapters 3 and 5, we observed that the athletes who participated in this project were reluctant to own that their failure to attain their athletic aspirations had something to do with their athletic performance, and they demonstrated a naiveté about the system of inequity. Most often, they pointed to their coaches as having failed them in providing playing opportunities, as well as the necessary exposure to, and contact with, college and university scouts. Evidently, this is in keeping with the prominent role that the coaches were playing in their lives for after all, their coaches were the ones who had assured them of their outstanding athletic abilities and skills, with little passing or no mention of their academic performance. Interestingly, in a schooling situation where athletic achievements should be regarded as secondary to academic achievement, it is their athletic aspirations and achievements that they tended to emphasize more. Coaches may very well have contributed to this situation. As educators, and not just as those concerned with the athletic performance of students, coaches need to not only encourage student athletes, boost their self-confidence, and support them in their aspirations and optimism, but also to assist them in thinking of the possibilities of life after high school. And in doing so, coaches need to help student athletes develop a critical understanding of how the inequities as well as racism, sexism, and classism may operate to produce hurdles and barriers that their determination, confidence and abilities may be unable to surmount. Such an education is necessary if student athletes are to effectively navigate their way through the educational system. They may just as easily rely on their academic abilities to take them to university as they rely on their athletic abilities. In what follows, I discuss how the coaches—Mick, Jerry, Jason, Alison, Bill, and Serena[4]—think about coaching and their roles in the lives of student athletes.

COACHES' PERSPECTIVES AND THEIR ROLES IN THE LIVES OF STUDENT ATHLETES

WHY COACH? "I LOVE THE COMPETITION"

Mick: I coach because I feel I have some knowledge of sport that I could pass on. And probably a more honest and also more selfish answer to that question would be that I have a competitive hunger that I need to feed. I love the competition and the nature of the chess master as coach, and depending on the sport you are coaching, you are part of the game. For example, in basketball your decision-

177

making has an immediate impact on the outcome of the game. As opposed to swimming, which I also coach, your impact is more relevant before the competition than during the swim meet. This is probably an answer that you'll never get. The first answer is the ideal, but the latter is the more honest answer.

Mick's "honest" response to the question about his interest in coaching is an indication that sports are not only for, and about the students but also for and about fulfilling his (and likely many other coaches') needs, interests, expectations, and ambitions. In addition, as in the case of Jerry, coaching provided the opportunity for him to continue playing hockey after he was injured, and in the process realized his ambition to become a coach. As he pointed out, playing hockey was:

one of the best times of my life, the best experiences. I didn't finish it, I got injured. That's basically when I stopped playing hockey and I started coaching, but, uhh, I loved it. It was kinda like what I wanted to do since I was six years old, from the day I started.

Such ambitions, the penchant for competition, and, by extension, the desire to win might explain why some coaches would recruit players (such as Jason, see note 2) whom they felt would make them winning "chess masters." However, none of the coaches who participated in this study admitted to recruiting players; in fact, they said that they disagreed with the practice, but they knew of coaches in their schools who engaged in the practice.

For instance, Mick revealed that at the school where he taught, there were coaches who would recruit football players based on the school's established reputation of producing graduates who won athletic scholarships to get "free university education in the United States." Hence, prospective student athletes were told that other schools with less reputable football programs would not provide them with "the chances of getting noticed," and any publicity they would get "are slim to none." Mick went on to indicate that he disagreed with this practice by saying "I would hope that their [the students'] entry to the school is based on ...." He smiled, and that smile became laughter among all of us in the conversation, as if to acknowledge that we all understood that it is academics that should be the focus of students' schooling. He continued:

Mick: That is the way it is supposed to work. Do students that can offer something else to the school get in as a result of their athletic prowess? Not if their academics are not at least average or standard. I mean you're not going to have somebody who can't read or write, White or Black, who is a phenomenal athlete get into the school because he is a good athlete.

Carl: Okay, let's talk generally about all athletes irrespective of race. Is it possible that at your school, there are athletes who come there just because they are just athletes … and wouldn't necessarily make …

Mick: You mean do they come through the cracks?

Carl: Yes …

Mick: Most definitely …

Carl: And do you know any of them?

Mick: Yes.

Carl: And how do they get in there? How do they manage to slip in?

Mick: I'd like to say they know the … coach …. You know we graduated one yesterday who should've never been there [at the school]. He is … [an] OFSAA medalist in track and field, transferred from a school in [Toronto to our school] in Grade Ten. He had a lot of academic difficulty, [but] managed to get his way through, probably with a 50-some odd average. And if he was not a good athlete, he probably would not have stayed at that school. So, yeah, we do have some other students like that …. It just so happens that quite often sadly, the kids who have academic difficulties [and] don't offer anything to the school get the boot, and those who, despite the fact [that they] are failing two courses, and if they are running track or playing football, they end up getting opportunities to stay because people are vouching for them, and often it is the coaches that are vouching for them.

Interestingly, while Mick hinted at disagreeing with the practices of recruiting and "vouching" for those student athletes who are perceived to be "offering something to the school," he did not criticize the practices, which, in all likelihood, are carried out with the tacit, if not explicit, support of administrators. Instead, Mick seemed to have passively accepted the fact that "this is how things are and it's not going to change." In fact, none of the coaches who participated in the study seemed ready to denounce the practices, which might imply that it is not simply what student athletes offer to the school, but also how much the needs, interests, and ambitions of the coach and athletes intersect. Mick did admit that he too would vouch for students if they offered a significant contribution to the athletic life of his school. For example, he mentioned a Grade Ten student from out of town who was attending his school to play hockey, and was having a "rough time" because of his financial and living situation. Mick indicated that if the situation arose where this student was "being kicked out of school because of academic performance," he would "easily" explain to the administration about the conditions under which the student was living, and ask that the student be given "a break." "The relationship between a coach and player," Mick went on to say, "is a lot stronger than a teacher and a student, or between administrator and a student, so it is easier for me to know more about a boy's personal life than it is for others, and that is how I can vouch for him."

Clearly, the recruiting and vouching for student athletes seem to be related to the ambitions and expectations of coaches: the students they recruit and for whom they vouch are the ones envisioned to make them and their schools proud (James, 2003c; Layden, 1995). Does it therefore follow that the ambitions of these coaches is premised on a win-at-all-cost philosophy? I put this question to the coaches who participated in this study:

Mick: There's no doubt about it, Carl, a lot of people who coach ... are not coaching for the kids. They are coaching because they are hoping to elevate their status in the coaching world, coach at a higher level, a better team ....

Jerry: [with reference to community and league hockey coaches] I know some of these coaches, we get paid out ... Coaches get paid for his development. So you find that bond, you find the superstar, you gonna make him go as far as you can 'cause money comes back to you years later. I know that happens. I know their agents will give thousands of dollars to whoever developed the kid from 12 years old.

Mick: [with reference to high school coaches] ... at high school it's if you're able to send a player to a Division One NCAA school,

> then ... the parent of a 13-year-old, or 14-year-old basketball phenomenon is going to say, "You should go to a so and so school. They have a good track record there; they have a good coach; they have NCAA potential" .... And what that does is that it builds your promo, you become more successful. Everyone loves to win—coaches, players—winning becomes important.

Interestingly, none of these male coaches admitted to having a win-at-all-costs philosophy, but they nevertheless agreed that such a philosophy did exist among their coaching colleagues. Does it mean, therefore, that as part of the fraternity, these male coaches hold that philosophy, but did not wish to admit it because intellectually they know it is hardly a progressive position? Is this philosophy particular to male coaches and/or to male athletes? Consider Alison's response to the question.

> Alison: And I always tell the girls from the beginning that, you know, skill development is important, umm, some strategy, and we work on that. If they can have fun while they're building new skills, then they build a social network and have some fun, and go away knowing more of the game, and have a better appreciation of the game and the effort that it takes. That's great, but I'm not a win-at-all-costs coach. Never have been, never will.

THE HIGH COST OF WINNING—"MY JOB IS TO TELL THEM THAT YOU'RE NOT GOING ANYWHERE"

> Mick: I teach 10 kids in my class who play triple A hockey, right? And those kids live, breathe, and their parents live, breathe hockey. And my job is to tell them that you're not going anywhere ... so that's where it becomes difficult, and division in hockey is a huge disparity.

Given the competitive ethos of sports and the "win-at-all-costs" philosophy of many coaches, it is understandable that many of their young male athletes, as well as their parents, would not merely play to know or appreciate the sport (as Alison suggested) but rather, to make it to the big leagues or win scholarships.

But as Mick suggested, there is the "difficult" reality of letting athletes know that "they're not going anywhere"—that the odds of them achieving their goals are quite slim. It is certainly commendable that Mick would be concerned with passing on this information to the students for, as Jerry related, from his community coaching experiences he was meeting young athletes, some of them Asian of immigrant backgrounds who were "ready for a nervous breakdown." It seems that some of the pressures that these athletes face had to do with their parents' desire that sports would help integrate them socially.

Jerry: Many of the kids I coach are very academically up there .... Kids last year I coached did tutorials Saturday mornings; they did different math classes .... If anything, I think these kids have a lot of pressure on them. They have lots of school, lots of homework, lots of hockey, they've got other recreational sports that they do, and they still go out with their friends to the park or wherever 15-year-olds go now. But they have full 70-hour weeks, and I can see some of them ready for a nervous breakdown at 15, but they push themselves and they do it and I've seen that and they're going nuts 'cause they're there for [a] 10 o'clock game and then they're going home at 12:30 to do some homework, and "I'm like, you're 15, what are you doing?" But they do it and they don't stop.

Carl: So why do you guys encourage them? Why don't you say "Don't come back?"

Jerry: They have this love of the game; some the talent .... I don't wanna tell them that if they are willing to come out, if they can do it, [and] if they can manage.

Carl: But at what cost?

Jerry: Well, I guess it depends on the child. For some, it's better for them [than being] out at the corner smoking drugs. They're out doing some activity with their friends and they're staying active; they're staying healthy. So either they're going to be out on the ice playing or they're going to be out with their friends doing something else, whatever it is. They're not going to be at home studying.

Carl: And what about the parents, who see them coming to a nervous breakdown. Do these parents encourage them to continue?

Jerry: One family last year actually pulled their kid out, an Asian family. Their son was one of my goalies, and she came to me and said

182

"We're going to have to take three weeks off." And you can really see it in the kid, he actually hurt himself. I don't know if it was a real injury or not, but he made himself believe that he hurt his back during the game he pulled himself out of, and he kinda went off and said, "I can't play, my back hurts." And so we spoke to the parent and she came up to me and said he just needs some time off and we had no problem with that. I completely understand. At 15 you shouldn't have to go though all that in your mind, but it does happen and he did. He went out. The team didn't have to know. As far as the team was concerned, he was injured.

Jerry's experiences with his athletes points to the extra efforts that some student athletes put into their sports in order to be successful. In addition to the obvious pressures from the additional coach (or coaches) and parents, there were the time pressures—the limited time that students had to complete their homework (after all, these are students who must also meet their academic requirements). Jerry suggested that he dealt with this situation by talking to the athletes' parents, and by suggesting to the athletes that their academic work should be their primary concern.

Jerry: We have a philosophy that your family comes first, your school comes second, and hockey comes third. So if you're not up to par, you're not going to play. How often that gets followed through is a different story 'cause a lot of these parents won't tell us. Then unless you can notice something in the dressing room, you're never going to know that these kids are failing courses, and they shouldn't be at a 10 o'clock hockey game, they should be home studying. But we don't get into any of that with the hockey coaches from [their] school.

To the question of what the classroom teacher does the next day when the student athletes attend class with their assignments incomplete, Mick (in his role of a classroom teacher) said, "When they try and tell you they couldn't get their homework done because ... they got home from school at 7 o'clock and they had to be at the rink at 8:30 for a 9:30 game, and got home at midnight ... You tell them, 'Well, too bad, you know school comes first.'" Mick admitted this expectation is "not easy" for these student athletes to hear. And to the question: what about both groups of coaches who supposedly have the best interests of the athletes at heart? Do they communicate with each other about the student athletes they coach? Both Jerry and Mick agreed that it would be good for such communication to take place, but as Jerry added, "In a perfect world, yes, but it's not going to happen" because their coaching is volunteer work. "I'm not getting paid," he said.

While the interviews with the coaches provided much insight into their philosophies and practices, it would have been useful to observe them in their interactions with their athletes. Had we conducted an ethnographic study, we would have had a chance to observe these significant interactions. As Morgan Campbell reported in his *Toronto Star* (2003) series of a Toronto high school basketball team (which was mostly black), such interactions are often filled with tensions and difficulties as coaches and team members position themselves to win games. Campbell (June 5, 2003, p. B1) observed that when team members were "complacent and resistant to change, they would 'mouth off' to the coach, criticized him at times in front of team members, and some would refuse to apologize for rude behaviours." The coach, Campbell writes, was dealing with a group of players who thought that they were "ready for the NBA, even though they still had a lot to learn." Despite such behaviour, which was in violation of rules and expectations, and sometimes even made the coach "too angry to sleep," he would still allow opportunities to play. Why was this? Was it because he was "soft"? Or is it because he could not afford for his team to lose games, which would happen if his star player or players were to sit out on disciplinary measures? Campbell offers this explanation:

> He doesn't get paid to coach basketball. He gets paid to teach. And when he's on the court he doesn't just want to coach a sport, he wants his players to learn a set of values, like teamwork, accountability, patience, perseverance, respect. Ever since he began coaching ... he has tried to instill these life skills into every player he has taught. But [he] prefers to use the power of persuasion, not a dictator's heavy fist (p. B1).

But at what cost?

RACIAL DIVERSITY AND THE SPORTS ETHOS: "I DON'T THINK WE LOOK AT ANY ONE GROUP DIFFERENTLY"

Susy: Do you think that racial factors affect the young women and their participation in sports in school?

184

Alison:[5]   Racial factors may come into play perhaps in terms of academic
            eligibility and perception that certain cultural groups do not
            perform academically .... But I think that's the perception thing,
            that certain races aren't academically high ....

Susy: So you think that's coming from people within the school?

Alison: I don't think it's perpetuated by the staff and the [school] policy
            per se, but I think there is a perception among the students that,
            you know, maybe all Black kids play basketball, and everybody
            else plays everything else. And you have a token White on a team,
            and so on and so forth .... But unfortunately for them, I don't
            think that's how—for sure I know that's not how I look at it and
            I don't think that the rest of the staff look at it that way. I don't
            see a kid of colour and say: "Oh, that kid's going to succeed," or
            "that kid's not." I just see a kid and a face and nothing else, and
            that kid performs, and that's what you expect. So I don't see that,
            but unfortunately for them, I think they perpetuate that whole
            self-fulfilling prophecy that, well, "I can't do it because I'm of this
            race, and I'm not going to succeed, and therefore I don't succeed
            because I do everything not to succeed." But I think that in terms
            of staff and administration, I don't think we look at any one group
            differently than another group. The policy is there for everyone
            .... And, uh, some kids, they cut themselves before they even give
            themselves a chance, but that's human nature.

From Alison's perspective, it was students' "faces" she saw and nothing else—
she did not see colour. But ironically she readily identified the colour of the
students who "perpetuate that whole self-fulfilling prophecy." By implication,
they were Black students, who, along with others, believed that basketball was
their game, and Whites had a "token" presence on the teams. So why the claim
that she did not see colour? It is possible that the message Alison is trying
to communicate is that she did not base her perceptions of, and interactions
with, students on race or colour as the students wished, hence she would not
appear to be racist? Nevertheless, she did concede that racial factors *may* play
a role in minority students' academic performance. But for the most part, she
claimed, suggesting that it is "unfortunate" that it is the students of colour
themselves (Black students in particular) who operate on the basis of colour,
want teachers and administrators to "see" and deal with them on that basis,

and, as a consequence, limit themselves academically. Why would students "perpetuate" or choose to negotiate school on the basis of race if doing so was meaningless in that setting? And how is it that Alison and her colleagues were oblivious to race? Educational scholars have documented the need of teachers like Alison to say that they are *blind* to colour, thus pretending that they are neutral and unbiased so that they are not accused of being prejudiced, racist, or discriminatory (Roman & Stanley, 1997; Sleeter, 1993; Solomon, Levine-Rasky, & Singer, 2003). The same can be said for coaches. Specifically, operating on the basis of the ethos of seeing the skills, abilities, and potential of athletes rather than race, class,[6] and/or ethnicity, then it is understandable that Alison would see disembodied, undifferentiated student athletes (see Paraschak, 2000; Fernández-Balboa, 2000).

This failure to recognize and understand how race operates in the lives of student athletes has implications not only for the coaching and educational processes, but also for the students' development in positive athletic environments. Given that race does matter in our society, and that bad experiences with racism can cause despair and anger, coaches must learn to understand the dynamics of racism. One example of racism is "racial slurs," which Jerry, a community "rep" hockey coach, said he had not "come across" among the members of his racially mixed hockey team. But he went on to say:

> Jerry: When I used to play ..., you get the odd racial slur thrown at you just 'cause they know who you are. But within our team, I don't see a problem at all. The second we step out of [our community], or somebody comes in to play us, you can hear it ... it's a six-game suspension now; it's kinda a stiff penalty if the referee hears it. But how often it gets heard, who knows? It's not called very often, but I know it happens, and if anything, I think it's more to aggravate that player, just to get under their skin.

That penalties for "racial slurs" are rarely given reflects the limited attention given by coaches for their minority players. In saying that "you get the *odd* racial slur thrown at you," and that this is not a "problem" because it is a matter of aggravating a "player just to get under their skin," Jerry indicated that for him this was not a serious problem. And even though he admitted to hearing racial slurs directed at players, particularly when his racially mixed team would play teams from communities that were homogeneously White, he still wondered about how often they got heard, specifically by referees. If racist comments are seen as little more than an intent to "aggravate" an opponent, it is understandable that Jerry (and other coaches and referees alike) would not expect players to be penalized. This is particularly true in a context where the ethos of competition and winning are dominant, and it is star players who might be given what Jerry considered a "stiff penalty." Furthermore, pretending not to hear racial slurs is consistent with coaches' conceptualization of athletes as an undifferentiated group where race, ethnicity, and sex do not affect their abilities. The idea then is not to acknowledge differences among players, which contributes to the myth of "sameness" among the players—that they are all players and "buddies." For their part, the minority players to whom these slurs are directed often do not complain (see Chapter 2) for fear of seeming unsportsman-like. In such a context, then, it is left to coaches to be sensitive to the impact of racism on an athlete's experience of the sport. Accordingly, coaches must act to help their marginalized players.

Unlike Alison and Jerry, Jason acknowledged that race played a role in the construction of athletes and their competence in particular sports.

Jason: Now that I have finished my studies and returned to my home community to teach and coach at the high school level, I see a clear connection between race, sport, and schooling. In my particular community, I do not have the opportunity to coach a racially diverse team. However, I still see how race plays a role and affects the perception of student athletes. My soccer team recently played a game and on the sidelines was an Asian student with a tensor bandage on his ankle and he did not play due to this injury. The players on my team immediately asked, "Does he play? He's good, eh?" "Why?" I asked. "Because of his skin colour?" And, yes, he is a very good soccer player. Without even putting on his cleats, my players concluded that this student would be an outstanding soccer player. Students have their own ideas pertaining to racial groups and athletic achievement. If a student is Portuguese, he must be a good soccer player. If a student is Black, he must be a good basketball player.

What is significant in Jason's comment is his naming of skin colour as the factor that his athletes were using to determine the athletic skills of the Asian player. Such assumptions are common. However, Jason did not say whether he challenged the player for his racialization. Should he have done so? Of course, but the fact that he was willing to show that he was aware of this practice suggests that (at least compared to the other coaches) he understands the role of colour in the perceptions and interactions of athletes, and probably would be willing to address the resulting issues.

CULTURE, GENDER, AND SPORTS ETHOS: "THEY'RE NOT PART OF THE SCHOOL LIFE ... THAT'S CULTURAL"

> Alison: I think there's a lot of girls that are protected by their family and go home right after school. And they don't have the opportunity to network with friends and get involved, nor do they have the chance to come and see an event in progress and say, "Well, maybe I'd like to try that." So they're taken right out of the school after school, and they're not part of the school life that way. I think that's discouraging. And part of that's cultural—maybe the families don't understand that school is more than just coming for your classes and going home. Short of giving [a] special invitation to these kids and their parents, it just goes on announcements on a daily basis.

In addition to race, coaches must also consider the role of gender in the cultural and athletic lives of students. I discussed in Chapter 4 how males tend to have an advantage over females as they receive more support and encouragement, as well as opportunities to participate. Nevertheless, it is not uncommon to find coaches like Alison who, as in the above comment, claim (with reference to Asian and South Asian female students) that their low participation rate in athletic activities is because of their "culture."[7] The same sentiment was expressed by Mick, who in referencing his wife's (a physical education teacher) experiences, noted that:

> in Canada, ... women and young girls who are of South Asian background, and from my wife's experience, umm, in the inner city of Toronto, their parents have absolutely no regard for the value, you know, in sport, for their young girls, umm .... and that is predominantly cultural. It's not economic, you know. You have responsibility at home at a young age and so that comes first ....

188

For Alison and Mick, then, the culture by which these students and their families operate—that is, the values, habits, practices, religious beliefs, expectations, and family responsibilities—is what the parents bring to Canada from their homeland. They believe that these females' parents are so entrenched in their "home" or "foreign" culture that there is little coaches can do to encourage them to participate in the athletic activities at school, "Short of giving [a] special invitation to these kids, and their parents," as Alison said in jest.[8]

This reasoning behind the under-representation of particular ethno-racial groups' participation in athletic activities is consistent with the multicultural principles and the athletic ethos that inform many coaches' thinking. Specifically, they reason that the school space is culturally neutral, and athletic activities accommodate all students interested in participating, regardless of their gender, ethnicity, and race. That is why Alison says that at her school, things are the same for male and females: both groups are given the "same" amount of money for their activities and can have "equal" numbers of games. She recalled that years ago the boys had more games and tournaments than the girls, but today, "there's a lot more equality." And if you took advantage of it [the opportunities provided], said Alison, "fine; if you didn't, so be it. But the opportunity was there and I think that's what really counts." This claim that the same treatment means equal opportunities for all student athletes ignores the role of gender, ethnicity, race, immigrant/citizenship, generation (first and/or second) to students' needs and aspirations. These differences must be taken into account for as Evans and Davies (1993) write:

> If, however, we take *equality* not only as "the condition of being equal in quantity, amount, value or intensity," but also as "the condition of being equal in dignity, privileges, power" (Bryne, 1985, p. 99), we are compelled to ask whether the planned provisions for different sorts of children in schools are equal at the level of what is invested in the process of its delivery and in their justly differentiated learning outcomes (p. 24).

In such a context, the low participation rate of Asians and South Asians cannot be taken simply as reflections of individual efforts and interests, or attributed to family influences and expectations; we must also address structural factors (see also Fleming, 2000; Raval, 1989; Tirone & Pedlar, 2000).

Addressing the barriers to participation in sports are well within the capacities of coaches, educators, and administrators, and for coaches this implies a re-conceptualization of what it means to play a sport, as well as maintaining a consciousness of, and sensitivity to, the gendered, raced, classed, and ethnic experiences and expectations of their students. So, for instance, Bill would need to revise his expectation that the Black Caribbean-Canadian females whom he coached be competitive and "give their all" to their basketball games.

Bill: Personally, I wanted them to win every night, and everybody wants to win, but I was just trying to tell the girls, "You know what? You gotta play every game like it's your last game." So I was trying to make them ... at anything they do, they gotta give their all because there might not be another chance, or there might not be another game, or there might not be another test, or you know? Whatever it was, just give their all so you can't say: "What if?" At the end of the day, you can't say: "What if I did this, what if I did this extra, or did this more? Would we have won, would I have passed the test?" or whatever .... That and just having fun, appropriating your teammates, you know, depending on people and trusting your teammates.

From Bill's perspective, he was treating the "girls" like players, the same as he treated males, and was "equally" demanding of them as he was of males (see also Simmons, 1999). This competitive approach, or male paradigm within which Bill was operating, prevented him from taking into account the fact that females have different expectations of their participation in athletics. According to Simmons (1999), "girls could be motivated to excel if properly coached" (p. 76).[9]

In addition to gender, other factors such as ethnic and class cultures also inform how coaches like Bill and Alison work with their athletes. In this regard, Alison, who coached the same athletes, would have to revisit her position about female athletes and commitment. She expected commitment from her players, and to this end, she said, "I've resorted now, at this point in my life, to tell kids up front, 'This is an extra for me as it is an extra for you.' My expectation is that I'm here, [and] so are you." While commitment, punctuality, and consistency are important, Alison should also note that cultural differences and responsibilities of students, as Jason pointed out, could make it difficult for some students to make the commitment that Alison expected.

Alison: In a traditionally White, middle-class community, I know that for the most part, students commit themselves to sports because they have the time and they want to. These students won't miss practices or games because they have to work 40 hours a week to help their parents and family survive. They can play soccer and hockey because they (or their parents) have the resources to allow them to.

COACH-ATHLETE RELATIONSHIPS: "YOU ALSO BECOME LOOKED AT IN THE KIDS' EYES AS THEIR ROLE MODEL"

Serena: Yeah, in coaching ... you spend a lot of time with the kids and you also become looked at in the kids' eyes as their role model .... You know, someone is teaching you something, or showing you something, so the kids ... see that the coach cares and so they often go to them 'cause sometimes ... some of the kids don't see their parents at all because they work night shifts and stuff like that so the coach becomes everything to them.

The idea of coaches acting as role models is now accepted as a by-product, as Serena stated, of the caring, interest, and concern that coaches show to players. And given the amount of time that coaches and young players interact with each other, sometimes even more than they do with their parents (at times acting almost like "stand-in" parents), it is understandable that they would develop a strong relationship. In fact, as Zirkel (2002) found, while role models generally provided students with a sense of their place within the society, "race- and gender-matched role models provided students with an increased sense of their own potential, value, and opportunities; and ... the role models themselves *cause* students to think more about their futures and to work harder to achieve their goals" (p. 373). It was also found that the relationships between role models and students were "stronger for students of colour than for White students; and they did not depend on the educational achievements of the role models themselves" (Zirkel, 2002, p. 374). In terms of coaches as role models, if, as Zirkel's research shows, race- and gender-matched role model relationships are more productive, given the understandings that a coach might have of the experiences and expectations of the young athlete, then White coaches may lack some elements that minority coaches could draw upon to support athletes[10] (see also James, 2005).

But this is not to suggest that White coaches cannot be good role models, and neither should we conclude that racial minority coaches are the most appropriate for minority student athletes. For whatever the background of coaches, their relationship with athletes will be productive if they are conversant with, and sensitive to, the cultural and social situation of the athletes, and to the educational structures that may operate as barriers and enablers (see Allen, 1994; James, 2000, Solomon, 1997). Furthermore, as Coakley (2002) writes, referring to Martia Golden's assertions about African-American youth in *Saving Our Sons* (1995):

> the rhetoric about role models often distracts attention away from the fact that young people need advocates, as well as models in their lives. Too often the call for role models is used by privileged White adults to justify why they should not be held responsible for providing moral and economic guidance for young people of colour (p. 27).

Coaches should learn to be concerned with the *whole* student—about the student's educational, social, economic, and cultural welfare—just as they are about the athlete's identities, skills, and abilities. Also, as advocates and role models, coaches must be conscious of the power differential in their relationship, and consciously operate in the best interest of athletes, encouraging their autonomy in decision-making in regard to their participation in athletics (Drewe, 2003).

Understandably, being a role model or an advocate is not unproblematic. As Jerry pointed out, negotiating the close relationships with young athletes is not always easy. As an example, he expressed concern with the compromising situations in which he had often found himself with information from his "minor" players.

Jerry: My biggest fear is that they tell me something that I don't want to hear, and they're still minors and then I have to turn around and report it or else it's on me as well. But I do listen, and they do have a closer bond. I have talked to some of them that they ask questions more, I guess, because I'm closer to their age, and they'll ask me questions about life in general, about the girls in their high school, ... about cigarettes and alcohol .... I get questions.

Close coach–athlete relationships sometimes can become difficult and problematic for coaches, and how they manage these relationships is critical to their effectiveness as coaches and teachers, as well as to the outcomes of the student athletes themselves. The story of the Toronto high school basketball team as reported by Morgan Campbell in the *Toronto Star* (February 9, 2003) is useful here to illustrate the difficulties and tensions inherent in some of the coach–athlete relationships. The head coach of the team described by Campbell appears very committed to his players. He is described as someone who helped the athletes through "problems that have nothing to do with basketball" and in his effort to assist one player who had been missing school, the coach worked with the school's vice-principal "to help sort things out," even volunteering to "deliver class assignments to the athlete's home, if he had to." The head and assistant coach were particularly close to the "star" player. At one time, that player was hospitalized because of a "life-threatening head injury" he sustained in an accident that left him in a coma for nine days. In his effort to provide support, the assistant coach visited the hospital daily, and while the player lay comatose, he "sprinkled holy water on his forehead and prayed that he would come out of the coma. The next day he awoke." Campbell writes that the head coach also visited, and would "help the player walk the halls at [the] hospital. He provided the shoulder that [the player] leaned on when he wasn't sure his legs would support him. He'd show up every night after school and the two men would just walk" (p. E4). But despite these close relationships, the coaches put significant efforts into building a respectable basketball team, and their support for the players' athletic aspirations, as well as their relationship with the players, was also one that was frustrating, tiring, and antagonistic enough to result in the "occasional sleepless night." In such a situation, one wonders if such coach–athlete relationships are indeed healthy, and how much the coach should "put up with" in order to help players. Should the behaviours of players, like the star player on this team, with "sporadic temper tantrums, outbursts, tirade, and cursing" be tolerated? What is accomplished, and what do players learn? Does tolerating such behaviours reflect the expectations that coaches have of minority working-class athletes who they think would not otherwise be in school? Or does this reflect a belief that athletics is the primary or only viable path to social and economic successes?

CONCLUSION: "SPORTS ARE SUCH AN EFFECTIVE TOOL FOR TEACHERS AND STUDENTS ALIKE"

Clearly, the relationships between coaches and student athletes are complex, varied, and interconnected, and are sustained by both the athletic culture—the philosophies, norms, values, etc.—of the school, as well as by the personal philosophies that coaches bring to the coaching process. It is important, therefore, for coaches to reflect critically on their relationships with athletes and their coaching pedagogies. For as Jones (2000) writes:

> through emphasizing constant self appraisal, flexibility, rigorousness and social awareness, such an approach is able to take account of the complex social pedagogical decisions that coaches face daily, while also getting coaches to ask critical questions about coaching. Such an approach is grounded in the assumption that coaching is an entirely personal process, with the effective application of broad pedagogical principles requiring considerable insights, even artistry (p. 39).

Having engaged in such critical appraisal herself, coach Susy Dabovic (2002, p. 32) writes:

> During my two years as a teacher and coach, due to my lack of awareness about equity issues, I had not given much consideration to whether I was providing an equitable program for the female athletes, or whether the young women in the school had the encouragement and opportunity to reach their full potential. I merely assumed that those women who were interested in playing sport did so, [and] those who did not either lacked the talent or the motivation. With my return to a position as an athlete and a student at York University, I become increasingly aware of my own marginalization in sport and in the larger society.

Obviously, students can and do benefit from their coaches, who can help them maximize their involvement in sports and in school. Jason's students are an example here.

Jason: As teacher/coach at the high school level, I see much of the same. The first really interesting experience I had as a coach came when I was a student teacher at an inner-city school in Toronto. I volunteered to help out with soccer. At first, the students just saw me as a figurehead, someone that was just there so they could play. Within days, however, many of the players found out that I had played competitive soccer at a very high level. They became intrigued, asking everything from the position I played, to how many times I could juggle the ball, to an overseas tournament I played in against an international team. I recognized immediately how this helped me build a positive relationship with these students not just on the pitch, but also in the classroom. Why were they so shocked that I had a successful background in soccer? It was clear that it was because I was a White [Anglo] man in a predominantly Portuguese school playing a traditionally "non-White" sport. This mattered little to me; I used this relationship successfully in the classroom to motivate the students. "We can talk about sports in the last five minutes if everyone gets their work done," I would say. It honestly worked, and the students responded positively to the fact that I was showing interest in their activities.

Ultimately, coaches should endeavour to maximize students' involvement in school, actively engaging them in the learning processes and encouraging them to develop a sense of responsibility for their educational outcomes. In this regard, the coach becomes a facilitator of the educational and athletic ambitions of the students, guiding and prompting them into appropriate academic and athletic paths. The academic environment should be structured such that students feel welcome to participate comfortably. In constructing such environments coaches must not only be personally aware of their own cultural values and expectations, but also be aware of, and sensitive to, those of the students. When this happens, then sports will have been, as Jason vows, an "effective tool":

I know that sport can keep students, regardless of colour or culture, interested in school and can motivate them to do well. I have just recently sat one of my starters out for disciplinary reasons. I know he will keep his nose clean because he wants to play, not sit out. Sport is such an effective tool for teachers and students alike. We just don't realize it yet.

NOTES

1. Clearly, the role of the high school coach is more complex than that of teachers and community or league coaches: they are both coaches and teachers, with a responsibility for the educational and academic welfare of all students. Furthermore, coaches spend more time with student athletes than teachers do with students (Drewe, 2003).

2. It is important to bear in mind that recruitment is based not on academic achievement but on perceived athletic ability and potential. Here is how Jason, a teacher-coach who participated in this study, said the recruitment process went for him. "My first real connection between sport and school was made when I was in Grade Eight and was attending a basketball camp sponsored by a public high school in my city. One of the coaches from the high school pulled me aside and asked me if I was going to attend his school. I told him "no," that I would be going to the local Catholic high school. He then called over a few of his assistants and proceeded to give a 10-minute presentation on the advantages of playing for him at his school. I quickly learned, even though I was only 13, that athletics might have its advantages in a high school setting."

3. In their study of male basketball players, Greenfield et al. (2002) found that African-American team members received preferential treatment from the coach, which made them feel that "they were superior players." This was also a reflection of how they were "socially constructed as being of a higher status than the rest of the team members" (p. 148).

4. **Mick**—White, about 30 years old, has been teaching at a private high school in Toronto for about five years, where he is head coach of basketball and also coaches swimming. A former baseball player, he has been coaching for about 6 years.
    Jerry—White, about 25 years old and a former hockey player, he is "a rep [representative] coach for community hockey" in a suburban area north of Toronto.
    Jason—White, about 27 years old, has been teaching for three years in a town east of Toronto. A former soccer player, he has been coaching soccer for about eight years, and now coaches basketball.
    Alison—White, about 50 years old and head of physical education, has been teaching for 26 years, and coached girls' basketball.
    Bill—Black, about 17 years old, played basketball and was assistant basketball coach for less than a year at the high school he attended in the west end of Toronto.
    Serena—South Asian, about 25 years old, was pursing her teaching degree. A rugby, soccer, and basketball player, she was a volunteer coach with middle and high school students in basketball and soccer.

5. Alison, the head basketball coach, worked with teams that were largely made up of Black females of Caribbean background.

6. Similar to her position that race did not have an effect on students' educational lives, Alison said the following of social class. "People talk about socio-economic—I think it's priorities. I don't think it has anything to do with socio-economic. You see some of those kids who you'd say might be poor or, you know, have less money to go around, but they have nice clothes, they have the cell phones, they're in nice cars. I don't buy that because if there's a will there's a way."

7. See Carroll & Hollinshead, 1993; Fleming, 2000; Nakamura, 2003; Raval, 1989; Talbani & Hasanali, 2000; Tirone & Pedlar, 2000.

8. Reference is often made to Muslim girls and their dress code as operating as a barrier to their participation in sports activities. For example, in her study of Muslim girls who attended school in southwestern Ontario, Nakamura (2003, p. 33) found that coaches and teachers were insensitive to their concerns and unaccommodating of their needs in terms of physical education uniforms and team activities. While some coaches would allow students to wear (for example) track pants, others would claim that "the uniform was mandatory or that everyone else would be wearing the appropriate clothing" (see also Carroll & Hollinshead, 1993, pp. 154–169).

9. Simmons (1999) also found that while male coaches felt that sex was an insignificant issue, "female coaches felt the girls benefited more from women's coaching than they did from men's coaching" (p. 76).

10. With reference to African-American student athletes, Lapchick (1995) notes that the coach is their "main contact, and the court frequently becomes the home where [they are] most comfortable" (p. 91). But Lapchick sees a disconnection in what the many White coaches can offer Black athletes. These White coaches hold "White values" of a White society, but these are not necessarily what will help Black athletes attain their aspirations.

7

PARENTAL CONCERNS, ATHLETIC PARTICIPATION, AND ACADEMIC ATTAINMENT

Dane is a Grade Six student who identified his favourite subjects in school as "gym and language" (in that order) and his favourite sports—the ones he played—as "football, baseball, and hockey." He also likes "sprint [track], long jump, and relays," and was known as a fast runner—"the fastest in the school and the region, one who comes in first in cross country against over 300 competitors," as his mother, Brenda, explained. However, this success was not reflected in Dane's end-of-year report. In fact, according to Brenda, his classroom teacher reported that "Dane is slipping in his academic work."

While Brenda was pleased with Dane's athletic accomplishments, and willingly supported his sport activities by attending sports meets and buying him sports fashionwear (he was wearing the latest pair of Nike running shoes when we met), she was concerned that Dane was putting "too much time and energy into athletics rather than his academic work." She threatened to stop him from participating in sports if his academic performance continued to be poor. When I asked for his response to his mother's concern, Dane replied that he knew "that academic work is important because you have to have an education to get a job." But even with this understanding, Dane asserted that he liked "sports better since it is more fun."

Brenda, an immigrant from the Caribbean, was well aware of the positive effects that sports had on Dane's schooling, but she was nevertheless concerned that her son, like many other Black male students (James, 1995; Solomon, 1992), was being stereotyped by coaches and teachers to be good athletes. As a result, she felt he was being encouraged to participate in sports more than academic activities. But while Brenda agreed that it is possible for students to successfully participate in sports and do well academically, she was still concerned that her son's athletic success was attained at the expense of his academic work, and that he would not realize his full academic potential and eventually make it to university.[1]

Is Brenda's concern with the potential negative effects that Dane's participation in sports could have on his academic performance and achievements justified? Is withdrawing Dane from sports an appropriate alternative for addressing the concern/problem?

This chapter examines the concerns of parents such as Brenda (particularly marginalized parents) who hold high educational and career aspirations for their children and, in so doing, discourage and/or prevent them from participating in athletic activities because they are concerned with a resulting academic underachievement. In examining this issue, I argue that while such concern is justifiable, disallowing them from participating in sports may not be the best solution. The reason for this is that involvement in athletics can help marginalized youth to build self-confidence and negotiate the structural constraints of inequity, stereotyping, racism, and discrimination within the school system.[2] Moreover, athletic activities—experienced through physical education and extracurricular activities—can be viewed as integral to the schooling process and complementary to the academic program, similar to music, computer, and chess clubs.

My argument is guided by the argument (see Introduction) that social inequality is based on (among other factors) class, race, ethnicity, gender, and citizenship/immigrant status. These factors are interconnected with related ideologies of classism, racism, and ethnocentrism, which structure the schooling situations and educational opportunities and outcomes of students. Within this context, educators and peers socially construct students as being more or less likely to succeed at athletics and/or academics. The resulting images that educators cultivate of student athletes have the effects of enabling or limiting their participation in schools, as well as their academic and athletic interests, performances, and aspirations. So, for example, if African students show interest and display great skills in athletic activities (see James, 2003b), and Asian students rarely get involved in athletic activities, but prefer academic pursuits (see Nakamura, 2003), educators—teachers and coaches—might believe this reflects the "ethnic cultures" of students (see Introduction). Such reading—that is, stereotyping or *profiling*—has the effect of regulating or managing the activities of these students and restricting them to educational activities that educators deem appropriate to, or consistent with, their "cultural selves." As a consequence, unable to participate in the full range of school programs and activities, these students also lose out on educational and career opportunities.

In this schooling context, then, parents need to be cognizant of the role athletic activities can play their children's lives, and need to critically interrogate the "good intentions" of educators who assess and rationalize students' athletic and academic abilities. It falls to parents to challenge the racist and ethnocentric practices and procedures that contribute to students' educational activities, performances, and achievements. They must advocate for equitable educational opportunities that will facilitate the participation of students in the full range of school programs and activities, particularly ones that enable them to better relate to the schooling process and to effectively negotiate the school system. Furthermore, since physical education and extracurricular athletic activities form a significant part of a school's overall curricular activities, then equitable education for racialized students would not be realized if parents discourage or disallow sport participation. The responsibility of parents, therefore, is to support their children's schooling interests and their engagement in activities that serve to *empower* them as they take advantage of all educational opportunities.

I refer to African, South-Asian, and Asian students' accounts of their athletic interests (and their parents' concerns, support, or non-support of their involvement in athletic activities) in my discussion of parental concerns. I then demonstrate how, concerns aside, athletics and academics can be complementary rather than contradictory. In the third section, I argue that the role of parents is to ensure equal educational opportunities for their children, and I conclude by suggesting that concerned parents need to enable, rather than frustrate or compromise, their own or their children's educational and occupational aspirations.

THE CONCERN: ENSURING THE ACADEMIC SUCCESS OF RACIALIZED STUDENTS

A close examination of parents concerned with their children's participation in athletic activities will reveal that they tend to be racial minorities and immigrants with a desire to create conditions that will produce "better" or "good" lives for their children, and ensure their upward social mobility in Canadian society (James 2002; Li 2001). Parents are also concerned with potential injuries, which not only could limit them athletically and academically, but could also limit their life chances. But as the following discussion reveals, while the various groups of parents share similar aspirations for their children, their concerns do vary according to their ethno-racial backgrounds, as well as by their economic, social, and cultural circumstances.

Canadian studies of Black students indicate that low teacher expectations, the tendency to stream Black students into basic and vocational educational programs, and teachers encouraging them to participate in athletic activities remain a concern for many Black parents. And while parents recognize that their children's involvement in sports is, for some, a means of coping with the alienating school system that has contributed to their disengagement and dropping out of school in significant numbers (BLAC, 1994; Brathwaite & James, 1996; Dei et al., 1996; James, 1990; Meta, 1989; Solomon, 1992), some, like Brenda, remain unconvinced that involvement in sports will reverse the trend and enable their children to attain their educational and career goals.[3] Parents continue to be doubtful, even though Black student athletes have demonstrated that through sports they have been able to develop friendships, gain recognition, educate their White peers, challenge stereotypes, and assume leadership responsibilities in schools. This parental doubtfulness, perhaps scepticism, seems to be well placed given the practices of teachers and coaches of overlooking poor class attendance, lack of discipline, and mediocre performance in academic subjects, assigning passing or generous grades to student athletes so that they can maintain their place on the school's sports teams (Campbell, 2003; James, 1996). And there are those student athletes like Greg (Chapter 5) and others (Chapter 3) who go from school to school, and remain in high school well beyond their five years primarily to play sports (see Solomon, 1992). The concern here is that without a sound academic background, parental aspirations may not be realized.

Lovell (1991) points out, with reference to African-Caribbean youth in Britain, that sports are often "a double edged sword": Black youth use sports to escape the consequence of racism, but sports also limit their academic performance, educational and career attainment, and social mobility, even within the sporting power structure (p. 69). Carrington (1983) also makes the point that for Black students in Britain, sports are sometimes used as a "convenient side-track" and "control mechanism" by teachers who have a tendency to view Black students stereotypically "as having skills of the body rather than skills of the mind" (p. 61). According to Parry and Parry (1991), teachers use this "coping strategy" to deal with Black youth "who have side-tracked the academic mainstream, which serves to reinforce both academic failure and unacceptable behaviours" (p. 169). In the Canadian context, and Toronto in particular, Black students, especially males, get recruited by high school coaches, gain entry into schools, and receive a significant number of awards because of their athletic contributions. But while on the one hand parents welcome these opportunities for their children, on the other, some are ambivalent and cautious because, as Harris (1994, p. 49) wrote with reference to Black high school basketball players in Washington, DC, coaches and teachers unwittingly contribute to the streaming

> of black males into an area that has few openings. In so doing, what they [educators] see as service to black males—pushing them into sport—is, in reality, a disservice to them because it fosters improbable expectations for athletics careers.

Harris (1991, p. 147) also contends that there is very little evidence to suggest that Blacks, more than Whites, "are 'hooked' on sport to the exclusion of academics," and while it is apparent that Blacks "suffer more scholastically from their participation in sport, the reasons for this are not due to emphasis on sport to the exclusion of scholastics."

Studies of South Asian and Asian students reveal that their parents view sport as a leisure activity, not very relevant to their children's educational life, and in this regard they emphasize academic subjects as a priority, and discourage their children from participation in physical education classes and/or extracurricular athletic activities (Chen & Hu, 1997; Nakumara, 2003; Li, 2001; Tirone & Pedlar, 2000). Fleming (1994) also mentions that Asian and South Asian parents tend to internalize the stereotype of sports inability, and in turn pass the stereotype on to their children who, as a result, become academically focussed. This may "take away" from their interest and attempts at trying non-academic activities such as sports. But while parents of both groups of students tend to value "subjects such as math and science" over physical education (Nakumara, 2003, p. 80), for some South Asian parents, specifically Muslims, religious beliefs and related dress code are also a basis for discouraging their children from sports participation (see also Carroll & Hollinshead, 1993). In their study of South Asian youth, Tirone and Pedlar (2000) found that parents expected their children to adhere to their cultural traditions, values, and beliefs. As immigrants, they perceived that their children's participation in "leisure activities" outside of their communities could lead to them adapting values and practices of the larger society, which are contrary to those of their ethnic cultural group. They also noted that "acceptance into the leisure activities of the greater society was more likely achieved by those participants who could look and behave like those in the dominant, white cultural groups" (Tirone & Pedlar 2000, p. 163). For these parents, the fact that their children wished to conform or assimilate into the dominant cultural group in order to "fit" into the society was a source of concern—a concern that their children would abandon or distance themselves from their ethnic cultural values, beliefs, and identification, and come to think of their culture as "inferior" or "old fashioned." An example of this thinking might be Jasminder in the movie *Bend It Like Beckham* (see Chapter 5). Recall how Jasminder struggled with wanting to play soccer and her parents did not give her permission to do so; they wanted her instead to be like her sister, and live up to the social and cultural values expected of young South Asian women.

In their study of the experiences of Asian boys in sports activities, McGuire and Collins (1998) found that parents' concern for their children's academic work *increased* as their children moved from primary to secondary school. They noted that in the primary school years, Asian parents "appeared keen to let their children play freely." But by high school, the parents' support for their children's participation in sports decreased or disappeared, while their emphasis on academic achievement increased. Based on his study of the expectations of Chinese immigrant parents (from China[4]) for their children's education, Li (2001) asserts that their high regard for formal education and their expectations of academic excellence for their children have to do with their cultural heritage deriving from Confucianism. Accordingly, parents sought to provide the academic grounding for their children that would secure educational, social, and economic success (and resulting family honour). But as Li goes on to point out, Chinese parents' emphasis on science and math education for their children is an adaptive response to the racist society in which they reside as immigrants. They believed that because of racism, their children are at a disadvantage in competing for jobs in areas such as arts, politics, and law, hence they "encourage their children to excel in science subjects so that they could take up professions in engineering and other fields where there is a high demand" (p. 486), and where their children will be able to "do better than the white majority" (p. 487). According to one respondent, "due to our cultural background and language barriers, we are placed in a disadvantaged situation. We can only show our strength in high-tech fields" (p. 487).[5]

Essentially, parents are concerned with ensuring their children's academic success, so that they will eventually attain the expected educational and career goals. While it is true that involvement in sports can potentially circumscribe the academic success of racial minority students, the issue is not sports involvement *per se*, but the educational system's racism, ethnocentrism, stereotyping, and discrimination.[6] Therefore, parents must object to the inequities in the schooling system, and not their children's interest or participation in sports. The concern should not be "fear" of their children losing their "culture," but how "their culture"—whatever it evolves into in Canadian society—gets recognized and incorporated into their sports activities. In this regard, parents should be advocating for a schooling system that capitalizes on the strengths, interests, skills, and competences of *all* students in ways that take into account their cultural and social situation and parental expectations. For after all, if students stand to benefit psychologically, physically, socially, culturally, and possibly economically from participating in athletic activities, as I discuss in the following section, then doing so cannot be considered a liability to academic success, but rather a valuable complement.

GETTING BEYOND THE CONCERNS: ATHLETICS CAN BE COMPLEMENTARY TO ACADEMICS

Apart from contributing to the good health and physical fitness of students, and as demonstrated with many of the participants in this study (see Chapters 2 to 5), participation in athletic activities also helps students build peer support, enhance their cultural and gender identities, and refrain from dropping out of school.[7] Furthermore, as Harris (1991, p. 124) asserts, athletic activities transmit to students "the importance of hard work, character development and team work"—values that are necessary complements for academic success. Therefore, contrary to the claim that participation in athletic activities is detrimental to student athletes' attainment of their academic goals, evidence indicates that such participation enhances academic performance and inspires high educational aspirations (Fejgin, 1995; James, 1996; Nakamura, 2003; Sabo, Melnick, & Vanfossen, 1993). With reference to male students in Britain of Caribbean background, Cashmore (1982) writes of a "spillover effect" of participation in sports on academic life. He suggests that student athletes' understanding of their capacities in one area will inspire "greater objectives" in others because "once exposed to the possibilities of achieving, the youth seeks to habitualize success" (Cashmore, 1982, p. 202). While it is true that females are less likely than males to participate in athletic activities, and consequently less likely to obtain the same degree of benefit from athletics, research has shown that when females do participate in athletics, they sometimes surpass their male counterparts (Yetman & Berghorn, 1993).[8]

In a longitudinal study of tenth-graders in the United States, Fejgin (1995) found that the educational aspirations of students who participated in athletics were similar to those who participated in academic clubs (p. 219). Her study also indicated that "students who were more involved in high school competitive sports had higher grades, a higher self-concept, higher educational aspirations, a more internal locus of control, and fewer discipline problems" (p. 223). Similarly, based on his study of the effects of participation in sports during the last two years of high school, Marsh (1993) found, after controlling for race, socio-economic status, sex, and ability level, that participation in sports had positive effects on the academic self-concept, educational aspiration, and attainment of students. "Participation in sport," writes Marsh (1993, p. 36), "leads to an increased commitment to, involvement with, or identification with school and school values ... [and] apparently adds to—not detracts from—time, energy, and commitment to academic pursuits." Fejgin (1995) further reasons that:

> Participation in sports teams requires adjustment to rigid rules, regulations, and practice times, as well as to the coach's authority .... Ongoing training of individuals to comply with these rules and to endure long hours of practice, while delaying the fulfilment of other physical and social needs, teaches the importance of and the rewards associated with such compliance, possibly making it easier to accept other school rules and formal authority. Furthermore, being on a school team means being recognized by the system as a "good citizen" who participates in community life beyond basic requirements. This may in turn create deeper commitment by the student, not only to the school's rules but also to the academic work that is its main mission (p. 225).

206

With such commitment to school, and ultimately to their academic work, it is understandable that student athletes would seek to take their sports and academic interests as far as they can. Indeed, many student athletes do eventually pursue post-secondary education—some do so on the basis of athletic scholarships, and go to colleges and universities in the United States where they play on sports teams, while others instead concentrate mainly on their academic work. (These latter students most often elect to attend Canadian universities.) But the fact remains that participation in athletic activities assists in providing students access to post-secondary education. On this basis, Hsia (1988) suggests, with reference to Asian-American students who are known for their hard-working and academically focused attitudes, that parents and students may overestimate the importance of academic excellence, especially when applying for universities and colleges. He goes on to say "when so many applicants are well-qualified academically, as in the case of Asian Americans, acceptance to the most selective institutions will most likely turn on non-academic factors" (Hsia 1988, p. 208) such as involvement in sports, which is perceived to contribute to the development of athletic, leadership, and other social skills among students. Clearly, then, high school athletic participation can and does lead, in many cases, to attendance at college and university. Therefore, as Marsh (1993, p. 38) argues, schools should promote extracurricular activities in general and sports in particular for "participation in sport is likely to have positive effects across a wide variety of educationally relevant outcomes for a diversity of students."

ENSURING EQUAL OPPORTUNITY AND ACADEMIC ATTAINMENT OF MARGINALIZED STUDENT ATHLETES

The evidence indicates that athletic participation positively affects students' academic performance and attainment. It also suggests that immigrants and racial minority students, especially Blacks, more than others in similar social and economic circumstances, tend to participate in athletic activities, and they use athletic activities to negotiate the school structures. And insofar as participation in athletic activities affords them opportunities to survive racist and discriminatory school structures, then it is logical that they would be attracted to sports as an important school activity. Furthermore, if participation in athletic activities provides immigrants and racial minority student athletes with a means by which they can meet their parents' expectations and aspirations, then it would be imprudent for them to ignore such opportunities. In this regard, parents cannot afford to ignore the salience of athletics in the educational lives of their children. To this end, parents have an important role to play in advocating for their children in such a way that educators recognize that their expectation is for sports to comply with their educational plans, programs, and aspirations—in other words, ensure that athletic activities enable rather than impede the academic success of their children.

Understandably, students' academic attainment will vary, depending on such things as how much they put into their academic work, their aspirations, the teaching-learning situation, the supports and accommodations of educators, and the expectations of, and supports from, parents. Also, such variation will be influenced by the stereotypes that teachers and coaches use to predict or determine students' athletic and academic potential. Such stereotyping sometimes take place because parents do not question the actions of teachers and coaches and, in some ways, not questioning is seen as tacit support for educators' assessment of students as more academically or athletically able—an assessment that might also be related to the self-fulfilling prophecy by which some coaches, teachers, and principals operate. The so-called "academic" students might never be encouraged to participate or excel in sport—for example, in the case of Amir in Chapter 5, his coach saw him more as an "academic" than an "athlete," and did not help him seek a US athletic scholarship. On the other hand, there are coaches and teachers who will go all out to support perceived "athletic" students who are members of school teams to ensure that low academic grades do not become a barrier to these student athletes' participation on sports teams. These practices contribute to suspicions about the integrity of the academic work of some student athletes; such suspicions result in the student not enjoying a fair assessment of his or her academic credentials. In such situations, parents must work with educators to address these systemic and individual practices, which otherwise undermine the academic capability of student athletes.

The situation for female athletes deserves special consideration as gender bias in school athletic activities tends to rob them of the opportunities, supports, and benefits that males receive. Also, while males have other avenues (e.g., community and recreational centres, clubs, the street, and other places), females, in many cases, must rely on the opportunities that schools provide. Attempts must be made to address this "male stream" orientation of sports (Kidd, 1995).

As Hall, Slack, Smith, and Whitson (1991) contend, while males and females may have equal rights to access physical education or extracurricular athletic programs in schools today, they do not have equal opportunities to learn and benefit from these activities. The needs and aspirations of females are different from those of males and must be recognized as such. Hence, parents must make specific efforts to encourage their daughters to get involved in athletic activities, taking into consideration their social circumstances and individual experiences (Lenskyj, 1994; Williams, 1993; Talbot, 1993).

In essence, as in all situations or contexts, the role of parents is vital in ensuring that their children realize academic success. In this regard, it is pertinent for parents to be guided by a view of equity, which holds that it is not enough for their children to have access to athletic activities,[9] but that the provision of such activities must necessarily take into account the interests and needs of their children in relation to their cultural backgrounds. Equity also means treating student athletes differently in terms of their ethnocultural variations and abilities, as well as encouraging them to diversify in sports, not only to broaden their athletic repertoire and demonstrate their diverse abilities and skills, but also to address "the volatile and divisive issue of sport specialization" (Hill, 1993, p. 113). Indeed, as Hill also argues, "it is healthier for young athletes to engage in a diverse set of activities" in order to develop "alternative identities" as well as to have a "cushion" from the stress that is inherent in sports participation (p. 113). Ultimately, parents will have to be active participants in all educational activities of their children, making sure that schools facilitate rather than negate their children's cultural background and social circumstances and, in turn, keep the cultural distance, as well as differences in aspirations between themselves and their children, to a minimum.

CONCLUSION

To begin, let us return to Dane. Clearly, his experience in school is not unique. Like many other Black students, Dane's education is taking place within a school system that is White, middle class, and Eurocentric (Ministry of Education and Training, 1993), run by White middle-class teachers and administrators who may be unaware of how school policies and practices alienate and silence Black youth. Unless this kind of racializing ideology in the school system is recognized and interrogated, it will continue to influence teachers' expectations that Dane will do better athletically than academically. As such, school for Dane and others like him is a less hospitable place. This is especially true when the gym and the playground are among the few spaces where these students can establish their sense of individuality and identity, enhance their status, and gain credibility. The problem with Dane and other minority student athletes is not that sports are or will become "too central to their schooling," or that they will spend too much time in the gym or on the playground; rather, it is how the educational system, the curriculum content, and teachers' pedagogical approaches stereotype minority students and/or render them invisible and silent. It is these issues that must be addressed, rather than how students have sought to cope with schooling.

Parents have a significant role to play in supporting their children's participation in school athletic activities. While it might seem appropriate for parents to discourage or limit these athletic activities if a child's academic work appears to be suffering as a result, such actions must be carried out with an awareness of the systemic problems that are responsible for the student's lack of success in the first place. In discouraging athletic participation, parents must be aware that taking away "the hook," that aspect of school life that contributes to the social, cultural, psychological, and intellectual development of the student, can be adverse to his or her educational process. For the evidence indicates that sports, accompanied by supportive parents, coaches, and teachers, can make the difference between a student failing and succeeding academically.[10]

The long-held belief of immigrant and minority group parents that academics is the main or sole means of succeeding in a racist society (James, 1995; Nakamura, 2003; Li, 2001), and that relying on sports is problematic since an injury could easily limit future achievement, is certainly supported by much evidence. However, the evidence also indicates that accommodating the needs, interests, and aspirations of minority and immigrant student athletes, and incorporating athletics into the school program, may well help school to be less alienating and more accessible and equitable.

NOTES

1. Taken from *The Possibility of Play: Black Youth, Athletics and Schooling*, by C. James, in K.S. Brathwaite & C.E. James (1996), *Educating African Canadians*, p. 259. Toronto: James Lorimer. Of course, all names, unless otherwise indicated, are pseudonyms.

2. Coakley & Donnelly, 2004; Fleming, 1994; Grey, 1992; James, 1995; Nakamura, 2003; Solomon, 1992.

3. It is worth noting that a Toronto Board of Education study showed that Black students, particularly those born in the Caribbean and Canada, participate in extracurricular activities more often than the rest of the student population (Cheng, Yau, & Ziegler, 1993).

4. Minichiello's (2001) study of Chinese secondary school students from Hong Kong reminds us of the variation in the situations, and hence parental expectations of Chinese students. While the parents tended to have similar educational expectations for their children, many Hong Kong immigrants, compared to those from mainland China, seemed to entertain the option of returning to Hong Kong to find employment. Hence, education for students from Hong Kong was not necessarily to prepare them to deal with Canadian racism or compete in the Canadian labour market but to attain a good job if or when they go to that country.

5. It is worth noting, as Chen and Hu (1997) found in their comparative study of the career choices of Asian-American and Caucasian students, that the encouragement of Asian children to value science and math courses in school is likely related to the fact that Asian parents themselves work in science, technology, or business-related professions. As a result, Asian children are more exposed and prepared for similar professions as opposed to sport related professions where Asian mentors are uncommon.

6. For instance, with reference to the situation of Black students in the United States for whom basketball seemed to be a unique centrality in their experience, Harris (1991) notes that "Black athletes are not poorer performers academically because of a disinterest in academics by themselves or their significant others, but rather, because they lack the resources—good schools, good programs, etc.—to compete with their white peers" (1991, p. 148).

7. Based on his study of US student athletes, McNeal (1995) found that athletic participation reduced the probability of dropping out by about 40 percent, and the probability was greatest for Blacks who were more likely to participate in athletics. We could infer here that the situation for Black students in Toronto might be similar since according to Cheng, Yau, and Ziegler (1993), compared to students from other ethno-racial groups, they too tend to participate in athletic/extracurricular in large numbers (proportionally speaking).

8. In their US-based study, Yetman and Berghorn (1993, p. 313) found that among Black basketball players, 29 percent of males and 43 percent of females earned college degrees. Not only did Black females do better than their male counterparts, but Black female athletes fared considerably better than the Black student body

as a whole.

9. Sports historian Bruce Kidd (1995) argues that access to physical activities is a basic human right of all Canadians, particularly when a physical activity contributes to good health.

10. Hsia, 1988; James, 1996; McNeal, 1995; Nakamura, 2003; Pittaway, 1994.

CONCLUSION:
TOWARD MORE INCLUSIVE SCHOOLING
FOR STUDENT ATHLETES

Claims that sport operates as a mechanism for the advancement and integration of all members of society, especially those groups who stand outside the mainstream are largely unfounded. One of the myths of ... society is that sportsmen and women are able to gain maximum reward and acceptance for their skills and ability. This "meritocratic" notion assumes that race, gender, ethnic background and economic status simply disappear on the sportsfield, that success is largely dependent on a combination of application, hard work, discipline, commitment and a certain amount of good fortune (Kell, 2000, p. 37).

T HIS "RACIAL BLINDNESS," AS KELL (2000) NOTES,[1] ASSUMES THAT ATHLETES are able to overcome social, cultural, and economic barriers to participation and prosperity in society on the basis of merit. But as Glenn Loury (2002) argues:

In matters of race, the most fundamental moral question is not about blindness at all. It is about ... "neutrality." Race-blindness means having no information about a person's race, while race-neutrality means having no interest in the racial aspect of a social disparity. Blindness asks about what a public decision-maker [coach or educator] can know; neutrality deals with the goals that a decision-maker [coach or educator] can rightly pursue .... (p. 13).

This distinction between blindness and neutrality, Loury insists, is crucial, especially if we are to meaningfully address the harmful effects of the social injustices experienced by racial minorities. Accordingly, "blindness" aside (after all, it is impossible to be indifferent or not see the race or colour of people), for coaches, educators, and others to see the over-representation of Black students in basketball (for example) as unproblematic[2] is to ignore their moral responsibilities to address the issues.

In our society the images of the working-class racial minority student athletes obtaining university and college scholarships, and eventually making it onto professional teams, as some coaches, athletes, media, educators, parents, and peers would have us believe, sustain the optimism and hopes of many athletes who come to believe that through sport, they are able to attain their ambitions. "This delightful belief," as Kell (2000) writes, fails to recognize the fact that sports continue to be organized around social, economic, cultural, and political structures that affirm and reinforce class, race, and gender boundaries (p. 38; see also Wilcox & Andrews, 2003). In this regard, it is necessary to consider these structures if indeed we are to empower student athletes to attain the acceptance, advancement, and opportunities they seek.

I return to the question posed in the Introduction: Are students really likely to benefit from their participation in athletic or sport activities in today's schools? Findings indicate that there are many ways in which sports are or can be beneficial to students. Participation in sports can, among other things, help students to develop self-confidence, discipline, and a healthy self-image. It can also inspire high educational and occupational aspirations, instill commitment to schooling, and foster a sense of identity—racial, ethnic, and/or athletic identity—through which students understand their relationship to others, to school, and to the world around them.

On the other hand, there are drawbacks. The self-confidence developed and nurtured through sports sometimes contributes to the formation of an athletic identity that can become so all-consuming that it limits or prevents student athletes from cultivating other social identities and attributes needed to navigate school and societal structures. Participating in sports can also give athletes a sense of over-optimism based on their belief in the merit system, and to this end, they will sometimes sacrifice their bodies and their futures in the name of "winning."

Essentially, there are a number of personal and material benefits to be earned from sports, but for the benefits to be realized, athletes must recognize the limitations and liabilities, and in turn modify irrational expectations of what sports can do for them. Such expectations can operate at the expense of success in other areas of life such as school life. Clearly, participation in sports can be good and bad, healthy and harmful, constructive and destructive. Whether the benefits of sports participation outweigh the disadvantages will ultimately be determined by how athletes, with the guidance and support of their coaches, parents, teachers, and peers, come to understand and negotiate the athletic, academic (or educational), and other societal structures they encounter.

Important to this understanding is how race, in accordance with racism, classism, sexism, mediates the schooling experience. It also affects academic performance, athletic participation, and educational aspirations and achievements of athletes, and racial minority athletes in particular. For all athletes, race (in relation to class, gender, and national origin) operates paradoxically to structure perceptions of athletic and academic abilities and skills, the basis of which is stereotyping (Kell, 2002). As discussed in Chapters 3 and 5, on the basis of their race (and holding other characteristics such as height and weight constant), athletes are either selected or rejected, encouraged or discouraged, from participating in specific sports or athletic activities. For example, on the basis of his colour, Greg (Chapter 5), a Black athlete, was well supported by his coaches, teachers, and peers to try for a US athletic scholarship. This was not the case for Amir, a South Asian athletic scholarship aspirant. In fact, Amir reports that his basketball abilities and skills were not taken seriously until he was vouched for (or sponsored) by his Black friend and teammate and "proved" himself (see also Odhiambo, 2003[3]).

The same scenario is reflected in the media accounts of a White Toronto high school basketball player (Chapter 3). Such stereotyping accounts for the fact that comparatively few Asians, South Asians, and other racialized students participate in athletic activities (see note 2). However, the privileges of White student athletes, such as David and Craig (Chapter 2), indicate that stereotypes do not limit them as much as it does racial minority athletes. In fact, notwithstanding class or financial resources, they demonstrate that they enjoyed a number of sporting options (see also Saul, 2004).

If racial minority athletes are to benefit from their participation in sports and athletic activities, they will need the guidance and support of coaches, teachers, and parents, who understand how race informs and structures their educational, social, and economic situations. So, those who work with these athletes cannot afford to be race-blind and, more importantly, race-neutral; for to be either is to negate the structural barriers against which these athletes struggle. Hence, it is imperative to address the raced aspect of these athletes' experiences, performance, interests, and aspirations.

In this regard, and consistent with the arguments against race-blindness and race-neutrality, I conclude by reflecting on the limits to student athletes' singular ambition and devotion to sports, and how this ambition obscures not only their academic and occupational opportunities and possibilities, but also their athletic ones. I suggest that while US university and college scholarship ambitions are valuable incentives to maintain their interests in school and make the school environment less alienating—hence more responsive to their needs, interests, and aspirations—as coaches concede, such aspirations are fantasies that will never be realized. And while there are "athletically friendly" high school programs that could open up possibilities and interests for students, financial and educational requirements sometimes operate as barriers.

Added to these issues or concerns is the competitive nature of sports and the determination of young athletes to follow their ambitions. To address this situation, with reference to my work in urban education, I reflect on how collaborative efforts between university faculty members, educators, coaches, and communities (Cutforth & Hellison, 2002) might be helpful to all concerned.

Significant to our discussion is the reality of the urban context in which many of today's student athletes are negotiating their way to stardom and success. Wilcox and Andrews (2003, p. 7) write, in reference to the United States, that there is a widening gulf of social, cultural, and economic inequality in today's heterogeneous cities. This has precipitated social fragmentation, segregation, polarization, and tensions as city dwellers affirm their right to take part in sporting and recreational activities, while sporting facilities increasingly are located beyond their economic and geographic reach. They continue:

> Of great significance here is the manner in which different groups and individuals have appropriated sport as a symbol of group affiliation and affirmation. From the affluent "soccer moms" of white America to the playground basketball tradition of America's black urban ghettos, the complex weave of socioeconomic status, gender, race, and space serves as a prime justification for the importance of better understanding the relationship between sport and the city (Wilcox & Andrews, 2003, p. 7).

In this context, therefore, schools have become an important space for not only providing access to sporting and recreational activities, but also for enabling marginalized student athletes to affirm their identities, to develop their abilities in sports, and to fashion their relationship to the school. Further, in many instances, sports have come to represent "the glue that [binds] the seams" (Wilcox & Andrews, 2003, p. 10) across the heterogenous student population of schools. This is sometimes the case for those student athletes and students generally who come to identify with a particular sport on the basis of racial and ethnic group affiliation, and in the process acquire a sense of group pride so frequently lacking in the often alienating school environment.

For many marginalized student athletes, school is not just a place of learning, but also a place expected to make learning meaningful, to facilitate and to support their aspirations, and to provide the means and opportunities toward the realization of their aspirations—particularly, as has been demonstrated in this work, aspirations such as winning scholarships to colleges and universities in the Unites States (with Canadian colleges and universities as a fallback). To this end, some student athletes attend school beyond their five years, and sometimes go from school to school[4] with the expectation of being made a "winner" through the development of their skills and exposure to US scouts. Also, there are those student athletes who move to the United States to complete high school and "as a means to improve their athletic appeal much earlier" (Leeder, 2001, p. S4). While some coaches encourage this practice, others are dismayed by it. In fact, writing of this practice among basketball players and "the chagrin" of their high school coaches, Leeder (2001, p. S4) quotes one coach as saying:

> Players aren't set straight early enough .... They're sold on the glitz of the NCAA .... Canadian schools don't present their package well enough to fight this .... [The fantasy] could damage them forever. There's more to high school life than just basketball. No one's selling them that.

Another coach is reported to have said, "the sad thing is that these kids think their basketball skills will get them somewhere. They forget about the classroom. In many cases, it's purely bad advice [to move to the United States]" (p. S4, see also Higgins, 2003).

Canadian student athletes do not have to go to school in the United States in order to attend athletically oriented schools. For as Branswell (1997) reports, about 50 public and private schools throughout Canada, including the National Sport School in Calgary, operate programs that are geared to meeting the athletic and educational needs, interests, and aspirations of students (see also Grossman, 2003, p. C3). At École Secondaire de Montagne in Quebec, where in 1997 almost 300 student athletes were enrolled in the program, Branswell notes that entering students are expected to have above-average grades "in order to ensure a high degree of success in the classroom" (p. 52). While this idea of grade requirements is a good merit incentive, it has the effect of limiting access to such programs for marginalized students struggling with inequitable schooling structures, alienating curriculum, and low teacher expectations. Notwithstanding limited financial resources, in such cases, grades could operate as barriers to their participation.

In Toronto, where schools require that players take a minimum number of courses, have passing grade point averages, attend classes regularly, and meet transfer requirements (that is, having approval from TDSSAA/OFSAA; see note 4), players, coaches, and teachers have given mixed reviews about the extent to which such eligibility requirement really operate in the interests of some students. For example, at one public school where these eligibility requirements must be approved by the player's teachers, basketball players pointed out that while they work hard to earn good grades in order to maintain eligibility and not to "let their team down" or "hurt the team on the court," they had little confidence in the system working for them. One player noted that eligibility requirements meant that players were at the "mercy" of teachers; hence, "if a teacher did not like any of the players, then they [teachers] had the power to prevent them from playing." For their part, teachers felt that the program is well intentioned and they have seen improvement in class attendance and assignments. There are those teachers, however, who appropriately expressed concern that the athletes who are not academically strong could lose their desire to be in school if prevented from playing on their sports teams. Coaches felt that such a program communicates to students that their main focus should be on their academic work and that "the school cares about how they do academically." As one coach correctly noted, some student athletes might merely focus on maintaining eligibility rather than fully applying themselves to their academic work. Once the basketball season ends, so would the incentive for staying in school and interest in their academic work.

There is no denying that all attempts must be made to encourage and support student athletes in their academic work, but as educators, we must do so recognizing that for many of these student athletes, sports are a centrality to their schooling life; this is especially true of those who, because of limited economic resources, perceive that it is through sports, more than academics, that they will be able to realize their ambitions. It is therefore understandable that these athletes would devote much of their time in school to practising and playing their sports in order to win at competitions—something they passionately uphold, and believe to operate on merit principles (see Chapters 4 and 5). In fact, these athletes, to quote bell hooks (1995, p. 23) writing about the character Arthur Agee in the movie *Hoop Dreams*, have "an almost religious belief in the power of competition to bring success." Further, as hook suggests, referencing feminist writer Mab Segrest, "the ethic of competition undergirds the structure of racism and sexism [and individualism] in the United States, that to be 'American' is to be seduced by the lure of domination by conquest, [and] by winning ..." (p. 23).

In the Canadian schooling context, and for student athletes in particular, winning at competition helps to mitigate the fear of failure and pervasive individualism, racism, and classism that constantly hound them. But it is a situation from which there is no escape, for to escape is to fail, so they keep playing in order to win (hook, 1995, p. 23). For racialized Canadians, winning establishes and/or reinforces their status as "good Canadians" (a good illustration of this would be the Nigerian-born Canadian wrestler Daniel Igali, who won gold in the 2000 Olympics; see Abdel-Shehid, 2004).[5]

Given what winning represents for these athletes, I wonder about the lengths to which they will go in their efforts to win. I think here of Ben Johnson, whose story is so well known that it need not be repeated here. However, it is a distinct possibility that he was so seduced by the lure of winning and caught up in the ethic of competition that he used a performance-enhancing drug in order to win and in the process be celebrated as a "Canadian." I am also persuaded by a recent CBC report (Canadian Broadcasting Corporation: 99.1 FM Toronto, Summer Sunday Edition, August 8, 2004) that indicates that steroid use among young athletes has been increasing because it is seen as getting them recognition, enhancing their potential to make money, and giving them a competitive edge. "It's a no brainer," the reporter declares. The point is that the use of performance-enhancing drugs is in some ways a consequence of the pressure for athletes to prove themselves—in order to achieve recognition as Canadians, they have to be no less than outstanding athletes. In light of this situation, we should be concerned about the extent to which today's student athletes resort to the use of such drugs in order to win (see also Bamberger & Yaeger, 1997).

Given these issues and experiences of racialized student athletes, it is important, as Cutforth and Hellison (2002, p. 106) advise, to "capitalize on the popularity of sport and physical activity" in an effort to make school meaningful, and to help them transfer their athletic skills and interests into their academic work. Accordingly, in my own work with teacher candidates whose practice teaching has been in racially and culturally diverse and economically disadvantaged school settings (commonly referred to as "urban" or "inner city" areas of Toronto), I have encouraged them to think critically of the contexts in which they teach.

I hope that they would come to recognize the subjectivities they bring to the teaching-learning process, challenge their power and privilege, understand the students' lives and communities from the students' perspectives, and develop a relevant class curriculum and "engaged pedagogy"(Preskill & Jacobvitz, 2001). The goal is to promote critical self-reflection, to assess critically our "good intentions," and to "make explicit the contradictions and paradoxes that are inherent in institutions, such as schools, which promise equality and inclusivity while producing and reproducing inequalities based on race, class, gender and other factors" (James, 2004, p. 16). For as Preskill and Jacobvitz (2001, p. 163) reason, "when teachers avoid self-study, they may unconsciously perpetuate stereotyping and bias in their own classroom practices."

I work with these ideas in the urban education course I teach to elementary, middle, and high school teacher candidates in a achool/university partnership program (James, 2004), and in the adolescence course I teach to high school teacher candidates in the consecutive education program. In their work with their host teachers, including physical education teachers, teacher candidates not only assist with classes, but also with coaching sports teams and with extracurricular athletic activities.

For both courses, an initial course assignment requires participants to conduct community visits to become familiar with the geography of the area, as well as, among other things, its demographic and socio-economic make-up. They observe the school grounds and play areas, noting the play activities and who participates in terms of gender, race, ethnicity, language, and age. In their work with students, participants are expected to recognize their students as authorities on their own lives, and hence best qualified to speak to their needs, interests, and aspirations.

Their role as teachers or teacher candidates is to facilitate open communication and to help students exercise voice and agency. In the end, it is the relationships that teachers are able to build with their students, in this case student athletes, that will enable teachers to "know" the athletes and assist them in putting in place an education or learning program that does not compromise or detract from their athletic ambitions—a program that opens up educational and occupational opportunities and possibilities, rather than limits them.

In the past year, through the partnership program, Grade Eleven students (the majority of whom are of racial minority backgrounds from local schools) have been spending their winter semester at the university where they take one course for which they receive a high school credit. For the remainder of the week the students have placements in particular educational/occupational areas of interest. I recall that two of these students were interested in athletics and elected to work in the kinesiology program in order to learn more about the subject and consider it as an option.

In the course on adolescents, teacher candidates complete a community practicum in which they engage with students outside of regular school activities. In many cases, candidates have participated in after-school programs in schools and community organizations, specifically in extracurricular athletic activities, including coaching sports teams, running music clubs, teaching dance classes, tutoring or helping students with their academic work, or simply "hanging" out with students in community centres. As one teacher candidate, who participated in athletic activities with youth at a community centre, said:

> Spending time with teens outside of school reminded me that studying in a classroom is only a small part of a student's life. In doing the community assignment, I was able to get to know students in completely different contexts, which helped to better understand and accommodate their needs (April 2003).

If some of the student athletes who participated in this project were given the opportunity to interact with teacher candidates or teachers who have had experience in "community-based education," it is possible that participants like Devin (in Chapter 5) would become acquainted with Canadian universities and learn more about what they have to offer.[6] (Recall that Devin was unaware of university programs in Canada.) It is likely that the research participants would be exposed to former student athletes, now teacher candidates of various ethnic, racial, and immigrant origins, who could talk from their experiences about their respective journey through school and university.

From these experiences, I have understood that when the education process enables students to reflect on the social realities of their lives and how cultural expectations shape their thinking, they come to envision and/or initiate "new social realities and new identities for themselves" (Preskill & Jacobvitz, 2001, p. 164). Moreover, when teaching and learning is made relevant to students, and when they learn about existing opportunities, then their attention to sports is unlikely to obscure the available opportunities in other fields. Sport, then, would cease to be their sole means of economic mobility (Simons & Butow, 1997). An example here is Devin, who, after our interview, contacted me to talk further about my suggestion that he consider pursuing teaching as a career and use his interests in athletics.

Today, Devin is completing his teaching degree. Indeed, as Cutforth and Hellison (2002, p. 112) write, with regard to "service learning experiences" in the university/community partnerships in which they are involved, "Physical education/kinesiology programs in higher education are well-positioned to direct more of their energies to their local communities, and to develop leaders in the youth development field—people willing to accept challenges and take risks" (see also Pitter, 2004).

Finally, I have shown through the stories of student athletes that contrary to the popular notion that equality of opportunity exists in the domain of sports, the experiences of marginalized or racialized student athletes reveal otherwise. In fact, what happens in sports reflects the "thinking and acting that support and legitimize the power structures and inequalities" in society and schooling in particular (Fejgin, 1994, p. 224). So simply having the athletic abilities, skills, and competence, and applying oneself to a chosen sport is no guarantee of achieving an ambition.

In this regard, and with reference to critical theorists, I have shown that the race culture discourse (and its derivative race-blindness and racial-neutrality) as informed by the Canadian ideology of multiculturalism continues to reproduce situations in which students' school participation reflects their positions in the social hierarchy of Canadian society. In other words, the pervasive inequitable structures and practices of society are to be found even in the educational and athletic systems, which claim to promote equality of opportunity as well as sensitivity to, and awareness of, differences. While participation in sports and athletic activities can indeed inculcate values such as discipline, hard work, respect, teamwork, leadership, goal-setting, fairness, and competition, for racialized student athletes, these values must also speak to their social and cultural context and circumstances. Thus, individuals such as coaches, teachers, parents, and mentors need to help them understand the realities of inequity. Similarly, they should be helped to disentangle education from athletics—an entanglement that, in many cases, has proven to be an impediment, if not a barrier, to their academic and educational performance. In light of these barriers, student athletes should be encouraged to participate in a diverse number of physical activities in order to broaden their athletic repertoire, so that they might escape the "volatile and diverse issues of sport specialization" (Hill, 1993, p. 113).

NOTES

1. Kell is referring to his native Australia; however, the same could be said of the situation in North America, and Canada in particular.

2. In his examination of the *Toronto Star*'s high school male and female "athletes of the week" over the 2003/2004 school year, Saul (2004) found clear differences in participation based on race. White males and females were almost exclusively represented in hockey. (The one exception was a male hockey player of Asian ancestry). The same is true for activities such as swimming, rugby, softball, baseball, field hockey, and surfing. Black males were represented as basketball, football, and track and field athletes, and, in one instance, soccer. And Black females were represented primarily as participating in basketball and track and field. Asians and South Asians were mostly absent from the weekly profiles of high school sports participation.

3. In his novel *Kipligat's Chance*, David Odhiambo (2003) tells the fictional story of John "Leeds" Kipligat, a Black 17-year-old, who emigrated with his parents from Kenya and was now living in a housing project in Vancouver, Canada. With his 16-year-old South Asian best friend, Kulvinder Sharma, also a Kenyan immigrant living with his mother in Vancouver, he joined a track club where they were coached by Sam Holt, a Black man and Olympian. The story is about how the friends used sports to negotiate their early years in Canada. It tells of the relationship they were able to form with the coach, who acted as their advocate,

and their belief that through excelling at running they would win scholarships to American universities and escape their dissatisfying life situations. For this reason, Leeds more than Kulvinder, trains hard in hopes of attaining his ambition. Eventually, Leeds earns a scholarship to a US university and Kulvinder, who at one time qualifies for the Canadian national junior track team, passes up the opportunity to attend a prestigious school in the US in order to remain in Vancouver with his fiancée and attend the University of British Columbia.

4. In their efforts to limit this practice, the Toronto District Secondary Schools Athletic Association (TDSSAA), in accordance with the Ontario Federation of School Athletic Association (OFSAA), the provincial governing body for high school sports, moved to restrict the participation of sixth-year players in athletic activities, and of "those who had not met transfer eligibility rules" (*Toronto Star*, February 22, 2002, p. D17).

5. Writing about the Aboriginals of Australia, Kell (2002, p. 55) explains that "their acceptance is dependent on their ability not to appear to be like the Aboriginal community but to be like 'one of us,' even though their appeal is often attributed to special qualities that only 'they' have; just as their vulnerability is equally attributed to 'their specific racial stereotypes.' At the same time that they are praised by the media for being "black magic," they can also be tagged as unpredictable and "lacking in the ethic of hard work." Arguably the same could be said of the situation of Black athletes in North America.

6. The partnership program between University of Toronto and Toronto Community Housing attempts to do just that. *Toronto Star* reporter Vivian Song (2004, July 28, p. B4) writes about the 2004 summer program in which some 300 young people, ages eight to 15, from the community housing communities competed for eight university track and field scholarship valued at $550. Through the program the young athletes, as the coach puts it, "rub shoulders with kids who want to be doctors, lawyers and rocket scientists." One 14-year-old male said that his involvement in track and field "gives you a reason to do well in school ...," and a 12-year-old stated "I'm here for the chance to be scouted. I want to go to college and get a good future."

REFERENCES

Abdel-Shehid, G. (2005). *Who Da Man?: Black Masculinities and Sporting Cultures.* Toronto: Canadian Scholars' Press.

Abdel-Shehid, G. (2003). In Place of "Race," Space: "Basketball in Canada" and the Absence of Racism. In R.C. Wilcox, D.L. Andrews, R. Pitter, & R.L. Irwin (eds.), *Sporting Dystopias: The Making and Meanings of Urban sport Cultures,* pp. 247–263. Albany: State University of New York Press.

Abdel-Shehid, G. (2002). Raptor Morality: Blacks, Basketball and National Identity. In S. Fogel & L. Thoman (eds.), *Changing Identities.* Toronto: Canadian Scholars' Press.

Abdel-Shehid, G. (2000). Writing Hockey through Race: Rethinking Black Hockey in Canada. In R. Walcott (ed.), *Rude: Contemporary Black Canadian Cultural Criticism,* pp. 69–86. Toronto: Insomniac.

Abdel-Shehid, G. (1997). "You da' Man": "Race," Sports Heroes and the Representation of Masculinities. Paper presented at the Feminist Graduate Colloquium (Toronto, York University).

Agnew, V. (2003). *Where I Come From.* Waterloo: Wilfrid Laurier University Press.

Alladin, M.I. (ed.) (1996). *Racism in Canadian Schools.* Toronto: Harcourt Brace.

Allen, A.L. (1994). On Being a Role Model. In D. Goldberg (ed.), *Multiculturalism: A Critical Reader,* pp. 180–199. Cambridge: Blackwell.

Anderson, G.L., Herr, K., & Nihlen, A.S. (1994). *Studying Your Own School: An Educator's Guide to Qualitative Practitioner Research.* Thousand Oaks, California: Corwin Press.

Andres, L., Anisef, P., Krah, H., Looker, D., & Thiessen, V. (1999). The Persistence of Social Science Structure: Cohort, Class and Gender Effects on the Occupational Aspirations and Expectations of Canadian Youth. *Journal of Youth Studies* 2(3), 261–282.

Andrews, D. (ed.) (2001). *Michael Jordan, Inc. Corporate Sport, Media Culture, and Late Modern America.* Albany: State University of New York Press.

Anisef, P., Axelrod, P., Baichman, E., James, C., & Turrittin, A. (2000). *Opportunities and Uncertainty: Life Course Experiences of the Class of '73.* Toronto: University of Toronto Press.

Anisef, P., & Kilbride, K.M. (eds.) (2003). *Managing Two Worlds: The Experiences and Concerns of Immigrant Youth in Ontario.* Toronto: Canadian Scholars' Press.

Anisef, P., Okihiro, N., & James, C. (1982). *Losers and Winners: The Pursuit of Equality and Social Justice in Higher Education.* Toronto: Butterworths.

Armour, K.M., & Jones, R.L. (2000). The Practical Heart Within: The Value of a Sociology of Sport. In R.L. Jones & K.M. Armour (eds.), *Sociology of Sport: Theory and Practice*, pp. 3–12. Essex: Longman.

Arnett, J.J. (2002). *Readings on Adolescence and Emerging Adulthood.* Englewood Cliffs, New Jersey: Prentice Hall.

Balk, D.E. (1995). *Adolescent Development: Early Years through Adolescence.* Monterey, California: Brooks/Cole.

Bamberger, M., & Yaeger, D. (1997). Over the Edge: Performance-Enhancing Drug Use. *Sports Illustrated* 86(15), April, 60–68.

Banet-Wiser, S. (2002). We Got Next: Negotiating Race and Gender in Professional Basketball. In M. Gatz (ed.), *Paradoxes of Youth and Sport*, pp. 93–102. Albany: State University of New York Press.

Barnard, R., Cosgrave, D., & Welsh, J. (1998). *Chips and Pop: Decoding the Nexus Generation.* Toronto: Malcolm Lester Books.

Bellaby, P. (1991). Histories and Sickness: Making Use of Multiple Accounts of the Same Process. In S. Dex (ed.), *Life and Work History Analysis: Qualitative and Quantitative Developments*, pp. 20–452. London: Routledge.

Billings, A., Denham, B., & Halone, K. (2002). Differential Accounts of Race in Broadcast Commentary of the 2000 NCAA Men's and Women's Final Four Basketball Tournaments. *Sociology of Sport Journal* 19, 315–332.

BLAC (Black Learners Advisory Committee). (1994). *BLAC Report on Education Redressing Inequality: Empowering Black Learners.* Halifax: Black Learners Advisory Committee.

Booth, D., & Tatz, C. (2000). *One Eyed: A View of Australian Sport.* Sydney: Allen & Urwin.

Bowlby, J., & McMullen, K. (2002). *At a Crossroads: First Results for the 18 to 20-Year-Old Cohort of the Youth in Transitions Survey.* Hull, Quebec: Human Resources Development Canada Publications Centre, Statistics Canada.

Boyd, M., & Grieco, E.M. (1998). Triumphant Transitions: Socioeconomic Achievements of the Second Generation in Canada. *International Migration Review* 32(4), 853–876.

Braddock, J.H. II, Royster, D., Winfield, L., & Hawkins, R. (1991). Bouncing Back: Sports and Academic Resilience among African-American Males. *Education and Urban Society* 24, 113–130.

Branswell, B. (1997). A Class of Their Own: Young Athletes Thrive in Schools That Cater to Their Demanding Schedules. *Maclean's* March, 110(11), 52–53.

Brathwaite, K.S. & James, C.E. (1996). *Educating African Canadians*. Toronto: James Lorimer.

Briggs, A., & Cobley, P. (1999). "I Like My Shit Sagged": Fashion, Black Music and Subcultures. *Journal of Youth Studies* 2(3), 337–352.

CAAWS (Canadian Association for the Advancement for Women in Sport). (1997). *How Parents Can Encourage Girls to Play Sport*. Fact Sheet. Gloucester: CAAWS.

Campbell, M. (2003). Stewart's Tough Journey to the NHL. *Toronto Star,* June 22, p. E8.

Campbell, M. (2003). Long Shots: The Final Hoops. *Toronto Star,* June 7, E4–E5.

Campbell, M. (2003). Time for a Hail Mary: Rifts and Resentments within the Team Threaten the Mavericks' Performance: Divided, They'll Fall. As a Crucial Game Approaches, the Coaches Can Only Plead—and Pray. *Toronto Star,* June 7, E1.

Campbell, M. (2003). Long Shots: Rising to the Occasion for the Big Boys. *Toronto Star,* June 6, B2.

Campbell, M. (2003). Long Shots: The Vanier Team Heads to the Championships. *Toronto Star*, June 6, F1–F2.

Campbell, M. (2003). Long Shots: The Power of Persuasion. *Toronto Star,* June 5, B1.

Campbell, M. (2003). Long Shots: Pressure on the Mavericks Grows: The Angry Young Prince. *Toronto Star,* June 4, B1.

Campbell, M. (2003). Long Shots: Vanier Player Drew Lomond's Change to Impress an NCAA Recruiter Gets Off to Rough Start. *Toronto Star*, June 3, A1.

Campbell, M. (2003). Long Shots: Why Vanier Mavericks' Smallest Player Is Gambling on His Future. *Toronto Star,* June 2, A1.

Campbell, M. (2003). Long Shots: Short-Sighted Ideas, But Very Tall Plans. *Toronto Star,* June 2, B1& B2.

Campbell, M. (2003). Long Shots: On a Cold Night, Pride Before a Fall. *Toronto Star,* June 1, A1 & A8.

Campbell, M. (2003). The Holy Wars: Tensions Rise Between the Teams and the Teammates as the Jean Vanier Mavericks Take on the Saints and Mother Teresa Scarborough High School Players Embark on a Long, Difficult Journey to an Ontario Championship. *Toronto Star*, May 31, A1, A18, & A19.

Campbell, M. (2003). Leaf Prospects Get C-Plus. *Toronto Star,* February 9, E2.

Canadian Press. (2002). Girl Goalie Sets History. *Toronto Sun.* January 23, 92.

Carrington, B. (1983). Sport As a Side-Track: An Analysis of West Indian Involvement in Extracurricular Sport. In L. Barton & S. Walker (eds.), *Race, Class and Education*, pp. 40–65. Sydney: Croom Helm.

Carrington, B., & McDonald, I. (eds.) (2001). *"Race," Sport and British Society.* London: Routledge.

Carroll, B., & Hollinshead, G. (1993). Equal Opportunities: Race and Gender in Physical Education: A Case Study. In J. Evans (ed.), *Equality, Education and Physical Education*, pp. 154–169. London: Falmer.

Carspecken, P.F. (1996). *Critical Ethnography in Educational Research: A Theoretical and Practical Guide.* New York: Routledge.

Cashmore, E. (1982). *Black Sportsmen.* London: Rouledge & Kegan Paul.

CBC (Canadian Broadcasting Corporation). (2004). (99.1 Toronto). Summer Sunday Edition, August 8.

Chadha, G. (Director). (2002). *Bend It Like Beckham* [Film]. Fox.

Chen, G., & Hu, X. (1997). Attitudes toward the Physical Education Profession: A Comparative Study of Career Choice in Asian-American and Caucasian students. *Journal of the International Council for Health, Physical-Education, Recreation, Sport, and Dance* 33(3), Spring, 28–32.

Cheng, M., Yau, M., & Ziegler, S. (1993). *Every Secondary Student Survey, Parts 1, 2 and 3.* Toronto: Research Services, Toronto Board of Eduction.

Clarke, G.E. (1998). White Like Canada. *Transition 73*, 98–109.

Clarkson, M. (2003). GTA a Hotbed for Hoops: High School Stars Reap Rewards of US Scholarships. *Toronto Star* (November 26), C2.

Coakley, J. (2002). Using Sports to Control Deviance and Violence Among Youth: Let's Be Critical and Cautious. In M. Gatz, M.A. Messner, & S.J. Ball-Rokeach (eds.), *Paradoxes of Youth and Sport.* New York: State University New York Press.

Coakley, J. (1998). *Sport in Society: Issues and Controversies.* Boston: McGraw-Hill.

Coakley, J., & Donnelly, P. (2004). *Sports in Society: Issues and Controversies.* First Canadian Edition. Toronto: McGraw-Hill Ryerson.

Codjoe, H.M. (2001). Fighting a "Public Enemy" of Black Academic Achievement— The Persistence of Racism and the Schooling Experiences of Black Students in Canada. *Race, Ethnicity and Education* 4(4), 343–375.

Cole, A.L., & Knowles, J.G. (2001). What Is Life History Research? *Lives in Context: The Art of Life History Research*, pp. 9–24. New York: Altamira Press.

Contena, S. (1993). *Rituals of Failure: What Schools Really Teach.* Toronto: Between the Lines.

Conway, J.K. (1999). *When Memory Speaks: Exploring the Art of Autobiography.* New York: Random House.

Cornelius, G. (1997). What Ever Happened to the White Athlete? *Sports Illustrated* December 87(23), 30–42.

Coté, J., & Allahar, A. (1994). *Generation on Hold: Coming of Age in the Late Twentieth Century.* Toronto: Stoddart.

Craig, C.L., Cameron, C., Russell, S.J., & Beaulieu, A. (2001). *Increasing Physical Activity: Supporting Children's Participation (2000 Physical Activity/Monitor).* Ottawa: Canadian Fitness and Lifestyle Research Institute.

Cummins, J. (1997). Minority Status and Schooling in Canada. *Anthropology and Education Quarterly* 28(3), 411–430.

Cutforth, N., & Hellison, D. (2002). Capitalizing on the Popularity of Sport and Physical Activity among Underserved Youth: Breaking New Ground in University/ Community Cultures. *University and Community Schools* 7(1–2), Fall-Winter, 106–112.

Dabovic, S. (2002). *Skirting Gender, Race and Class: Women and (In)equity in Sport.* Graduate Program in Education, York University, Toronto.

Danesi, M. (1994). *Cool: The Signs and Meanings of Adolescence.* Toronto: University of Toronto Press.

Davidson, A.L. (1996). *Making and Molding Identity in Schools: Student Narratives on Race, Gender and Academic Engagement.* New York: State University of New York Press.

Davis, B. (2004). *Teaching Tough Kids.* Toronto: Our Schools/Our Selves.

Davison, K. (2000). Masculinities, Sexualities and the Student Body. In C.E. James (eds.), *Experiencing Difference*, pp. 44–52. Halifax: Fernwood.

Day, R. (2000). *Multiculturalism and the History of Canadian Diversity.* Toronto: University of Toronto Press.

Dei, G.S. (1996a). *Anti-Racism Education: Theory and Practice.* Halifax: Fernwood.

Dei, G.S. (1996b). Black/African Canadian Students' Perspectives on School Racism. In M.I. Alladin (ed.), *Racism in Canadian schools*, pp. 42–61. Toronto: Harcourt Brace.

Dei, G.S., & Calliste, A. (eds.) (2000). *Power, Knowledge and Anti-Racism Education.* Halifax: Fernwood.

Dei, G.S., Holmes, L., Mazzuca, J., McIsaac, E., & Zine, J. (1997). *Reconstructing "Drop-Out": A Critical Ethnography of the Dynamics of Black Students' Disengagement from School.* Toronto: University of Toronto Press.

Denham, B.E., Billings, A.C., & Halone, K.K. (2002). Differential Accounts of Race in Broadcast Commentary of the 2000 NCAA Men's and Women's Final Four Basketball Tournaments. *Sociology of Sport Journal* 19, 315–32.

Denzin, N.K. (1996). *Interpretive Ethnography: Ethnographic Practices for the 21st Century.* Thousand Oaks: Sage.

Desai, S., & Subramanian, S. (2003). Colour, Culture and Dual Consciousness: Issues Identified by South Asian Immigrant Youth in the Greater Toronto Area. In P. Anisef & K.M. Kilbride (eds.), *Managing Two Worlds: The Experiences and Concerns of Immigrant Youth in Ontario*, pp. 118–162. Toronto: Canadian Scholars' Press.

Dimmons, S. (2002). Minority Report: More Talk Has Yet to Translate into More Action for African-American Coaching Hopefuls. *Sunday Sun*, December 8, S14–S15.

Dodds, P. (1993). Removing the Ugly "Isms" in Your Gym: Thoughts for Teachers on Equity. In J. Evans (ed.), *Equality, Education and Physical Education*, pp. 20–39. London: Falmer.

Donnelly, P. (2002). *Taking Sport Seriously: Social Issues in Canadian Sport* (Second Edition). Toronto: Thompson Educational.

Drewe, S.B. (2003). What Do Coaches Have to Say about Ethical Issues in Sport? *Why Sport?: An Introduction to the Philosophy of Sport*, pp. 101–120. Toronto: Thompson Educational.

Drewe, S.B. (2003). The Coach–Athlete Relationship: How Close Is Too Close? *Why Sport?: An Introduction to the Philosophy of Sport*, pp. 187–200. Toronto: Thompson Educational.

Dua, E. (1999). Canadian Anti-Racist Feminist Thought: Scratching the Surface of Racism. In E. Dua & A. Robertson (eds.), *Scratching the Surface: Canadian Anti-Racist Thought*, pp. 7–31. Toronto: Women's Press.

Duffy, A. (1996). The Superstars of the Hoop Court. *Toronto Star*, March 25, A6.

Duffy, A. (1996). Chasing the Dream of Hoop Fame. *Toronto Star*, March 24, A6.

Duffy, A. (1996). Metro's School of Hoop Dreams. *Toronto Star*, March 23, A22.

Dunn, R. (2002). Growing Good Citizens with a World-Centered Curriculum. *Educational Leadership*, October, 10–14.

Dyck, N. (2000). Parents, Kids and Coaches: Constructing Sport and Childhood in Canada. In N. Dyck (eds.), *Games, Sports and Cultures*, pp. 137–161. Oxford: Oxford International.

Eitle, T., & Eitle, D. (2002). Race, Cultural Capital, and the Educational Effects of Participation in Sports. *Sociology of Education*, April, 75(2), 123–146.

Eitle, T., & Eitle, D. (2002a). "Just Don't Do It: High School Sports Participation and Young Female Adult Sexual Behavior." *Sociology of Sport* 19, 403–418.

Eitzen, D.S., & Sage, G.H. (1997). *Sociology of North American Sport*. Madison: Brown & Benchmark.

Entine, J. (2000). *Taboo: Why Black Athletes Dominate Sports and Why We're Afraid to Talk about It*. New York: Public Affairs.

Errande, A. (2000). "But Sometimes You've Not Part of the Story": Oral Histories and Ways of Remembering and Telling. *Educational Researcher* 29(2), 16–27.

Evans, J., & Davies, B. (1993). Equality, Equity and Physical Education. In J. Evans (ed.), *Equality, Education and Physical Education*, pp. 11–27. London: Falmer.

Ewing, M.E, Cano-Overway, L.A., Branta, C., & Seefledt, V. (2002). The Role of Sports in Youth Development. In M. Gatz, M. Messner, A. Michael, & S.J. Ball-Rokeach (eds.), *Paradoxes of Youth and Sport*. New York: State University of New York Press.

Fair Play: Current Facts on Women's Sports. www.womensportsfoundation.org/cgi-bin/iowa/shop/equity/index.html

Farber, P., Provenzo, E.F. Jr., & Holm, G. (eds.) (1994). *Schooling in the Light of Popular Culture*. New York: State University of New York Press.

Fejgin, N. (1995). Participating in High School Competitive Sports: A Subversion of School Mission or Contribution to Academic Goals? *Sociology Sport Journal* 11(3), 211–230.

Fenton, J., Bryna, K., & Lawrence, T. (2000). *On the Move: Increasing Participation for Girls and Women in Recreational Sport and Physical Activity*. Vancouver: Canadian Association for the Advancement of Women and Sport and Physical Activity (CAAWS).

Fenton, J., Frisby, W., & Luke, M. (1999). Multiple Perspectives of Organizational Culture: A Case Study of Physical Education for Girls in a Low-Income Multiracial School. *Avante* 5(2), 1–22.

Fenton, J., Kopelow, B., Viviani, C., & Millar, S. (2000). *On the Move: Increasing Participation of Girls and Women in Recreational Sport and Physical Activity*. Vancouver: Canadian Association for the Advancement of Women and Sport and Physical Activity.

Fernández-Balboa, J.-M. (2000). Discrimination: What Do We Know and What Can We Do About It? In R.L. Jones & K.M. Armour (eds.), *Sociology of Sport: Theory and Practice*, pp. 134–144. Essex: Pearson.

Fields, C.D. (2001). National Student Athlete Day Gives Top Billing to Academic Achievement. *Black Issues in Higher Education* 18(2), March, 14.

Finley, B. (2002). Who's Afraid of Title IX: That's What We Asked the Panel Appointed by the Bush Administration to Determine the Law's Future. *Sports Illustrated for Women* 4(8), December, 57.

Fleming, S. (2001). Racial Science and South Asian and Black Physicality. In B. Carrington & I. MacDonald (eds.), *"Race", Sport and British society*, pp. 105–120. London: Routledge.

Fleming, S. (1994). Sport and South Asian Youth: The Peril of "False Universalism" and Stereotyping. *Leisure Studies* 13, 159–177.

Fleming, S. (1991). Sport, Schooling and Asian Male Youth Culture. In G. Jarvie (ed.), *Sport, Racism and Ethnicity*, pp. 30–57. London: Falmer.

Fleras, A., & Elliott, J. (1992). *The Challenge of Diversity: Multiculturalism in Canada*. Scarborough: Nelson Canada.

Fontana, A., & Frey, J.H. (1994). Interviewing: The Art of Science. In N.K. Denzin & Y.S. Lincoln (eds.), *Handbook of Qualitative Research*, pp. 361–376. Thousand Oaks: Sage.

Fredricks, J., Alfeld-Lira, C., Hruda, L., Eccles, J., Patrick, H., & Ryan, A. (2002). A Qualitative Exploration of Adolescents' Commitment to Athletics and the Arts. *Journal of Adolescent Research* 17(1), 68–97.

Frey, D. (1994). *The Last Shot: City Streets, Basketball Dreams*. New York: Houghton Mifflin.

Fulgiani, A.J., Yip, T., & Tseng, V. (2002). The Impact of Family Obligation on the Daily Behavior and Psychological Well-Being of Chinese-American Adolescents. *Child Development* 73, 306–318.

Gabor, P., Thibodeau, S., & Manychief, S. (1997). Taking Flight? The Transition Experiences of Native Youth. In B. Galaway & J. Hudson (eds.), *Youth in Transition: Perspectives on Research and Policy*, 79–89. Toronto: Thompson Educational.

Galaway, B., & Hudson, J. (eds.) (1996). *Youth in Transition: Perspectives on Research and Policy*. Toronto: Thompson Educational.

Garrod, A.C., Smulyan, L., Powers, S.I., & Kilkenny, R. (2002). *Adolescent Portraits: Identity, Relationships, and Challenges*. Toronto: Allyn & Bacon.

Gaskell, J., McLaren, A., & Novogrodsky, M. (1989). *Claiming an Education: Feminism and Canadian Schools*. Toronto: Our School/Our Selves.

Gatz, M., Messner, M. A., & Ball-Rokeach, S. J. (eds.) (2002). *Paradoxes of Youth and Sport*. Albany: State University of New York Press.

Gause, C.P. (2003). *Book Review on Greg Dimitriadis., Performing Identity/Performing Culture: Hip Hop as Text Pedagogy, and Lived Practice*. January (1), 134–140.

Geertz, C. (1973). Thick Description: Towards an Interpretive Theory of Culture. In *The Interpretation of Cultures*, pp. 3–30. New York: Basic Books.

Gender Equity in Coaching (Coaching Association of Canada). www.coach.ca/women/e/resources/books.htm

Gerdy, J.R. (1997). A Suggestion for College Coaches: Teach by Example. *Black Issues in Higher Education* August 14(12), 28.

Gibbons, S., Wharf Higgins, J., Gaul, C., & Van Gun, G. (1999). Listening to Female Students in High School Physical Education. *Avante* 2, 36–52.

Giroux, H.A. (1996). *Fugitive Cultures: Race, Violence, and Youth*. New York: Routledge.

Graveline, F.J. (1998). *Circle Works: Transforming Eurocentric Consciousness*. Halifax: Fernwood.

Greenfield, P., Davis, H.M., Suzuki, L.K., & Boutakides, I.P. (2002). Understanding Intercultural Relations on Multiethnic High Sports Teams. In M. Gatz, A. Messner, A. Michael, & S.J. Ball-Rokeach (eds.), *Paradoxes of Youth and Sport*, pp. 141–159. Albany: State University of New York Press.

Greenstone, D. (2002). White Men Can't Pass, *PopPolitics.com* (April 11).

Grey, M.A. (1992). Sport and Immigrants, Minority and Anglo Relations in Garden City (Kansas) High School. *Sociology of Sport Journal* 9(3), 255–270.

Griffin, P.S. (1996). Changing the Game: Homophobia, Sexism and Lesbian in Sport. In D.S. Eitzen (ed.), *Sport in Contemporary Society: An Anthology*, pp. 392–409. New York: St. Martin's.

Grossman, D. (2004). *Toronto Star*'s Annual All Star Basketball Team. *Toronto Star.* February 18, C4.

Grossman, D. (2003). Howorun Is Two Good. *Toronto Star,* March 11, E9.

Grossman, D. (2003). Basketball Brains: These High School Students Excel in the Classroom as Well as on the Court. *Toronto Star*, February 25, E1 & E4.

Grossman, D. (2003). Program Provides Flexibility for Student athletes. *Toronto Star*, February 18, C8.

Grossman, D. (2003). An Elite Juggling Act: Program Provides Flexibility for Student Athletes. *Toronto Star,* February 18, C8.

Grossman, D. (2003). Watt's Happening: Unselfish Star Takes First-Year Squad to the Top. *Toronto Star,* February 11, E8.

Grossman, D. (2003). Playing on the Boys' Team Not a "Big Deal" for Shakti. *Toronto Star*, February 4, E10.

Grossman, D. (2003). Teen Hurdles to No. 2 on the World List: Pickering Student. *Toronto Star,* January 14, E4.

Grossman, D. (2003). Program Provides Flexibility for Student Athletes. *Toronto Star*, February 18, C8.

Grossman, D. (2002). No Sixth Year for Athletes: Governing Bodies Crack Down on Extended Careers. *Toronto Star.* February 22, D17.

Grossman, D. (2002). Tathan Family Courts Success. *Toronto Star*, November 5, E7.

Grossman, D. (2002). More Students in Sports: Despite Cutback Numbers on Rise Survey Reveals. *Toronto Star*, October 22, D6.

Grossman, D. (2002). High School Year in Review. *Toronto Star,* July 2, C6.

Grossman, D. (2002). Commerce Player Boast Major Talent: Cuban-Born Star Hopes to Follow Grandpa to Pros. *Toronto Star,* May 10, D11.

Grossman, D. (2002). Monarchs Want Their Crown. *Toronto Star*, February 17, D17.

Grossman, D. (2002). High School Basketball All-Stars. *Toronto Star*, February 15, C18.

Grossman, D. (2002). Afghan Wrestling Star Finds Refuge in Canada. *Toronto Star*, January 25, E08.

Grossman, D. (2002). Silver Lining for Silverthorn. *Toronto Star,* January 11, C8.

Grossman, D. (2001). Players Cut Because of Bad Grades. *Toronto Star*, January 11, C13.

Grossman, D. (2000). School Gives James a Second Shot. *Toronto Star,* June 9, E1 & E4.

Gruneau, R., & Whitson, D. (1993). *Hockey Night in Canada: Sport, Identities and Cultural Politics.* Toronto: Garamond.

Haig-Brown, C., Hodgson-Smith, K.L., Regnier, R., & Archibald, J. (1997). *Making the Spirit Dance Within: Joe Duquette High School and an Aboriginal Community.* Toronto: Our Schools/Our Selves, James Lorimer.

Hall, A., Slack, T., Smith, G., & Whitson, D. (1991). *Sport in Canadian Society.* Toronto: McClelland & Stewart.

Hammersley, M., & Atkinson, P. (1992). *Ethnography: Principles in Practice.* New York: Rouledge.

Hanmer, T.J. (1996). *The Gender Gap in Schools: Girls Losing Out.* Springfield, New Jersey: Enslow Publishers.

Hanson, S. & Kraus, R. (1999). Women in Male Domains: Sport and Science. *Sociology of Sport Journal,* 16, 92–110.

Harris, O. (1994). Race, Sport and Social Support. *Sociology of Sport Journal* 11, 40–50.

Harris, O. (1991). Athletes and Academics: Contrary or Complementary Activities? In G. Jarvie (ed.), *Sport, Racism and Ethnicity,* pp. 124–149. London: Falmer.

Harrison, Jr., L., Azzarito, L., & Burden, Jr., J. (2004). Perceptions of Athletic Superiority: A View From the Other Side. *Race, Ethnicity and Education* 7(2), 149–166.

Hatchell, H. (2004). Privilege of Whiteness: Adolescent Male Students' Resistence to Racism in an Australian Classroom. *Race, Ethnicity and Education* 7(2), 99–114.

Hawkins, R., Royster, D.A., & Braddock, J.H. II (1992). *Athletic Investment and Academic Resilience among African-American Females and Males in the Middle Grades.* Urban Child Research Center, Cleveland State University. Research Report No. 3, pp. 1–23.

Hay, J., & Donnelly, P. (1996). Sorting out the Boys from the Girls: Teacher Perceptions of Student Physical Ability. *Avante* 2, 36–52.

Head, W. (1975). *The Black Presence in the Canadian Mosaic.* Toronto: Ontario Human Rights Commission.

Henry, A. (1998). *Talking Back: African Canadian Women Teachers' Lives and Practice.* Albany: State University of New York Press.

Henry, A. (1995). Growing up Black, Female, and Working Class: A Teacher's Narrative. *Anthropology & Education Quarterly* 26(3), 279–305.

Henry, A. (1993). Missing: Black Self-Representation in Canadian Educational Research. *Canadian Journal of Education* 18(3), 206–222.

Henry, F. (1994). *The Caribbean Diaspora in Toronto: Learning to Live with Race.* Toronto: University of Toronto Press.

Higgins, D. (2003). Who's Got Now: Canada's Top High School Ballers In Pursuit of Hoop Dreams. *Peace Magazine* 66, June 26–28.

Hill, G. (1993). Youth Sport Participation of Professional Baseball Players. *Sociology of Sport* 10, 107–114.

Hoffman, A. (1995). Women's Access to Sport and Physical Activity. *Avante* 1, 77–92.

Hollands, R. (2002). Divisions in the Dark: Youth Cultures, Transitions and Segmented Consumptions Spaces in the Night-time Economy. *Journal of Youth Studies* 5(2), 153–171.

Honora, D. (2003). Urban African American Adolescents and School Identification. *Urban Education* January 38(1), 58–77.

hooks, b. (1995). Dreams of Conquest; Hoop Dreams and the Oscar. *Sight and Sound*, April, 22–23.

hooks, b. (1994). *Teaching to Transgress: Education as the Practice of Freedom*. Boston: South End Press.

Howell, C. (2001). *Blood, Sweat, Cheers: Sport and the Making of Modern Canada*. Toronto: University of Toronto Press.

Hsia, J. (1988). *Asian Americans in Higher Education and at Work*. Hillsdale, New Jersey: Lawrence Erlbaum Associates.

Humburt, M.L. (1995). One the Sidelines: The Experiences of Young Women in Physical Education Classes. *Avante* 1(2), 58–77.

International Working Group on Women and Sport (IWG). (2002). *Investing in Change: The Montreal Tool Kit: A Legacy of 2002 World Conference*. Hull: Conference Secretariat. http://www.canada2002.org

James, C.E. (2005). Constructing Aspirations: The Significance of Community in the Schooling Lives of Children of Immigrants. In L. Pease-Alvarez & S. Schecter (eds.), *Learning, Teaching and Community*. Mahwah: Lawrence Erbaum.

James, C.E. (2004). Urban Education: An Approach to Community-Based Education. *Intercultural Education* 15(1), 15–32.

James, C.E. (2003a). *Seeing Ourselves: Exploring Race, Ethnicity and Culture*. Toronto: Thompson Educational.

James, C.E. (2003b). Schooling, Basketball and US Scholarship Aspirations of Canadian Athletes. *Race, Ethnicity and Education* 6(2), 124–144.

James, C.E. (2003c). "It Can't Be Just Sports": Schooling Academics and Athletic Scholarship Expectations. *Orbit—Anti-Racism Practices and Inclusive Schooling* 33(3), 33–35.

James, C.E. (2002a). Achieving Desire: Narrative of a Black Male Teacher. *Qualitative Studies in Education* 15(2), 171–186.

James, C.E. (2002b). "You Can't Understand Me": Negotiating Teacher–Student Relationships in Urban Schools. *TESL (Association of Teachers of English as a Second Language of Ontario)* 28(2), 8–20.

James, C.E. (2001). Multiculturalism, Diversity, and Education in the Canadian Context: The Search for an Inclusive Pedagogy. In C.A. Grant & J.L. Lei (eds.), *Global*

235

Constructions of Multicultural Education: Theories and Realities, pp. 175–204. Mahwah, NJ: Lawrence Erlbaum Associates.

James, C.E. (1996). The Possibility of Play: Black Youth, Athletics and Schooling. In K.S. Brathwaite & C.E. James (eds.), *Educating African Canadians*, pp. 259–283. Toronto: Lorimer.

James, C.E. (1995). Negotiating School through Sports: African Canadian Youth Strive for Academic Success. *Avante* 1(1), 20–36.

James, C.E. (1990). *Making It: Black Youth Racism and Career Aspirations*. Oakville: Mosaic Press.

James, K. (2000). A Letter to a Friend. In C.E. James (ed.), *Experiencing Difference*, pp. 44–52. Halifax: Fernwood.

Johal, R. (2002). *The World Is Ours: Second Generation South Asian Youths Reconcile Conflicting Expectations*. Toronto: Faculty of Education, York University.

Johnson, S., & Meinhof, U.H. (1997). *Language and Masculinity*. Oxford: Blackwell.

Jones, R.L. (2000). Toward a Sociology of Coaching. In R.L. Jones & K.M. Armour (eds.), *Sociology of Sport: Theory and Practice*, pp. 33–43. Essex: Pearson Education.

Jordon G., & Weedon, C. (1995). *Cultural Politics: Class, Gender, Race and the Postmodern World*. Oxford: Blackwell.

Kalchman, L. (2002). Free Phones Hanging up Scholarships: Women's League Scrambles over Question of "Pay." *Toronto Star*, November 27, E2.

Katz, J. (1996). Masculinity and Sports Culture. In R.E. Lapchick (ed.). *Sport in Society: Equal Opportunity or Business as Usual*, pp. 101–105. Thousand Oaks: Sage.

Kell, P. (2000). *Good Sports: Australian Sport and the Myth of the Fair Go*. Annandale: Pluto Press Australia.

Kelly, J. (1998). *Under the Gaze: Learning to Be Black in a White Society*. Halifax: Fernwood.

Kerr, G. A. (1996). The Role of Sport in Preparing Youth for Adulthood. In B. Galaway & J. Hudson (eds.), *Youth in Transition: Perspectives on Research and Policy*, pp. 293–301. Toronto: Thompson Educational.

Kidd, B. (1995). Confronting Inequality in Sport and Physical Activity. *Avante* 1(1), 1–19.

Kidd, B. (1987). Sport and Masculinity. In M. Kaufman (ed.), *Beyond Patriarchy: Essay by Men*. Toronto: Oxford University Press.

King, K. (2002). Special Report: High School Sports: Part II: The Ultimate Jock School. *Sports Illustrated*, November 25, 98(21), 48–54.

Kumashiro, K. (2001). "Posts" Perspectives on Anti-Oppressive Education in Social Studies, English, Mathematics, and Science Classrooms. *Educational Researcher* 30(3), 2–12.

Kumashiro, K.K. (2000). Toward a Theory of Anti-Oppressive Education. *Review of Educational Research* 70(1), 25–54.

Lapchick, R. (2001). *Smashing Barriers: Race and Sport in the New Millennium.* Boston: Madison Books.

Lapchick, R.E. (1995). Race and College Sport: A Long Way to Go. *Race & Class* 36(4), 87–94.

Lapchick, R.E. (ed.) (1995). *Sport in Society: Equal Opportunity or Business as Usual.* Thousand Oaks: Sage.

Larter, S., Cheng, M., Capps, S., & Lee, M. (1982). *Post-Secondary Plans of Grade Eight Students and Related Variables 165.* Toronto: The Board of Education for the City of Toronto.

Lather, P. (1991). *Getting Smart: Feminist Research and Pedagogy with/in the Postmodern.* New York: Routledge.

Layden, T. (1995). Leap of Faith. *Sports Illustrated* 83(9), 105–107.

Leaman, O., & Carrington, B. (1985). Athleticism and the Reproduction of Gender and Ethnic Marginality. *Leisure Studies* 4, 205–217.

Lee, S. (2003). Model Minorities and Perpetual Foreigners. In M. Sadowski (ed.), *Adolescents at School: Perspectives on Youth, Identity and Education*, pp. 41–49. Cambridge: Harvard University Press.

Lee, S. (1996). Unravelling the "Model-Minority" Stereotype: Listening to Asian Americans as the Model Minority: An Analysis of the Popular Press Image in the 1960s and 1980s. In G.Y. Okihiro, S. Hune, A.A. Hansen, & J.M. Liu (eds.), *Reflections on Shattered Windows: Promises and Prospects for Asian American Studies*, pp. 165–174. Pullman: Washington State University Press.

Leeder, D. (2001). Growing Number of Basketball Players Leaving High School Early to Head South: Teachers' Dispute, Lure of NCAA Glory Combine to Rob Toronto of Top Talent. *Globe and Mail*, Saturday, January 13, S4.

Lenskyj, H.J. (2003). *Out on the Field: Gender, Sport and Sexualities.* Toronto: Women's Press.

Lenskyj, H.J. (1994). Jocks and Jills: Women's Experiences in Sport and Physical Activity. In G. Finn (ed.), *Limited Edition.* Halifax: Fernwood.

Li, J. (2001). Expectations of Chinese Immigrant Parents for their Children's Education: The Interplay of Chinese Tradition and the Canadian Context. *Canadian Journal of Education* 26(4), 477–494.

Lopiano, D. (1995). Growing Up with Gender Discrimination in Sport. In R.E. Lapchick (ed.), *Sport in Society: Equal Opportunity or Business as Usual*, pp. 83–95. Thousand Oaks: Sage.

Loury, G.C. (2002). When Color Should Count. *New York Times*, July 28, Section 4, 13.

Lovell, T. (1991). Sport, Racism and Young Women. In G. Jarvie (ed.), *Sport, Racism and Ethnicity*, pp. 58–73. London: Falmer.

MacDonald, G. (2003). Stuck in the 'Hood: Hip-hop Language Is Everywhere, Thanks to Advertisers Anxious to Capitalize on the Power of Cool and Rake in Those Tween Dollars. *Globe and Mail,* January 11, p. R8.

Macleod, J. (1991). *Ain't No Makin' It: Leveled Aspirations in a Low-Income Neighbourhood.* Boulder: Westview.

Maguire, J., Jarvie, G., Mansfield, L., & Bradly, J. (2002). *Sport Worlds: A Sociological Perspective.* Champagne, Illinois: Human Kinetics.

Marsh, H.W. (1993). The Effects of Participation in Sport During the Last Two Years of High School. *Sociology of Sport Journal* 10, 18–43.

Martin, R., & Miller, T. (1999). *Sport Cult*. Minneapolis: Regents of the University of Minnesota.

Mazurek, K. (1987). Multiculturalism, Education and the Ideology of Meritocracy. In T. Wotherspoon (ed.), *The Political Economy of Canadian Schooling*, pp. 141–163. Toronto: Methuen.

McCall, N. (1997). The Revolution Is about Basketball. In N. McCall (ed.), *What's Going On: Personal Essays*, pp. 3–16. New York: Random House.

McGuire, B., & Collins, D. (1998). Sport, Ethnicity and Racism: The Experience of Asian Heritage Boys. *Sport, Education and Society* 3(1), 79–88.

Mckay, J., Messner, M., & Sabo, D. (2000). *Masculinities, Gender Relations, and Sport: Research on Men and Masculinities.* Thousand Oaks: Sage.

McLaren, P. (1994). *Life in Schools*. New York: Longman.

McNeal, J., & Ralph, B. (1995). Extracurricular Activities and High School Dropouts. *Sociology of Education* January, 68, 62–81.

Meta, F.G. (1989). *The Black Youth of Toronto: Exploration of Issues.* Ottawa: Policy & Research, Multiculturalism & Citizenship/Government of Canada.

Metcalfe, A. (2003). Sport and Canadian Culture. In K.G. Pryke & W.C. Soderlund (eds.), *Profiles of Canada*, pp. 179–199. Toronto: Canadian Scholars' Press.

Milne, S. (1998). *White Student Responses to Increasing Racial Diversity in School.* MEd. Thesis. Toronto: Department of Graduate Studies, York University.

Minichiello, D. (2001). Chinese Voices in a Canadian Secondary School Landscape. *Canadian Journal of Education* 26(1), 77–96.

Ministry of Education. (1993). *Changing Perspectives: A Resource Guide for Antiracist and Ethnocultural-Equity Education.* Toronto: Queen's Printer for Ontario.

Ministry of Education. (1992). *Antiracism and Ethnocultural Equity in School Boards: Guidelines for Policy Development and Implementation.* Toronto: Queen's Printer for Ontario.

Ministry of Education and Training. (1993). *Antiracism and Ethnocultural Equity in School Boards: Guidelines for Policy Development and Implementation.* Toronto: Queen's Printer for Ontario.

Moodley, K. (1999). Antiracist Education through Political Literacy: The Case of Canada. In S. May (ed.), *Critical Multiculturalism: Rethinking Multicultural and Antiiracist Education*. London: Falmer.

Morse, J.M. (1994). Designing Funded Qualitative Research. In N.K. Denzin & Y.S. Lincoln (eds.), *Handbook of Qualitative Research*, pp. 220–233. Thousand Oaks: Sage.

Mosely, P. A., Cashman, R., O'Hara, J., & Weatherburn, H. (1997). *Sporting Immigrants.* Crows Nest: Walla Walla Press.

Munro, P. (1998). *Subject to Fiction: Some Teachers' Life Narratives and the Cultural Politics of Resistance.* Philadelphia: Open University Press.

Nakamura, Y. (2003). *Finding a Way, Finding the Self: The Journeys of Nine Physical Educational Students Pursuing "Non-Traditional" Paths.* Toronto: Graduate Department of Exercise Science, University of Toronto.

Nelson, M.B. (2002). *We Are All Athletes.* New York: Dare Press.

Nelson, M.B. (1995). *The Stronger Women Get, the More Men Love Football: Sexism and the American Culture of Sports.* New York: Avon Books.

Odhiambo, D.N. (2003). *Kipligat's Chance.* Toronto: Penguin Canada.

Ormsby, M. (1997). A Tall Order: Toronto's Jamaal Magloire Pursues His Dream in Hoops Hotbed. *Toronto Star*, February 8, C1.

Palmer, H. (ed.) (1997). *"... But Where Are You Really from?": Stories of Identity and Assimilation in Canada.* Toronto: Sister Vision.

Paraschak, V. (2000). Knowing Ourselves through the "Other": Indigenous Peoples in Sport in Canada. In R.L. Jones & K.M. Armour (eds.), *Sociology of Sport: Theory and Practice*, pp. 153–216. Essex: Longman.

Parry, J., & Parry, N. (1991). Sport and the Black Experience. In G. Jarvie (ed.), *Sport, Racism, and Ethnicity*, pp. 150–174. London: Falmer.

Paul, J. (2002). Hoops Is Happiness: Canada Represents a New Beginning for Congo High Schooler. *Toronto Sun*, January 11, p. S7.

Paul, J. (2002). Nothing but Net Gains: Marion Academy Star Making the Grade on Court and in Class. *Toronto Sun*, January 9, 81.

Phelan, P., Locke, A., & Cao, H.T. (1991). Students' Multiple Worlds: Negotiating the Boundaries of Family, Peer, and School Cultures. *Anthropology and Education Quarterly* 22, 224–250.

Phinney, J., Madden, T., & Ong, A. (2000). Cultural Values and International Values Discrepancies in Immigrant and Non-Immigrant Families. *Child Development* 77, 528–529.

Pittaway, K. (1994). Scoring a Touchdown in the Classroom. *Home & School* November, pp. 24–25.

Pitter, R. (2004). Sport, Recreation Programming and Youth Development. In J. Phillip & B. Kidd (eds.), *From Enforcement and Prevention to Civic Engagement:*

Research Colloquium on Community Safety. Toronto: Department of Criminology, University of Toronto.

Plaza, D. (1998). Strategies and Strategizing: The Struggles for Upward Mobility among University Educated Caribbean-Born Men in Canada. In M. Chamberlain (ed), *Globalized Identities: New Directions in the Study of Caribbean Migration*, pp. 249–266. London: Routledge.

Pon, G. (2000). Beamers, Cells, Malls and Cantopop: Thinking through the Geographies of Chineseness. In C.E. James (ed.), *Experiencing Difference*, pp. 222–34. Halifax: Fernwood.

Portes, A., & McLeod, D. (1999). Educating the Second Generation: Determinants of Academic Achievement among Children of Immigrants in the United States. *Journal of Ethnic and Migration Studies* 25(3), 373–396.

Preskill, S.L., & Jacobvitz, R.S. (2001). *Stories of Teaching: A Foundation for Educational Renewal*. Upper Saddle River: Merrill Prentice-Hall.

Price, S.L. (1997). Whatever Happened to the White Athlete? *Sports Illustrated* December 8 (87), n. 23(12), 30–51.

Prince, A., & Silva-Wayne, S. (eds.) (2004). *Feminisms and Womanisms: A Women's Studies Reader*. Toronto: Women's Press.

Pronger, B. (1992). *The Arena of Masculinity: Sports, Homosexuality, and the Meaning of Sex*. Toronto: University of Toronto Press.

Raval, D. (1989). Gender, Leisure and Sport: A Case Study of Young South Asian Descent—a Response. *Leisure Studies* 8, 237–240.

Reid, C., Dyck, L., McKay, H., & Frisday, W. (2000). *The Health Benefits of Physical Activity for Girls and Women*. Vancouver: British Columbia Centre of Excellence for Women's Health.

Reuters. (2003). James' New SUV: Teen's Luxury Hummer Sparks Probe. *Toronto Star*, January 14, E5.

Rodriguez, T.D. (2002). Oppositional Culture and Academic Performance among Children of Immigrants in the USA. *Race, Ethnicity and Education*, December, 5(2), 199–213.

Rollin, L. (1999). *Twentieth-Century Teen Culture by the Decades: A Reference Guide*. London: Greenwood.

Roman, L.G., & Eyre, L. (1997). *Dangerous Territories: Struggles for Difference and Equality*. New York: Routledge.

Roman, L.G., & Stanley, T. (1997). Empires, Emigrants, and Aliens: Young People's Negotiations of Official and Popular Racism in Canada. In L.G. Roman & L. Eyre (eds.), *Dangerous Territories: Struggles for Difference and Equality in Education*, pp. 205–231. New York: Routledge.

Rosser, S.V. (2001). Are There Feminist Methodologies Appropriate for the Natural Sciences and Do They Make a Difference? In M. Leferman & I. Bartsch (eds.), *The Gender and Science Reader*, pp. 123–144. New York: Routledge.

Sabo, D., Melnick, M.J., & Vanfossen, B.E. (1993). High School Athletic Participation and Postsecondary Education and Occupational Mobility: A Focus on Race and Gender. *Sociology of Sport Journal* 10, 44–56.

Sadowski, M. (ed.) (2003). *Adolescents at School: Perspectives on Youth, Identity, and Education.* Cambridge: Harvard Education Press.

Sailes, G.A. (1991). The Myth of Black Sports Supremacy. *Journal of Black Studies* 21(4), 480–487.

Sandoz, J., & Winans, J. (eds.) (1999). *Whatever It Takes: Women on Women's Sport.* New York: Farrar, Straus and Giroux.

Saul, R. (2004). *Profiles in "Success": Black Student Athletes and Their Representations in Toronto Media.* Toronto: Graduate Studies in Education, York University.

Schempp, P.G., & Oliver, K.L. (2000). Issues of Equity and Understanding in Sport and Physical Education: A North American Perspective. In R.L. Jones & K.M. Armour (eds.), *Sociology of Sport: Theory and Practice*, pp. 145–152. Essex: Longman.

Shadd, A. (2001). "Where Are You Really From?": Notes of an "Immigrant" from North Buxton, Ontario. In C.E. James & A. Shadd (eds.), *Talking about Identity: Encounters in Race, Ethnicity and Language*, pp. 10–16. Toronto: Between the Lines.

Shogan, D. (ed.) (1993). *A Reader in Feminist Ethics.* Toronto: Canadian Scholars' Press.

Shrosphire, K.L. (2002). *Race, Youth, Athletes and Role Models.* In M. Gatz, M.A. Messner, & S.J. Ball-Rokeach (eds.), *Paradoxes of Youth and Sport.* New York: State University of New York Press.

Siegel, D. (1994). Higher Education and the Plight of the Black Male Athlete. *Journal of Sport & Social Issues* 18(3), 107–223.

Simmons, P. (1999). *Gender Issues and Equity within Canadian High School Sport.* Graduate Program in Education, York University, Toronto.

Simons, J., & Butow, D. (1997). Improbable Dream: African-Americans Are a Dominant Presence in Professional Sports: Do Blacks Suffer as a Result? *US News & World Report.* Monday, March 24, 122(11), 46–52.

Sixty Minutes (1997). Sunday, October 26, 7–8 pm.

Slavin, R.E. (1991). *Educational Psychology: Theory into Practice.* Boston: Allyn and Bacon.

Sleeter, C. (1993). How White Teachers Construct Race. In C. McCarthy & W. Crichlow (eds.), *Race, Identity and Representation in Education*, pp. 151–171. New York: Routledge.

Smith, D. (2003). The LeBron Phenomenon: Hype over Teen Hits Incredible Level. *Toronto Star*, May 21, E3.

Smith, D. (2003). Alston Savours Another Chance to Play: Ball-Handling Wizard a Hero in Harlem. *Toronto Star*, January 13, E1–E4.

Smith, D. (2002). Young Hoops Starts Getting an Early Boost. *Toronto Star,* May 10, D8.

Solomon, R.P. (1997). Race, Role Modelling, and Representation in Teacher Education and Teaching. *Canadian Journal of Education* 22(4), 395–410.

Solomon, R.P. (1992). *Black Resistance in High School: Forging a Separatist Culture.* Albany: State University of New York Press.

Solomon, R.P., Levine-Rasky, C., & Singer, J. (2003). *Teaching for Equity and Diversity: Research to Practice.* Toronto: Canadian Scholars' Press.

Song, V. (2004). Future Stars on Track for Scholarships: U of T Meet Draws 300 Teens. *Toronto Star*, July 28, B4.

Sparkes, A. (2002). *Telling Tales in Sport and Physical Activity: A Qualitative Journey.* Champagne, Illinois: Human Kinetics.

Sparkes, A.C. (2000). Illness, Premature Career-Termination, and the Loss of Self: A Biographical Study of an Elite Athlete. In R.L. Jones & K.M. Amour (eds.), *Sociology of Sport: Theory and Practice*, pp. 13–32. Essex: Longman.

Spence, C. (1999). *The Skin I'm In: Racism, Sports and Education.* Halifax: Fernwood.

Sperber, M. (1995). Affirmative Action for Athletes. *Education Digest* 61, December, 57–59.

Sport Canada. (1999). *Sport Gender Snap Shot 1997–1998.*

Sport Canada. (2001). *Sport Participation in Canada 1998 Report.*

Sports Digest.(2003). High School Sensation Draws Record Crowd. *Toronto Star*, January 21, E9.

Staples, B. (1994). The Cruelest Game: High School Players in Coney Island Buy a Ticket out of the Ghetto on a Train That Doesn't Run. *The New York Times,* Book Review Section, 1, 66 & 68.

Starkman, R. (2002). Relax, It's Just a Game. *Toronto Star*, November 28, C03.

Starkman, R. (2002). Jumper Going Onward and Upward. *Toronto Star*, July 23, E9.

Sullivan, P.J. (1999). Strategies to Increase Self-Confidence in Youth in Sport and Physical Activity. *Manitoba Physical Education Journal* 22(4), April, 21–23.

Talbani, A., & Hasanali, P. (2000). Adolescent Females between Tradition and Modernity: Gender Role Socialization in South Asian Immigrant Culture. *Journal of Adolescence* 23, 615–627.

Talbot, M. (1993). A Gendered Physical Education: Equality and Sexism. In J. Evans (ed.), *Equality, Education and Physical Education*, pp. 74–89. London: Falmer.

Tate, M. (1993). *A Study of Racism and Exploitation in Intercollegiate Athletics.* Unpublished M.A. Thesis, Mount Pleasant, Central Michigan University.

Tatum, B. (1997). *"Why Are All the Black Kids Sitting Together in the Cafeteria?" and Other Conversations about Race.* New York: Basic Books.

Taylor Gibbs, J. (1996). Triple Marginality: The Case of Young African-Caribbean Women in Toronto (Canada) and London (England). *Canadian Social Work Review* 13(2), 143–156.

Thomas, C.E. (1988). Criteria for Athlete Autonomy in a Paternalistic Sport Model. In S. Ross & L. Charette (eds.), *Persons, Minds and Bodies*, pp. 191–202. North York: University Press of Canada.

Thornton, A.D. (2003). Driving the Lane against the Raptor: The Production and Racialization of (Transgressive) Subjects on the Streets of Toronto. In R.C. Wilcox, D.L. Andrews, R. Pitter, & R.L. Irwin (eds.), *Sporting Dystopias: The Making and Meanings of Urban Sport Cultures*, pp. 265–279. Albany: State University of New York Press.

Tilley, S. (2003). "Challenging" Research Practice: Turning a Critical Lens on the Work of Transcription. *Qualitative Inquiry* 9(5), 750–773.

Tirone, S., & Pedlar, A. (2000). Understanding the Leisure Experiences of a Minority Ethnic Group: South Asian Teens and Young Adults in Canada. *Society and Leisure* 23(1), 145–169.

Toronto Board of Education. (1993). *Report on 1991 Toronto Every Secondary Student Survey.* Toronto: Toronto Board of Education.

Tyyskä, V. (2001). *Long and Winding Road: Adolescents and Youth in Canada Today.* Toronto: Canadian Scholars' Press.

Varpatolai, A. (1996). Canadian Girls in Transitions to Womanhood. In B. Galaway & J. Hudson (eds.), *Youth in Transition: Perspectives on Research and Policy.* Toronto: Thompson Educational Publishing.

Vertinsky, P.A., & Captain, G. (1998). More Myth Than History: Representation of the Black Female Athlete's Athletic Ability. *Journal of Sport History* 25(3), 532–561.

Walcott, R. (1997/2003). *Black Like Who?* Toronto: Insomniac.

Warikoo, N. (2004). Race and the Teacher-Student Relationship: Interpersonal Connections Between West Indian Students and Their Teachers in a New York City High School. *Race, Ethnicity, and Education* 7(2), 135–148.

Waters, M. (1996). The Intersection of Gender, Race and Ethnicity in Identity Development of Caribbean American Teens. In B.J. Ross-Leadbeater & N. Way (eds.), *Urban Girls: Resisting Stereotypes, Creating Identities*, pp. 65–81. Albany: State University of New York Press.

Weiler, K., (1995). Freire and a Feminist Pedagogy of Difference. In J. Holland, M. Blair, & S. Sheldon (eds.), *Debates and Issues in Feminist Research and Pedagogy*, pp. 23–44. Philadelphia: Multilingual Matters & Open University.

White, P., & Young, K. (eds.) (1999). *Sport and Gender in Canada.* Toronto: Oxford University Press.

Wilcox, R.C., & Andrews, D.L. (2003). Sport in the City: Cultural, Economic, and Political Portraits. In R.C. Wilcox, D.L. Andrews, R. Pitter, & R.L. Irwin (eds.),

Sporting Dystopias: The Making of Urban Sport Cultures, pp. 1–16. Albany: State University of New York Press.

Williams, A. (1993). Who Cares about Girls? Equality, Physical Education and the Primary School Child. In J. Evans (eds.), *Equality, Education and Physical Education*, pp. 125–138. London: Falmer.

Wilson, T. (2002). The Paradox of Social Class and Sports Involvement: The Roles of Cultural and Economic Capital. *International Review for the Sociology of Sport* 37(1), 5–16.

Wolff, A. (2002). Special Report: The High School Athlete. *Sports Illustrated* 97(20), November 18, pp. 74–78.

Wood, M. (2002). *Black Canadian Girls: An Absented Presence in Canadian Educational Theorizing*. Graduate Program in Education, York University, Toronto.

Woolfolk, A.E. (1990). *Educational Psychology*. Englewood Cliffs, New Jersey: Prentice-Hall.

Wright, R. (2001). *Hip and Trivial: Youth Culture, Book Publishing and the Greying of Canadian Nationalism.* Toronto: Canadian Scholars' Press.

Wyn, J., & White, R. (2000). Negotiating Social Change: The Paradox of Youth. *Youth & Society* 32(2), 165–183.

Yetman, N.R., & Berghorn, F.J. (1993). Racial Participation and Integration in Intercollegiate Basketball: A Longitudinal Perspective. *Sociology of Sport Journal* 10, 301–314.

Zhou, Min. (1997). *Segregation Assimilation: Issues, Controversies and Recent Research on the New Second Generation.* Cambridge: Harvard University Press.

Zimmerman, J., & Reaveille, G. (1998). *Raising Our Athletic Daughters.* New York: Doubleday.